EASY to BUILD
Expandable HOME PLANS

STARTER HOME

"EXPANDED" HOME

CREATIVE HOMEOWNER®, Upper Saddle River, New Jersey

Home Plans Editor: Kenneth D. Stuts, CPBD

Design and Layout: iiCREATiVE (David Kroha, Cindy DiPierdomenico, Judith Kroha)

Cover Design: David Geer

Vice President and Publisher: Timothy O. Bakke
Production Coordinator: Sara M. Markowitz

Current Printing (last digit)
10 9 8 7 6 5 4 3 2 1

Easy-to-Build, Expandable Home Plans
Library of Congress Control Number: 2009923715
ISBN-10: 1-58011-467-9
ISBN-13: 978-1-58011-467-7

CREATIVE HOMEOWNER®
A Division of Federal Marketing Corp.
24 Park Way
Upper Saddle River, NJ 07458
www.creativehomeowner.com

Note: The homes as shown in the photographs and renderings in this book may differ from the actual blueprints. When studying the house of your choice, please check the floor plans carefully.

PHOTO CREDITS

Front cover: *top* plan 721007, page 11; *bottom* plan 722007, page 105 **page 1:** *top* plan 721006, page 43; *bottom* plan 722006, page 192 **page 3:** *top* plan 721008, page 62; *center top* plan 722008, page 147; *center bottom* plan 721043, page 95; *bottom* plan 722043, page 189 **page 4:** plan 721069, page 49 **page 5:** *top* plan 723069; *bottom* plan 722069, page 188 **page 10:** 721005, page 109; **pages 22–23:** *all* Phillip H. Ennis Photography, design: Anne Cooper Interiors **pages 24–25:** *all* Phillip H. Ennis, design: Audio Design Assoc./Justin Baxter **page 26:** *both* Phillip H. Ennis, design: Beverly Ellsley **page 27:** Phillip H. Ennis, design: Blodgett Designs **page 28:** *top* Phillip H. Ennis, design: Siskin-Valls, Inc.; *bottom* Phillip H. Ennis, design: Rita Grants **page 29:** Phillip H. Ennis **page 52:** Alan Shortall Photography **page 53:** *top* Mark Lohman; *center* Leonard Lammi, design: Cheryl Casey Ross; *bottom* Phillip Clayton Thompson, design: Nancy Setterquist **page 54:** *top both* Jessie Walker, design: Claire Golan; *bottom* courtesy of York Wallcoverings **page 55:** Leonard Lammi, design: Cheryl Casey Ross **page 56:** *top* Tria Giovan Photography; *bottom* Mark Lohman **page 58:** *top left* Mark Samu; *top right* Brian Vanden Brink, design: Atlantic Kitchens; *bottom right* courtesy of American Orlean; *bottom left* Brian Vanden Brink, design: Atlantic Kitchens **page 59:** *top left* Brian Vanden Brink, design: Atlantic Kitchens; *top right & bottom left* Mark Lohman; *bottom right* Phillip Clayton Thompson, design: Nancy Setterquist. **pages 82–83:** *both* George Ross/CH **page 84:** Christine Elasigue/CH **page 85:** *top right* George Ross/CH; *bottom* Christine Elasigue/CH **page 86:** *bottom left* George Ross/CH; *top & bottom* Christine Elasigue/CH. **pages 87–89:** Christine Elasigue/CH. **page 118:** courtesy of Kraftmaid Cabinetry **page 119:** *top* courtesy of Merillat; *bottom* courtesy of Kraftmaid Cabinetry **pages 120–121:** *left & top right* courtesy of Kraftmaid Cabinetry; *bottom right* courtesy of American Orlean **pages 122–123:** *top left* Wellborn Cabinet; *top right* courtesy of Kraftmaid Cabinetry; courtesy of Diamond Cabinets **page 124:** *top* courtesy of Wellborn Cabinet; *bottom* courtesy of Diamond Cabinets **page 125:** *top right* courtesy of Rev-A-Shelf; *bottom right* courtesy of Merillat; *top left* courtesy of Iron-A-Way. **page 150:** Crandall & Crandall **pages 151–153:** *all* courtesy of McHale Landscape Design **pages 154–155:** *all* Crandall & Crandall **page 156:** courtesy of Owens Corning Cultured Stone **page 157:** *top* Crandall & Crandall; *bottom* courtesy of KitchenAid **page 176:** Eric Roth **page 177:** *both* courtesy of GarageTek **page 178:** *top* Tony Giammarino/Giammarino & Dworkin, stylist: Christine McCabe; *bottom* courtesy of Rubbermaid **page 179:** *top* courtesy of Gladiator; *inset* courtesy of GarageTek **page 180:** *top* Bradley Olman; *bottom* courtesy of The Container Store **page 181:** *top left & bottom* courtesy of GarageTek; *top right* Mark Lohman **page 182:** *top* Eric Roth, architect: Ben Nutter; *bottom right* courtesy of Osram-Sylvania; *bottom left* melabee m miller, design/builder: Doyle Builders **page 183:** Eric Roth, architect: Ben Nutter **page 204:** Mark Samu **page 205:** *left* courtesy of Fypon; *right* Jessie Walker **page 206:** *left* courtesy of Focal Point Architectural Products; *right* Jessie Walker **page 207:** *left* courtesy of White River Hardwoods/Woodworks; *right* courtesy of Fypon **page 208:** courtesy of Celotex **page 209:** *top* courtesy of Georgia Pacific; *bottom* courtesy of Fypon **page 210:** courtesy of Fypon **page 211:** *top* courtesy of Fypon; *bottom* courtesy of LG **page 229:** plan 722026, page 219 **page 233:** *top* plan 721062, page 37; *center* plan 721024, page 30; *bottom* plan 721036, page 79 **page 240:** *top* plan 721038, page 41; *center* plan 721049, page 99; *bottom* plan 722018, page 164

Contents

YOUR NEW HOME–LET'S BUILD IT TOGETHER

Easy-to-Build, Expandable Home Plans

You'll appreciate the easy-to-build standard frame construction of these single-story "starter" homes and two-story "move-up" homes and the smart thinking behind them.

- All plans have been designed to use a single plate height and dimensional lumber without the use of trusses. This makes them easier and less expensive to build than many other starter and move-up homes.
- Three foundations are included to suit your lot and local site conditions: slab on grade, crawl space, and full basement.
- Perhaps most importantly, as a cost-saving measure, each one-story house has been structurally designed in advance to accommodate a future second-floor addition, if you choose to build one, with no alterations to the basic supporting structure required. The basement girders and first-floor headers have been engineered to carry the additional load, and the ceiling is designed to be the future second-story floor system. You can purchase the one-story plan, and then purchase the second-story addition later. Or you can buy the two-story plan at the start.
- Any of these affordable plans can be built with all the national brands you'll find at Lowe's. That's everything you need, from framing lumber to siding and from flooring to paint.
- Visit our Web site, www.ultimateplans.com, and click on the "Easy To Build" link for complete details on this program.

Free Material Take-off

With your plans you'll receive, free, the "Material Take-off" (a builder's material and time estimate for building the plan), a $345 value. (See page 234 for more details on this program.) In addition to the complete take-off of materials, we will also include free upgrades for millwork, kitchen cabinets, plumbing, and lighting fixtures. This complete package will be sent to your local Lowe's store, and a representative will contact you with a price quote for the materials. If you buy a minimum of $5,000 in merchandise from Lowe's, you will be eligible to receive a $345 Lowe's gift card. The free Material Take-off and the Lowe's gift card comprise the "Value Savings" of $690. This offer cannot be combined with any other offer. Visit our Web site, www.ultimateplans.com, and click on the "Easy To Build" link for complete details on this program.

The Lowe's Advantage

You can ALSO save 10% (up to $500) off your first building materials purchase. You will receive details on this program with your order. This offer is good for a single purchase of any in-stock or Special Order merchandise (maximum discount $500) over and above or separate from the purchase required for the Lowe's gift card mentioned above. Not valid on previous sales; service or installation fees; the purchase of gift cards; or any products by Fisher & Paykel, Electrolux, John Deere, or Weber.

3-D Framer's Walk-Through

Step-by-step 3-D framing instructions from foundation sill plate to roof sheathing are available for all plans in this collection at a cost of $545. This plan-specific "slide show" will be deliverd in PDF format for easy viewing. The 3-D framer's walk-through enables you to "virtually tour" your dream house in the framing stage of construction. This is a valuable tool when framing the home, and it can save you time and money. It will show you stud lengths, plate heights, header size and location, plus girder size and location.

1

The Starter Home—Small and "Easy to Build." Each one-story house has been structurally designed in advance to accommodate a future second-floor addition.

While home ownership is still the American dream, building your own home can be one of life's most satisfying adventures. Looking for a place to start? You've found it.

2

When you are ready to expand, purchase the Second Story Addition Plan. No alterations to the basic supporting structure are required. The basement girders and first-floor headers have been engineered to carry the additional load, and the ceiling is designed to be the future second-story floor system.

3

Two-story version of the home. You can purchase the one-story plan, and then purchase the second-story addition later. Or you can buy the two-story plan at the start.

Getting Started

Maybe you can't wait to bang the first nail. Or you may be just as happy leaving town until the windows are cleaned. The extent of your involvement with the construction phase is up to you. Your time, interests, and abilities can help you decide how to get the project from lines on paper to reality. But building a house requires more than putting pieces together. Whoever is in charge of the process must competently manage people as well as supplies, materials, and construction. He or she will have to

- Make a project schedule to plan the orderly progress of the work. This can be a bar chart that shows the time period of activity by each trade.
- Establish a budget for each category of work, such as foundation, framing, and finish carpentry.
- Arrange for a source of construction financing.
- Get a building permit and post it conspicuously at the construction site.
- Line up supply sources and order materials.
- Find subcontractors and negotiate their contracts.
- Coordinate the work so that it progresses smoothly with the fewest conflicts.

Hiring a Builder to Handle Construction

A builder or general contractor will manage every aspect of the construction process. Your role after signing the construction contract will be to make regular progress payments and ensure that the work for which you are paying has been completed. You will also consult with the builder and agree to any changes that may have to be made along the way.

Leads for finding builders might come from friends or neighbors who have had contractors build, remodel, or add to their homes. Real-estate agents and bankers may have some names handy but are more likely familiar with the builder's ability to complete projects on time and budget than the quality of the work itself.

Contracts

Lump-Sum Contracts

A lump-sum, or fixed-fee, contract lets you know from the beginning just what the project will cost, barring any changes made because of your requests or unforeseen conditions. This form works well for projects that promise few surprises and are well defined from the outset by a complete set of contract documents. You can enter into a fixed-price contract by negotiating with a single builder on your short list or by obtaining bids from three or four builders. If you go the latter route, give each bidder a set of documents and allow at least two weeks for them to submit their bids. When you get the bids, decide who you want and call the others to thank them for their efforts. You don't have to accept the lowest bid, but it probably makes sense to do so since you have already honed the list to builders you trust. Inform this builder of your intentions to finalize a contract.

Cost-Plus-Fee Contracts

Under a cost-plus-fee contract, you agree to pay the builder for the costs of labor and materials, as verified by receipts, plus a fee that represents the builder's overhead and profit. This arrangement is sometimes referred to as "time and materials." The fee can range between 15 and 30 percent of the incurred costs. Because you

ultimately pick up the tab—whatever the costs—the contractor is never at risk, as he is with a lump-sum contract. You won't know the final total cost of a cost-plus-fee contract until the project is built and paid for. If you can live with that uncertainty, there are offsetting advantages. First, this form allows you to accommodate unknown conditions much more easily than does a lump-sum contract. And rather than being tied down by the project documents, you will be free to make changes at any point along the way. This can be a trap, though. Watching the project take shape will spark the desire to add something or do something differently. Each change costs more, and the accumulation can easily exceed your budget. Because of the uncertainty of the final tab and the built-in advantage to the contractor, you should think twice before entering into this form of contract.

Contract Content

The conditions of your agreement should be spelled out thoroughly in writing and signed by both parties, whatever contractual arrangement you make with your builder. Your contract should include provisions for the following:
- The names and addresses of the owner and builder.
- A description of the work to be included ("As described in the plans and specifications dated . . .").

Some Final Words

Having a positive attitude is important when undertaking a project as large as building a home.

Stay Flexible. Expect problems, because they certainly will occur. Weather can upset the schedule you have established for subcontractors. A supplier may get behind on deliveries, which also affects the schedule. An unexpected pipe may surprise you during excavation. Just as certain, every problem that comes along has a solution if you are open to it.

Be Patient. The extra days it may take to resolve a construction problem will be forgotten once the project is completed.

Express Yourself. If what you see isn't exactly what you thought you were getting, don't be afraid to look into changing

- Notify inspectors at the appropriate milestones.
- Make payments to suppliers and subcontractors.

You as the Builder

You'll have to take care of every logistical detail yourself if you decide to act as your own builder or general contractor. But along with the responsibilities of managing the project, you gain the flexibility to do as much of your own work as you want and subcontract out the rest. Before taking this path, however, be sure you have the time and capabilities. Do you also have the time and ability to schedule the work, hire and coordinate subs, order materials, and keep ahead of the accounting required to manage the project successfully? If you do, you stand to save the amount that a general contractor would charge to take on these responsibilities, normally 15 to 30 percent of the construction cost. If you take this responsibility on but mismanage the project, the potential savings will erode and may even cost you more than if you had hired a builder in the first place. A subcontractor might charge extra for having to return to the site to complete work that was originally scheduled for an earlier date. Or perhaps because you didn't order the windows at the beginning, you now have to pay for a recent cost increase. (If you had hired a builder in the first place he or she would absorb the increase.)

The next step is to narrow your list of candidates to three or four who you think can do a quality job and work harmoniously with you. Phone each builder to see whether he or she is interested in being considered for your project. If so, invite the builder to an interview at your home. The meeting will serve two purposes. You'll be able to ask the candidate about his or her experience, and you'll be able to see whether or not your personalities are compatible. Go over the plans with the builder to make certain that he or she understands the scope of the project. Ask if they have constructed similar houses. Get references, and check the builder's standing with the Better Business Bureau. Develop a short list of builders, say three, and ask them to submit bids for the project.

- The date that the work will be completed if time is of the essence.
- The contract price for lump-sum contracts and the builder's allowed profit and overhead costs for changes.
- The builder's fee for cost-plus-fee contracts and the method of accounting and requesting payment.
- The criteria for progress payments (monthly, by project milestones) and the conditions of final payment.
- A list of each drawing and specification section that is to be included as part of the contract.
- Requirements for guarantees. (One year is the standard period for which contractors guarantee the entire project, but you may require specific guarantees on certain parts of the project, such as a 20-year guarantee on the roofing.)
- Provisions for insurance.
- A description of how changes in the work orders will be handled.

The builder may have a standard contract that you can tailor to the specifics of your project. These contain complete specific conditions with blanks that you can fill in to fit your project and a set of "general conditions" that cover a host of issues from insurance to termination provisions. It's always a good idea to have an attorney review the draft of your completed contract before signing it.

Working with Your Builder

The construction phase officially begins when you have a signed copy of the contract and copies of any insurance required from the builder. It's not unheard of for a builder to request an initial payment of 10 to 20 percent of the total cost to cover mobilization costs, those costs associated with obtaining permits and getting set up to begin the actual construction. If you agree to this, keep a careful eye on the progress of the work to ensure that the total paid out at any one time doesn't get too far out of sync with the actual work completed.

What about changes? From here on, it's up to you and your builder to proceed in good faith and to keep the channels of communication open. Even so, changes of one sort or another beset every project, and they usually add to its cost.

Light at the End of the Tunnel. The builder's request for a final inspection marks the end of the construction phase—almost. At the final inspection meeting, you and the builder will inspect the work, noting any defects or incomplete items on a "punch list." When the builder tidies up the punch list items, you should reinspect. Sometimes, builders go on to another job and take forever to clean up the last few details, so only after all items on the list have been completed satisfactorily should you release the final payment, which often accounts for the builder's profit.

it. Or you may spot an unforeseen opportunity for an improvement. Changes usually cost more money, though, so don't make frivolous decisions.

Finally, watching your home go up is exciting, so stay upbeat. Get away from your project from time to time. Dine out. Take time to relax. A positive attitude will make for smoother relations with your builder. An optimistic outlook will yield better quality work if you are doing your own construction. And though the project might seem endless while it is under way, keep in mind that all the planning and construction will fade to a faint memory at some time in the future, and you will be getting a lifetime of pleasure from a home that is just right for you.

"FREE"*
Garage Plans

*Only with home plans that do not include a garage.

Maybe you selected a home plan that does not have an attached garage, but you would like a 2-car garage. If your building lot has room for a detached garage, please select one pictured here for FREE. See the home plan page to determine whether your plan qualifies for the FREE garage plan.

Plan #721076

Dimensions: 20' W x 20' D
Square Footage: 400
Material Take-off Included: Yes
Price Category: DD

Images provided by designer/architect.

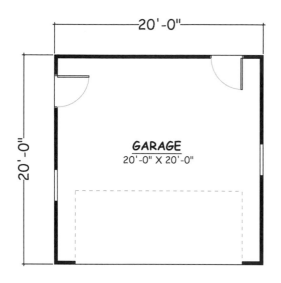

20'-0"

20'-0"

GARAGE
20'-0" X 20'-0"

Copyright by designer/architect.

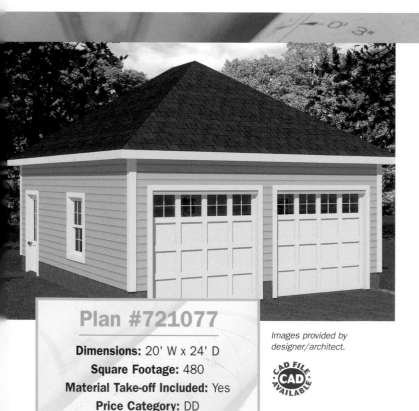

Plan #721077

Dimensions: 20' W x 24' D
Square Footage: 480
Material Take-off Included: Yes
Price Category: DD

Images provided by designer/architect.

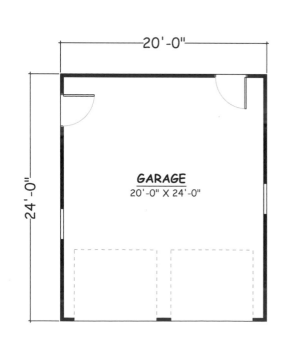

20'-0"

24'-0"

GARAGE
20'-0" X 24'-0"

Copyright by designer/architect.

- Select a garage plan with a style to match your home plan.
- A FREE Material Take-off is included with all FREE garage plans. See page 234 for more details.
- If the plan you selected has a garage and you need more storage space, all garage plans are also for sale. See page 237 for pricing.

Customers who *purchase* a garage plan recieve a FREE Material Take-off, a $125 value. In addition, if you buy a minimum of $2,000 in merchandise from Lowe's, you will be eligible to receive a $125 Lowe's gift card. More details will be included in your plan package.

Plan #721078

Dimensions: 22' W x 24' D
Square Footage: 528
Material Take-off Included: Yes
Price Category: DD

Images provided by designer/architect.

Copyright by designer/architect.

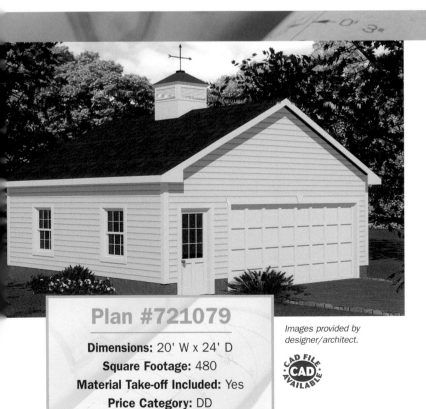

Plan #721079

Dimensions: 20' W x 24' D
Square Footage: 480
Material Take-off Included: Yes
Price Category: DD

Images provided by designer/architect.

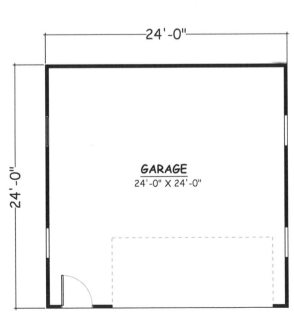

Copyright by designer/architect.

Ten Steps You Should Do Before Submitting Your Plans For a Permit

1. Check Your Plans to Make Sure That You Received What You Ordered

You should immediately check your plans to make sure that you received exactly what you ordered. All plans are checked for content prior to shipping, but mistakes can happen. If you find an error in your plans call 1-800-523-6789. All plans are drawn on a particular type of foundation and all details of the plan will illustrate that particular foundation. If you ordered an alternate foundation type. It should be included immediately after the original foundation. Tell your builder which foundation you wish to use and disregard the other foundation.

2. Check to Make Sure You Have Purchased the Proper Plan License

If you purchased prints, your plan will have a round red stamp stating, "If this stamp is not red it is an illegal set of plans." This license grants the purchaser the right to build one home using these construction drawings. It is illegal to make copies, doing so is punishable up to $150,000 per offense plus attorney fees. If you need more prints, call 1-800-523-6789. The House Plans Market Association monitors the home building industry for illegal prints.

It is also illegal to modify or redraw the plan if you purchased a print. If you purchased prints and need to modify the plan, you can upgrade to the reproducible master, PDF file or CAD file—call 1-800-523-6789. If you purchased a reproducible master or CAD file you have the right to modify the plan and make up to 10 copies. A reproducible master or CAD files comes with a license that you must surrender to the printer or architect making your changes.

3. Complete the "Owner Selection" Portion of the Building Process

The working drawings are very complete, but there are items that you must decide upon. For example, the plans show a toilet in the bathroom, but there are hundreds of models from which to choose. Your individual selection should be made based upon the color, style, and price you wish to pay. This same thing is true for all of the plumbing fixtures, light fixtures, appliances, and interior finishes (for the floors. walls and ceilings) and the exterior finishes. The selection of these items are required in order to obtain accurate competitive bids for the construction of your home

4. Complete Your Permit Package by Adding Other Documents That May Be Required

Your permit department, lender, and builder will need other drawings or documents that must be obtained locally. These items are explained in the next three items.

5. Obtain a Heating & Cooling Calculation and Layout

The heating and cooling system must be calculated and designed for your exact home and your location. Even the orientation of your home

can affect the system size. This service is normally provided free of charge by the mechanical company that is supplying the equipment and installation. However, to get an unbiased calculation and equipment recommendation, we suggest employing the services of a mechanical engineer.

6. Obtain a Site Plan

A site plan is a document that shows the relationship of your home to your property. It may be as simple as the document your surveyor provides, or it can be a complex collection of drawings such as those prepared by a landscape architect. Typically, the document prepared by a surveyor will only show the property boundaries and the footprint of the home. Landscape architects can provide planning and drawings for all site amenities, such as driveways and walkways, outdoor structures such as pools, planting plans, irrigation plans, and outdoor lighting.

7. Obtain Earthquake or Hurricane Engineering if You Are Planning to Build in an Earthquake or Hurricane Zone

If you are building in an earthquake or hurricane zone, your permit department will most likely require you to submit calculations and drawings to illustrate the ability of your home to withstand those forces. This information is never included with pre-drawn plans because it would penalize the vast majority of plan purchasers who do not build in those zones. A structural engineer licensed by the state where you are building usually provides this information.

8. Review Your Plan to See Whether Modifications Are Needed

These plans have been designed to assumed conditions and do not address the individual site where you are building. Conditions can vary greatly, including soil conditions, wind and snow loads, and temperature, and any one of these conditions may require some modifications of your plan. For example, if you live in an area that receives snow, structural changes may be necessary. We suggest:

(i)Have your soil tested by a soil-testing laboratory so that subsurface conditions can be determined at your specific building site. The findings of the soil-testing laboratory should be reviewed by a structural engineer to determine if the existing plan foundation is suitable or if modifications are needed.

(ii)Have your entire plan reviewed by your builder or a structural engineer to determine if other design elements, such as load bearing beams, are sized appropriately for the conditions that exist at your site.

Now that you have the complete plan, you may discover items that you wish to modify to suit your own personal taste or decor. To change the drawings, you must have the reproducible masters, PDF files or CAD files (see item 2). We can make the changes for you. For complete information regarding modifications, including our fees, go to www.ultimateplans.com and click the "resources" button on the home page; then click on "our custom services."

9. Record Your Blueprint License Number

Record your blueprint license number for easy reference. If you or your builder should need technical support, the license number is required.

10. Keep One Set of Plans as Long as You Own the Home

Be sure to file one copy of your home plan away for safe keeping. You may need a copy in the future if you remodel or sell the home. By filing a copy away for safe keeping, you can avoid the cost of having to purchase plans later.

Images provided by designer/architect.

Plan #721007

Dimensions: 56' W x 32' D
Levels: 1
Heated Square Footage: 1,030
Bedrooms: 2
Bathrooms: 1½
Foundation: Crawl space, slab or basement
Material Take-off Included: Yes
Price Category: B

The open design of this ranch house is ideal for the young family that wants a home that will grow with them.

Features:

- **Porch:** This wraparound covered porch provides the perfect place for a swing or rocker. It will become a favorite spot for the family to gather during the day or in the evenings to watch outdoor activities.

- **Foyer:** This spacious foyer, with dual coat closets and a powder room, provides an elegant entrance into an open floor plan.

- **Dining Room:** Conveniently located, this welcoming dining room is easy to reach through either the kitchen or the foyer.

- **Kitchen:** This large kitchen has a breakfast bar that will be used all day long. It also features easy access to the utility room and the formal dining room.

- **Deck:** The rear deck is accessible through sliding glass doors from the living room, extending the living and entertaining area to include the great outdoors.

CAD FILE CAD AVAILABLE

Copyright by designer/architect.

DECK
12'-0" X 8'-0"

KITCHEN
16'-6" X 9'-6"

LIVING ROOM
15'-6" X 11'-0"

BEDROOM 1
11'-0" X 11'-0"

GARAGE
18'-0" X 21'-0"

DINING
10'-10" X 11'-8"

FOYER
10'-10" X 8'-6"

BEDROOM 2
9'-0" X 9'-8"

PORCH
37'-8" X 6'-0"

32'-0"

56'-0"

YOU CAN EXPAND THIS HOUSE!

For the ever-growing family, this home is designed to be expanded. When you're ready to "grow" the house you can purchase its second floor addition, Plan #723007. To see the finished 2-story version go to page 105

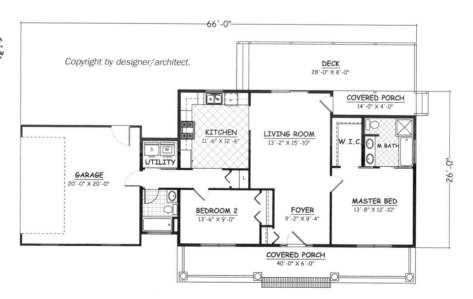

Images provided by designer/architect.

Plan #721028

Dimensions: 66' W x 26' D
Levels: 1
Heated Square Footage: 1,085
Bedrooms: 2
Bathrooms: 2
Foundation: Crawl space, slab or basement
Material Take-off Included: Yes
Price Category: B

The covered porch and transomed windows add to this home's curb appeal.

CAD FILE AVAILABLE · CAD ·

Features:

• Covered Porch: This large covered entry porch, with its elegant columns, offers shelter from the elements and has enough room for a small seating area.

• Living Room: This room opens from the foyer and is connected to the kitchen through a cased opening. It features sliding glass doors that open onto a rear deck and French doors that lead to a covered porch. This living room truly invites indoor and outdoor entertaining.

• Kitchen: This eat-in kitchen is just steps away from the utility room and a full bath. It also opens up to the living room, which allows for easy traffic flow when entertaining guests.

• Deck: This deck at the rear of the house has a covered area that is perfect for enjoying your morning coffee or for socializing outdoors in the summer.

• Master Suite: This master suite enjoys a private bath that includes a tub, separate shower, and a dual vanity. The room also features a large walk-in-closet and is situated away from the other bedroom to ensure privacy.

Floor plan

Copyright by designer/architect.

66'-0"

DECK
28'-0" X 8'-0"

COVERED PORCH
14'-0" X 4'-0"

KITCHEN
11'-6" X 12'-6"

LIVING ROOM
13'-2" X 15'-10"

W.I.C.

M.BATH

UTILITY

GARAGE
20'-0" X 20'-0"

BEDROOM 2
13'-6" X 9'-0"

FOYER
9'-2" X 9'-4"

MASTER BED
13'-8" X 12'-10"

26'-0"

COVERED PORCH
40'-0" X 6'-0"

YOU CAN EXPAND THIS HOUSE!

For the ever-growing family, this home is designed to be expanded. When you're ready to "grow" the house you can purchase its second floor addition, Plan #723028. To see the finished 2-story version go to page 136.

Images provided by designer/architect.

Plan #721052

Dimensions: 70' W x 25' D
Levels: 1
Heated Square Footage: 1,150
Bedrooms: 3
Bathrooms: 2
Foundation: Crawl space, slab or basement
Material Take-off Included: Yes
Price Category: B

You will love the features in this cozy traditional-style home.

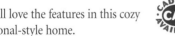

Features:

- **Covered Porch:** Turned columns add charm and grace to this spacious front entry porch. The ample size of the porch will allow for the placement of a small seating area, perfect for enjoying warm summer evenings.

- **Entry Foyer:** Open to the living room, this entry foyer immediately welcomes all into the home.

- **Kitchen:** This kitchen is designed with efficiency in mind. Just a step away is a utility room housing the washer and dryer, ensuring that the multitasking that is often required with today's active lifestyles is made much simpler.

- **Dining Room :** Adjacent to the kitchen, this dining room also features sliding glass doors leading to the generous sized rear deck.

- **Master Suite:** Separate from the secondary bedrooms in the home, this master suite provides a quiet area to retreat to after a long day.

The fluent lines and thoughtful design make this home one that is both affordable and easy to build. Because of these wonderful elements, this home can also be expanded to meet the needs of the growing family.

Copyright by designer/architect.

YOU CAN EXPAND THIS HOUSE!

For the ever-growing family, this home is designed to be expanded. When you're ready to "grow" the house you can purchase its second floor addition, Plan #723052. To see the finished 2-story version go to page 111.

Plan #721011

Dimensions: 56' W x 38' D

Levels: 1

Heated Square Footage: 1,167

Bedrooms: 3

Bathrooms: 2

Foundation: Crawl space, slab or basement

Material Take-off Included: Yes

Price Category: B

Images provided by designer/architect.

• **Kitchen:** This large L-shaped kitchen features ample counter space and modern conveniences. The adjacent dining room is just steps away, making family dinners a snap.

• **Deck:** The large deck is perfect for quiet morning breakfasts or outdoor summer entertaining.

• **Master Suite:** This master suite has a tray ceiling and large windows, creating a bright and airy space that makes relaxing a joy. It also offers a private bath with a dual vanity and a large walk-in-closet.

This two-story cottage style house makes it the perfect first home for a young family.

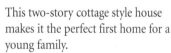

Features:

• **Living Room:** The living room is part of an open floor plan. The rooms flow into one another, creating a space that is light and airy, making it seem larger than it is.

• **Dining Room:** This space adjoins the kitchen and has a set of sliding glass doors that open onto a large deck. It's perfect for dining inside or out.

Copyright by designer/architect.

DECK
12'-0" X 10'-0"

KITCHEN
12'-8" X 12'-0"

DINING ROOM
13'-0" X 12'-0"

BATH #1
10'-4" X 5'-0"

W.I.C.

MASTER SUITE
13'-6" X 12'-6"

GARAGE
17'-4" X 14'-10"

LIVING ROOM
13'-0" X 13'-2"

BEDROOM #3
11'-8" X 9'-4"

BEDROOM #2
10'-2" X 12'-4"

28'-0"

56'-0"

YOU CAN EXPAND THIS HOUSE!

For the ever-growing family, this home is designed to be expanded. When you're ready to "grow" the house you can purchase its second floor addition, Plan #723011. To see the finished 2-story version go to page 101.

Plan #721066

Dimensions: 40' W x 44' D
Levels: 1
Heated Square Footage: 1,198
Bedrooms: 3
Bathrooms: 2
Foundation: Crawl space, slab or basement
Material Take-off Included: Yes
Price Category: B

Images provided by designer/architect.

This moderately sized home with clean and simple lines is filled with many amenities to fit the lifestyle of a busy family.

Features:

• Covered Porch: Not only will this expansive front-entry porch offer you shelter from the elements, the space is also large enough to fit a small seating area, a perfect spot for relaxing after dinner.

• Dining Room: This dining room has ample space for entertaining. After dinner, guests can step through the sliding glass doors leading to the backyard for some after-dinner activities.

• Kitchen: This well-designed kitchen, with such features as a double sink and a snack bar, is sure to please the family cook. The snack bar is a perfect spot for informal meals.

• Master Suite: Relax at the end of the day in this lovely master suite featuring a large walk-in closet and a private bathroom. The bathroom has a luxurious feel, with such amenities as a whirlpool tub and a dual vanity, and is sure to leave you feeling rejuvenated.

• Secondary Bedrooms: Two additional bedrooms flank the spacious foyer, and a full bathroom completes the home.

This comfortable home, with its thoughtful design, is not only affordable to build but is also ideally set for future expansion.

Copyright by designer/architect.

YOU CAN EXPAND THIS HOUSE!

For the ever-growing family, this home is designed to be expanded. When you're ready to "grow" the house you can purchase its second floor addition, Plan #723066. To see the finished 2-story version go to page 193.

Plan #721030

Dimensions: 72'7" W x 26' D

Levels: 1

Heated Square Footage: 1,200

Bedrooms: 3

Bathrooms: 2

Foundation: Crawl space, slab or basement

Material Take-off Included: Yes

Price Category: B

A feeling of spaciousness is generated in this home by its generous rooms and excellent design.

CAD FILE AVAILABLE

Features:

- Living Room: This large room is open to the kitchen and offers sliding glass doors to the rear deck. The open floor plan will ensure that it becomes the central gathering place for the entire family.

- Dining Room: Directly across from the kitchen, this dining room also has a set of sliding glass doors onto the large deck.

- Kitchen: The large pantry and plenty of extra storage space will keep the cook organized. The rest of the family will enjoy the companionship that the snack bar encourages.

- Master Suite: Privacy is assured in this master suite, as it is separated from the main part of the house. A separate bath and his and her walk-in closets add convenience as well as luxury.

- Master Bath: This space features a sunlit whirlpool tub, separate shower, private toilet room, and dual sink vanity. These amenities will soothe you at the end of a busy day.

- Secondary Bedrooms: Two additional bedrooms, a full bath, and a utility room complete the private areas of the home.

DECK
16'-0" X 8'-0"

LIVING ROOM
12'-10" X 12'-0"

KITCHEN
12'-4" X 12'-2"

M. BATH
13'-8" X 7'-10"

W.I.C.

UTILITY

GARAGE
20'-0" X 20'-0"

MASTER BED
13'-8" X 12'-10"

W.I.C.

FOYER
5'-0" X 7'-0"

BEDROOM 2
10'-0" X 9'-6"

BEDROOM 3
10'-0" X 9'-6"

BATH 2

PORCH
8'-0" X 4'-0"

72'-8"

26'-0"

YOU CAN EXPAND THIS HOUSE!

For the ever-growing family, this home is designed to be expanded. When you're ready to "grow" the house you can purchase its second floor addition, Plan #723030. To see the finished 2-story version go to page 116.

Images provided by designer/architect.

Plan #721035

Dimensions: 40' W x 50' D

Levels: 1

Heated Square Footage: 1,200

Bedrooms: 3

Bathrooms: 2

Foundation: Crawl space, slab or basement

Material Take-off Included: Yes

Price Category: B

This delightfully charming traditional-style ranch invites the outdoors in.

Features:

- Covered Porch: With its understated columns and brick accents, this porch welcomes you into this charming home.

- Living Room: Columns at each of its entry ways give this living room an added touch of elegance.

- Kitchen: This tidy kitchen has a large counter-top eating area and is open to the family room, allowing for interaction between the cook and the rest of the family.

- Family Room: Large windows and a set of sliding glass doors make this family room bright and inviting.

- Rear Deck: Spanning the length of the house, this wonderful outdoor space certainly connects the homeowners with nature. The family room and the two secondary bedrooms each feature sliding glass doors leading out to the deck.

- Master Suite: This master suite features its own bath with a dual vanity, which provides comfort and privacy.

Copyright by designer/architect.

YOU CAN EXPAND THIS HOUSE!

For the ever-growing family, this home is designed to be expanded. When you're ready to "grow" the house you can purchase its second floor addition, Plan #723035. To see the finished 2-story version go to page 173.

Images provided by designer/architect.

Plan #721032

Dimensions: 40'2" W x 51'6" D

Levels: 1

Heated Square Footage: 1,224

Bedrooms: 3

Bathrooms: 2

Foundation: Crawl space, slab or basement

Material Take-off Included: Yes

Price Category: B

CAD FILE AVAILABLE — CAD

This quaint home is perfect for a young family who is just starting out.

Features:

- **Great Room:** Sliding glass doors, which add natural light, grace the rear of this great room. These doors also access an expansive covered patio area, making outdoor living a part of the everyday.

- **Kitchen:** This kitchen has plenty of counter space, which makes mealtime prep a joy. An attached utility area houses the washer and dryer, aiding in today's multitasking lifestyle.

- **Master Suite:** Featuring a private bath and separated from the other bedrooms in the home, this master suite will ensure the comfort and privacy you seek.

- **Bedrooms:** Two additional moderately sized bedrooms help to complete this already comfortable home.

Copyright by designer/architect.

YOU CAN EXPAND THIS HOUSE!

For the ever-growing family, this home is designed to be expanded. When you're ready to "grow" the house you can purchase its second floor addition, Plan #723032. To see the finished 2-story version go to page 137.

Plan #721040

Dimensions: 56'6" W x 50' D
Levels: 1
Heated Square Footage: 1,226
Bedrooms: 3
Bathrooms: 2
Foundation: Crawl space, slab or basement
Material Take-off Included: Yes
Price Category: B

This delightful three-bedroom house is the perfect starter home.

Features:

- Covered Porch: The stately porch columns add elegance to the entrance of the home.

- Entry: Step through the front door and be welcomed immediately into the heart of the home. The area is spacious and has a free-flowing nature, allowing for easy passage between rooms.

- Family Room: Gracious in nature and connected to the dining room, entry, and kitchen, this family room will surely be the gathering spot for all.

- Kitchen: This spacious kitchen is open to the dining room and located close to the expansive family room. Its layout makes organization and meal preparation simple.

- Master Suite: Located at the rear of the home, this master suite features a private bath with a double vanity. The suite also has French doors that lead to a generously sized deck. This outdoor space offers you a place of respite for morning coffee or for sitting on a warm summer evening.

- Secondary Bedrooms: Two moderately sized bedrooms and a full bathroom round out this home.

Images provided by designer/architect.

Copyright by designer/architect.

YOU CAN EXPAND THIS HOUSE!

For the ever-growing family, this home is designed to be expanded. When you're ready to "grow" the house you can purchase its second floor addition, Plan #723040. To see the finished 2-story version go to page 140.

Plan #721056

Dimensions: 59' W x 39'1" D

Levels: 1

Heated Square Footage: 1,244

Bedrooms: 3

Bathrooms: 2

Foundation: Crawl space, slab or basement

Material Take-off Included: Yes

Price Category: B

- **Master Suite:** This master suite features a large walk-in closet and a private bathroom, ensuring privacy and comfort.

- **Secondary Bedrooms:** Two more moderately sized bedrooms and a full bathroom help to round out the home.

Simple and thoughtful design elements make this home affordable to build and one that can be easily expanded to meet the demands of a growing family.

This charming three-bedroom home offers a nice balance between public and private areas.

Features:

- **Kitchen:** This galley-style kitchen provides plenty of counter and cabinet space, making this space easy to organize. The kitchen is also connected to the utility room, which houses the washer and dryer, helping to make the multitasking that is often required with today's active families much easier to complete.

- **Breakfast Nook:** Open to the kitchen and the living room, this cozy breakfast nook will be the main area for everyday family meals. The room also features a French door leading out to a covered porch that will surely have you enjoying many meals outdoors.

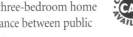

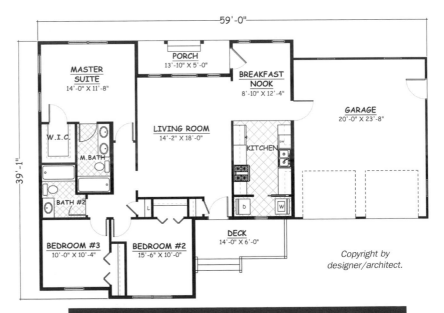

Copyright by designer/architect.

YOU CAN EXPAND THIS HOUSE!

For the ever-growing family, this home is designed to be expanded. When you're ready to "grow" the house you can purchase its second floor addition, Plan #723056. To see the finished 2-story version go to page 170.

Images provided by designer/architect.

Plan #721059

Dimensions: 54' W x 42' D

Levels: 1

Heated Square Footage: 1,260

Bedrooms: 3

Bathrooms: 2

Foundation: Crawl space, slab or basement

Material Take-off Included: Yes

Price Category: B

tasking that is often required with today's active families much easier to complete.

- **Master Suite:** Set apart from the secondary bedrooms in the home is this lovely master suite. The suite features a large walk-in closet and a private bathroom ensuring privacy and comfort.

- **Secondary Bedrooms:** Two additional moderately sized bedrooms and a full bathroom help to round out the home.

Thoughtfully designed, this home is affordable to build and can be expanded to meet the demands of a growing family.

If a traditional-style home makes you feel comfortable, you will love this spacious three-bedroom home.

Features:

- **Covered Porch:** This cozy covered entry to the home provides you with shelter from the elements.

- **Foyer:** This wide entry foyer leads you to the dining room and the family room situated at the rear of the home.

- **Dining Room:** Open to the kitchen and the foyer, and connected to the family room through a cased opening, this lovely space will be the main area for everyday family meals.

- **Kitchen:** This galley-style kitchen provides plenty of counter and cabinet space, making it easy to organize. The kitchen is also connected to the utility room, which houses the washer and dryer, helping to make the multi-

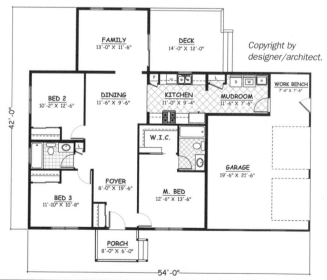

Copyright by designer/architect.

YOU CAN EXPAND THIS HOUSE!

For the ever-growing family, this home is designed to be expanded. When you're ready to "grow" the house you can purchase its second floor addition, Plan #723059. To see the finished 2-story version go to page 166.

Adding a Room

Do you need more living area? Do your domestic dreams include a home office, a deluxe media room, or perhaps a downstairs hangout for wild and crazy teens? Look no further than under your feet. That's right, your humble basement. In most cases, even the most ambitious project costs only a fraction of what you would spend to build an addition. Estimates for building aboveground average about $150 a foot; remodeling a basement, on the other hand, usually costs only $75 per foot—that's a 50-percent savings.

The lower cost shouldn't surprise you. After all, a basement is fully enclosed and already comes with walls, a floor, and a ceiling. There's no need to spend major dollars breaking ground for an addition or to move to a new house in order to have that special hobby room or that extra bedroom.

What's more, no matter how grand your plan, remodeling your basement provides a major head start over new construction when it comes to heating and cooling the new space, powering a media room or home office, or meeting the

CREATIVE HOMEOWNER

DESIGN IDEAS FOR
basements

WAYNE KALYN
Principle Photography
PHILLIP H. ENNIS

The following article was reprinted from *Design Ideas for Basements* (Creative Homeowner 2004).

A basement space, opposite, can be fun, decorative, and reflective of all of your interests.

Don't settle for a plain living space. Enliven the room with glamour and flavor, left, that will make it unforgettable to guests. Decorate it with an over-the-top theme or exotic accessories.

Adding details to the room, such as an arched median and decorative wallcoverings, below, will leave family and friends wondering whether they are really in a basement.

SMARTtip

Basic Basement Types

The type of basement you have may set up different challenges to overcome in your design, whether it is finishing surfaces, providing sources of ventilation, or choosing windows and doors that may be required by the new International Residential Code (IRC).

A standard basement is surrounded by below-ground walls, with maybe 20 percent of the walls above grade. There might be small windows at the very top or none at all. You can access or exit this basement only through an interior stairway. There is very little light and limited air circulation. A concern may be the coolness of all that concrete, especially in winter.

A walk-out basement has at least one wall that is above grade. This allows more light into the interior. With windows and doors, a walk-out basement has more air circulation than a standard basement. Also, interior and exterior stairs provide greater access into and out of the basement, which makes this space highly usable for bedrooms.

A grand staircase can be a preview, above, of the lush amenities downstairs.

Set the mood, left, with a surround-sound system built into the wall.

A theater-sized screen, opposite, allows you to watch your favorite movie in plush style.

additional plumbing needs of a bathroom or kitchen. The utilities are accessible and can be easily upgraded or adapted to accommodate your design needs.

Heating and cooling are usually a breeze. Basements are naturally cool in summer so air conditioning is often not required. Basements retain some of the residual heat from the furnace that warms up the main and upstairs living space. In colder areas, adding a few panels of baseboard heating can fill in the chilly gaps.

Upstairs, Downstairs

As increasing numbers of people spend more time at home. Experts agree that they see their living space in a new way. People have come to realize that their homes are designable real estate that can meet changing needs and passions, rather than static rooms with rigid roles. And basements are, in

SMARTtip
Future Uses of New Space

People and families change and, along with them, the rooms they inhabit. Before you commit to your basement's final design, make sure that you think through what you might need when the kids move out, you retire, or (gulp) your mother-in-law comes to live with you. The space you use for a playroom now may be converted into a guest suite or a home workshop in the future. Save time and money later by making sure the necessary wiring, plumbing, and mechanical work is roughed in before you cover the walls.

In order to imagine all of the possibilities, do some blue-sky thinking about 5 or 10 years down the line and create a checklist of possible needs for future configurations of your basement space.

many ways, the perfect space for that kind of flexible thinking and designing. The very shape of a basement—a long, shoe-box-like room running the length of the house—is equivalent to a blank slate, beckoning you to leave your design imprint on it, whether your are creating a large space for the entire family or a suite of medium-sized rooms that serve an array of practical purposes.

In fact, the amorphous quality of a basement actually cries out for creativity and the kind of architectural interest and dimension that can transform it from unappealing to inviting.

Think beyond knotty pine paneling and bean-bag chairs, and envision something more sophisticated. You can easily upgrade and enliven a boxy basement, for instance, by varying the height and angle of wall and ceiling planes. Mix materials, textures, and finishes on walls and ceilings. Include a greenhouse bumpout to bring the light and the outdoors into the space.

Let's assume your basement is dry and mold-free. The choice of furniture, accessories, and window treatments can be limitless, and often no different from those you would use in the rest of the house.

SMARTtip

Adding Molding

Keep moldings simple in a basement with lower ceilings. Elaborate moldings around the ceiling or floor can shorten the height of the room.

Stone, ironwork, and rough-hewn beams create an Old World look in this setting, inset.

Dinner is set in this romantic, softly lit wine cellar that was created in a remodeled basement, left.

Rooms of Opportunity

While some designers espouse tying the basement design into the home's overall style, others view basement conversions as a license to be daring. If you've always wanted to try a different look, go for it in the basement. Down-under spaces aren't seen from other levels, so there's no reason to take your design cues from upstairs. Here are some possibilities.

Family Room. This all-purpose living space is probably the easiest and least expensive way to add square footage to your home. You usually won't have to fiddle with or upgrade plumbing or worry about special egress windows. The main concern is keeping the space dry, and selecting finishes for walls, floors, and ceilings that suit your taste and vision. Whether you are looking for space for the kids' toys and games or just a place where you can watch television, listen to music, or dance away the night, a family room is an ideal choice.

Home Office. If you telecommute and need privacy and quiet to get your work done, designing a home office in the out-of-the-way basement is a no-brainer. Just make sure to include enough electrical circuits to power all of your equipment as well as any add-on technology in the future.

Wine Cellar. You might have always wanted one to house your collection of, say, Merlots or Syrahs, but couldn't find the right spot in your main living space. A cool, dark base-

ment provides a perfect climate for your vintage hobby.

Crafts Studio or Home Workshop. Perhaps you have a desire to take up landscape painting, to do some major crafting, or to try woodworking, but don't want to mess up the upstairs rooms or fill the house with paint fumes and dust. A downstairs arts-and-craft studio or home workshop, equipped with a quiet but powerful exhaust fan and a wall of storage bins, can solve both problems and provide the privacy to enable you to complete your masterpiece. You might even combine this space with a laundry room, a trend that's called a "home studio."

Media Room. You don't need a fortune to create a highly entertaining media room for family and friends. It's easy to darken an already dim basement and to increase sound absorption with the right floor, wall, and ceiling materials. If you

order direct: 1-800-523-6789

are ambitious, include a snack bar or kitchenette, complete with a refrigerator, sink, and microwave oven, so that you don't have to miss a moment of the movie.

Spa or Gym. After a long day's journey back from work, wouldn't it be relaxing to soak in a hot tub or melt away the tension in a sauna? Or reinvigorate yourself with a run on the treadmill or elliptical trainer? Look to your basement, again. The concrete-slab floor requires no additional structural reinforcement to handle the substantial weight of a hot tub, which can weigh more than 4,000 pounds when filled to capacity, or heavy gym machines. Saunas—which usually come as prefabricated packages, complete with walls, floor, and ceiling—are the perfect amenity for a windowless corner of the basement, and can often be tied into existing household circuits.

Bedroom. A basement is perfect for an extra bedroom. It typically has a bare minimum of natural light, and it's cool and quiet—a recipe for a good night's sleep.

Extra Bathroom or Kitchen. Adding an extra bathroom to a basement can free up space and thin out traffic upstairs and, when it's located near water-supply lines and a drain system, is easy and inexpensive to build. For the exact same reasons, adding a small kitchen won't break the bank.

SMARTtip

Sizing Up Rooms

While there is no perfect-sized room—it depends on your needs and the space you have to work with—the U.S. Department of Housing and Urban Development (HUD) has come up with some recommendations, which are listed below. The minimum net floor area refers to the space within the enclosed walls and excludes built-in features such as cabinets and closets.

	Minimum Area	Minimum Size	Preferred
Master Bedroom	n/a	n/a	12 x 16 ft.
Bedroom	80 sq. ft.	8 x 10 ft.	11 x 14 ft.
Family Room	110 sq. ft.	10.5 x 10.5 ft.	12 x 16 ft.
Living Room	176 sq. ft.	1 x 16 ft.	12 x 18 ft.
Great Room	n/a	n/a	14 x 20 ft.
Bathroom	35 sq. ft.	5 x 7 ft.	5 x 9 ft.

Workout time flies by while watching your favorite TV shows, opposite top.

An extra bathroom in the basement can be glamorous, opposite bottom.

A basement bedroom is the ideal getaway from the upstairs traffic, above.

Images provided by designer/architect.

Plan #721024

Dimensions: 61'3" W x 31' D

Levels: 1

Heated Square Footage: 1,268

Bedrooms: 3

Bathrooms: 2

Foundation: Crawl space, slab or basement

Material Take-off Included: Yes

Price Category: B

Featuring front and rear covered porches, this charming ranch home takes on a county feel.

Features:

• Family Room: Upon entering through the front door, you are welcomed immediately into the heart of the home. This generously sized room is open to both the kitchen and the dining room, serving as the gathering place for all.

• Dining Room: This dining room features sliding glass doors to a rear covered porch. Dining will be a pleasure, whether you choose to eat indoors or outdoors.

• Master Suite: A large walk-in closet and private bath help to add both privacy and comfort to this already lovely room.

• Bedrooms: Two additional bedrooms and a hall bath complete this charming home.

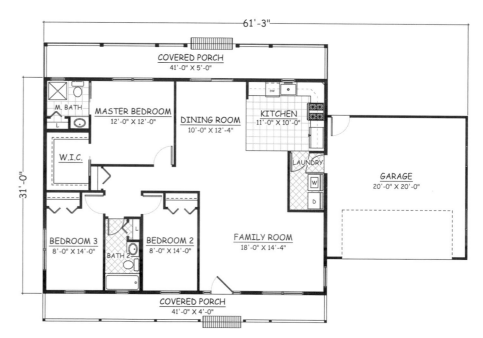

Copyright by designer/architect.

order direct: 1-800-523-6789

Rear Elevation

YOU CAN EXPAND THIS HOUSE!

For the ever-growing family, this home is designed to be expanded. When you're ready to "grow" the house you can purchase its second floor addition, Plan #723024. To see the finished 2-story version go to page 191.

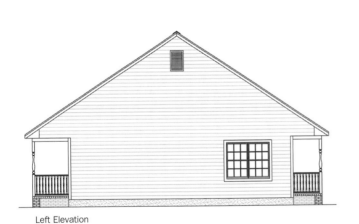

Left Elevation

Right Elevation

SMARTtip

Hydro-seeding

An alternative to traditional seeding is hydro-seeding. In this process, a slurry of grass seed, wood fibers, and fertilizer is spray-applied in one step. Hydro-seeding is relatively inexpensive. Compared with seeding by hand, hydro-seeding is also very fast.

Plan #721071

Dimensions: 51'8" W x 60' D
Levels: 1
Heated Square Footage: 1,260
Bedrooms: 3
Bathrooms: 2½
Foundation: Crawl space, slab or basement
Material Take-off Included: Yes
Price Category: B

The splendid design of this ranch home will please those with even the most discerning tastes.

Features:

- Foyer: A welcoming and cozy area, this foyer features tiled flooring and a moderately sized coat closet for added convenience.

- Family Room: Step from the foyer into this gracious family room, certain to be a gathering spot for all. The ample size of the room is perfect for evenings of family enjoyment, as well as for entertaining guests.

- Kitchen: This kitchen includes a generously sized pantry, ample counter space, and an abundance of cabinets, making it a cook's dream.

- Master Suite: This master suite will be a welcome retreat after a long day. This gracious space is sure to delight, with its

expansive walk-in closet and private bathroom, which features an oversized tub, a separate shower, and dual vanities, providing additional comfort to the room. A French door leading to the rear deck continues the relaxation to the outdoors.

Copyright by designer/architect.

YOU CAN EXPAND THIS HOUSE!

For the ever-growing family, this home is designed to be expanded. When you're ready to "grow" the house you can purchase its second floor addition, Plan #723071. To see the finished 2-story version go to page 130.

Plan #721067

Dimensions: 49'7" W x 29'5" D
Levels: 1
Heated Square Footage: 1,293
Bedrooms: 3
Bathrooms: 2
Foundation: Crawl space, slab or basement
Material Take-off Included: Yes
Price Category: B

Images provided by designer/architect.

Optional Free Garage: If you would like an optional FREE 2-car garage plan, select one from page 8 or 9.

This three-bedroom ranch home is thoughtfully designed, providing a nice balance between common and private areas in the home.

Features:

- **Foyer:** Step from the covered entry into this comfortable foyer, which features a nicely sized coat closet. This room gently ushers you to the main areas of the home.

- **Kitchen:** With a moderately sized pantry and thoughtful design, this kitchen will be easy to organize.

- **Master Suite:** Separated from the secondary bedrooms in the home is this spacious master suite. The suite features a generously sized walk-in closet and a private bathroom. The private bathroom, featuring dual vanities, an oversized tub, and a separate shower, will provide you with the comfort and privacy you seek.

- **Secondary Bedrooms:** Each of the additional two bedrooms features large windows, making the rooms bright and cheery. These secondary bedrooms are also just steps away from a centrally located bathroom for convenience.

Thoughtful design makes this home affordable to build, and one that can be easily expanded to meet the demands of a growing family.

Copyright by designer/architect.

YOU CAN EXPAND THIS HOUSE!

For the ever-growing family, this home is designed to be expanded. When you're ready to "grow" the house you can purchase its second floor addition, Plan #723067. To see the finished 2-story version go to page 132.

Plan #721061

Dimensions: 65'6" W x 35'4" D
Levels: 1
Heated Square Footage: 1,294
Bedrooms: 3
Bathrooms: 2
Foundation: Crawl space, slab or basement
Material Take-off Included: Yes
Price Category: B

Images provided by designer/architect.

You'll love the open layout and excellent design of this spacious-feeling home.

CAD FILE AVAILABLE

Features:

- Covered Porch: This covered porch at the front entry is wide enough for a small sitting area or perhaps to display a few planters that will provide additional curb appeal to the home.

- Living Room: From the covered entry you step directly into this gracious living room. Open to the dining room at the rear, it is certain to be the gathering spot for all.

- Dining Room: Open to both the living room and the kitchen, this dining room will certainly host many a dinner party. A set of French doors at the rear of the room that lead to a deck will allow the entertaining to continue to the great outdoors.

- Kitchen: The simple and thoughtful design of this kitchen will make the preparing of meals a joy. Open to the dining room and the living room, it invites interaction between the chef, family members, and guests.

- Master Suite: This generously sized master suite with an immense walk-in closet and a private bathroom will offer you a bit of respite from the everyday. The private bathroom features a dual vanity, an oversized tub, and a separate shower, ensuring comfort and privacy.

With its free-flowing nature, this home remains affordable to build and still offers room for expansion.

Copyright by designer/architect.

YOU CAN EXPAND THIS HOUSE!

For the ever-growing family, this home is designed to be expanded. When you're ready to "grow" the house you can purchase its second floor addition, Plan #723061. To see the finished 2-story version go to page 113.

Plan #721033

Dimensions: 51'4" W x 41'2" D

Levels: 1

Heated Square Footage: 1,295

Bedrooms: 3

Bathrooms: 2

Foundation: Crawl space, slab or basement

Material Take-off Included: Yes

Price Category: B

Images provided by designer/architect.

The brick facade on this lovely ranch home gives it a country feel.

Features:

- **Entry:** This simple entry ushers you directly into the home, making you and your guests feel welcome.

- **Great Room:** Just steps from the foyer and connected to the dining room, this great room will become the heart of the home. This gracious space is enhanced with sliding glass doors to a rear deck, offering you an expanded area for gathering and entertaining.

- **Dining Room:** Adjacent to the kitchen and the great room, this dining room is perfect for entertaining, whether it' informal family meals or elegant dinner parties.

- **Kitchen:** Efficiently designed, this kitchen will make mealtime tasks simple and pleasurable. With a utility room just steps away, the room also offers busy families a way to multitask.

- **Master Suite:** This lovely master suite, complete with a private bath and a large walk-in closet, will offer peace and comfort after a long day.

YOU CAN EXPAND THIS HOUSE!

For the ever-growing family, this home is designed to be expanded. When you're ready to "grow" the house you can purchase its second floor addition, Plan #723033. To see the finished 2-story version go to page 104.

Plan #721044

Dimensions: 26' W x 50' D
Levels: 1
Heated Square Footage: 1,300
Bedrooms: 3
Bathrooms: 2
Foundation: Crawl space, slab or basement
Material Take-off Included: Yes
Price Category: B

Optional Free Garage: If you would like an optional FREE 2-car garage plan, select one from page 8 or 9.

CAD FILE AVAILABLE

The design of this single-family home is reminiscent of colonial row homes.

Features:

- **Foyer:** The entry foyer is generously sized and is adjacent to the family room.

- **Family Room:** From the foyer you step directly into the heart of this home. Gracious in its size, this family room features a lovely set of double windows that will bathe the room in natural light.

- **Kitchen:** The L-shaped layout of this kitchen keeps the traffic flowing and provides abundant counter space, making meal prep easy and more enjoyable. This kitchen also includes a large panty, which makes organization a breeze.

- **Master Suite:** This large master suite features a walk-in closet and a private bath. The bath adds comfort and privacy to an already delightful space.

- **Secondary Bedrooms:** The additional two bedrooms in the home are moderately sized and are just steps away from a centrally located full bathroom.

The straightforward design of this home keeps it affordable to build.

YOU CAN EXPAND THIS HOUSE!

For the ever-growing family, this home is designed to be expanded. When you're ready to "grow" the house you can purchase its second floor addition, Plan #723044. To see the finished 2-story version go to page 146.

Images provided by designer/architect.

Plan #721062

Dimensions: 52' W x 42' D

Levels: 1

Heated Square Footage: 1,305

Bedrooms: 3

Bathrooms: 2

Foundation: Crawl space, slab or basement

Material Take-off Included: Yes

Price Category: B

If you are looking for a home that will make the whole family comfortable, this is the one for you.

Features:

- **Foyer:** From the front porch you enter into this cozy foyer that both welcomes and guides you back to the generously sized living room.

- **Dining Room:** Connected to both the living room and the kitchen and featuring large windows, this dining room has a bright and airy feel, making mealtime a pleasant experience.

- **Kitchen:** This galley-style kitchen features a pantry and a utility closet, making storage as well as multitasking much simpler.

- **Master Suite:** Featuring a large walk-in closet and a private bathroom, this generously sized master suite is certain to leave you feeling relaxed and renewed. The bathroom features an oversize tub, a separate shower, and dual vanities, providing comfort and privacy to the suite.

- **Secondary Bedrooms:** With two additional bedrooms and a full bathroom, this home offers each and every member of the family the space and privacy that they deserve.

This simple and thoughtful design will allow this home to be affordably built while still offering room for expansion.

Copyright by designer/architect.

YOU CAN EXPAND THIS HOUSE!

For the ever-growing family, this home is designed to be expanded. When you're ready to "grow" the house you can purchase its second floor addition, Plan #723062. To see the finished 2-story version go to page 167.

Plan #721041

Dimensions: 50' W x 47'10" D
Levels: 1
Heated Square Footage: 1,310
Bedrooms: 3
Bathrooms: 2
Foundation: Crawl space, slab or basement
Material Take-off Included: Yes
Price Category: B

Images provided by designer/architect.

This thoughtfully designed three-bedroom house will welcome family and guests to your home.

CAD FILE AVAILABLE

Features:

- Entry: Step through the front door into a spacious foyer.

- Dining Room: Open to the kitchen and family room, this dining room is perfect for entertaining. This room also features a set of sliding glass doors that open to an expansive rear deck, ensuring many nights of outdoor dining.

- Kitchen: Featuring a large pantry and plenty of counter space, this kitchen will surely please the family chef. A computer desk, along with the thoughtfully located mud-room that houses a washer and a dryer, helps to make the multitasking that is necessary with today's active lifestyle much easier.

- Master Suite: Located at the rear of the home, this master suite features a private bath with a double vanity for comfort. A large walk-in closet and a linen closet provide generous storage space.

- Secondary Bedrooms: Two additional moderately sized bedrooms and an additional full bathroom round out this home.

Thoughtful in its layout, this home certainly will please all members of the family and can be affordably expanded if family dynamics change.

YOU CAN EXPAND THIS HOUSE!

For the ever-growing family, this home is designed to be expanded. When you're ready to "grow" the house you can purchase its second floor addition, Plan #723041. To see the finished 2-story version go to page 169.

Copyright by designer/architect.

Images provided by designer/architect.

Plan #721021

Dimensions: 40' W x 48'9" D

Levels: 1

Heated Square Footage: 1,311

Bedrooms: 3

Bathrooms: 2

Foundation: Crawl space, slab or basement

Material Take-off Included: Yes

Price Category: B

This charming cottage-style home is perfect for the small family who values spending time together.

CAD FILE AVAILABLE

Features:

- **Covered Porch:** The front covered entry porch, featuring turned columns, is just the place to welcome family and friends home.

- **Kitchen:** This tidy kitchen features a snack bar that will get lots of use for impromptu family dining.

- **Family Room:** This family room is open to the kitchen and is bright and airy. It's sure to be the central gathering place of the home. Sliding glass doors open to a rear porch that spans the entire width of the house.

- **Bedrooms:** A spacious master suite and two additional bedrooms complete the space.

Copyright by designer/architect.

YOU CAN EXPAND THIS HOUSE!

For the ever-growing family, this home is designed to be expanded. When you're ready to "grow" the house you can purchase its second floor addition, Plan #723021. To see the finished 2-story version go to page 202.

Images provided by designer/architect.

Plan #721050

Dimensions: 31' W x 42'5" D
Levels: 1
Heated Square Footage: 1,315
Bedrooms: 3
Bathrooms: 2
Foundation: Crawl space, slab or basement
Material Take-off Included: Yes
Price Category: B

Optional Free Garage: If you would like an optional FREE 2-car garage plan, select one from page 8 or 9.

CAD FILE AVAILABLE

The brick accent on the covered porch welcomes you into this home, which is designed to fit on a narrow lot.

Features:

- **Covered Porch:** This lovely entry to the home is gracious enough for the placement of a small sitting area, a spot to gather on a warm summer evening.

- **Kitchen:** Sure to please the family cook, this room is wonderfully designed with ample counter space and a plethora of cabinets. The room also features a utility closet housing the washer and dryer.

- **Breakfast Nook:** This cozy breakfast nook, located right off the kitchen, will be bathed in natural light from its many windows and single French door. The French door at the rear of the room leads you out to a generously sized rear deck, a perfect spot for summer meals.

- **Master Suite:** Set at the rear of the home with its own hallway, the master suite features a large walk-in closet, a private bathroom, and a French door leading to the rear deck. The bathroom is sure to add to the comfort and privacy of an already lovely space.

DECK
18'-0" X 8'-0"

MASTER SUITE
12'-0" X 15'-10"

BREAKFAST NOOK
12'-4" X 7'-10"

KITCHEN
11'-0" X 14'-0"

BEDROOM #2
15'-6" X 10'-0"

LIVING ROOM
14'-4" X 19'-2"

BEDROOM #3
15'-6" X 9'-8"

PORCH
31'-0" X 8'-0"

42'-5"

31'-0"

Copyright by designer/architect.

YOU CAN EXPAND THIS HOUSE!

For the ever-growing family, this home is designed to be expanded. When you're ready to "grow" the house you can purchase its second floor addition, Plan #723050. To see the finished 2-story version go to page 194.

Plan #721038

Dimensions: 70'6" W x 27'4" D
Levels: 1
Heated Square Footage: 1,324
Bedrooms: 3
Bathrooms: 2
Foundation: Crawl space, slab or basement
Material Take-off Included: Yes
Price Category: B

Images provided by designer/architect.

Designed for the young family, this home has a good balance between private and public spaces. Its simple layout allows for easy expansion.

Features:

- **Great Room:** Enter immediately into the heart of this home. This expansive space is open to both the dining room and the kitchen, making it the gathering spot for all.

- **Kitchen:** The family cook will surely be pleased with the layout of this kitchen. Open to the dining room, it features a stand-alone island with countertop seating, which enables the cook to interact with others while preparing meals.

- **Dining Room:** Connected to both the kitchen and great room, this space will be to host to many dinner parties as well as serve for the everyday family dinners. Sliding doors that lead to a gracious rear deck will encourage outdoor dining, as well.

- **Master Suite:** Being set apart from the secondary bedrooms in the home gives this lovely room a touch more privacy. The suite includes a private bath to add comfort.

- **Secondary Bedrooms:** Moderately sized, these rooms are just off the great room and have their own hallway, as well as a centrally located bathroom.

Designed for the young family, this home has a good balance between private and public spaces. Its simple layout allows for easy expansion.

CAD FILE AVAILABLE

YOU CAN EXPAND THIS HOUSE!

For the ever-growing family, this home is designed to be expanded. When you're ready to "grow" the house you can purchase its second floor addition, Plan #723038. To see the finished 2-story version go to page 196.

Plan #721037

Dimensions: 49' W x 50'3" D

Levels: 1

Heated Square Footage: 1,328

Bedrooms: 3

Bathrooms: 2

Foundation: Crawl space, slab or basement

Material Take-off Included: Yes

Price Category: B

Images provided by designer/architect.

The thoughtful design of this home makes it affordable to build. The home can also expand to the meet the needs of a growing family.

This charming three-bedroom home is the perfect starter home for a young family.

Features:

- **Living/Dining Room:** Step through the entry directly into this gracious space. These open areas provide the home with a continuous flow between both rooms, making this the central gathering spot for all.

- **Kitchen:** This kitchen's U-shaped design offers plenty of counter and cabinet space, making organization easy.

- **Master Suite:** This room will provide you with the comfort and solace you seek. The en-suite bath features a vanity with dual sinks and an oversize tub that's perfect for soaking in after a long day.

- Bedrooms: Two additional bedrooms and a full bathroom help to complete the home.

Copyright by designer/architect.

YOU CAN EXPAND THIS HOUSE!

For the ever-growing family, this home is designed to be expanded. When you're ready to "grow" the house you can purchase its second floor addition, Plan #723037. To see the finished 2-story version go to page 141.

Plan #721006

Dimensions: 62' W x 32' D

Levels: 1

Heated Square Footage: 1,334

Bedrooms: 2

Bathrooms: 2

Foundation: Crawl space, slab or basement

Material Take-off Included: Yes

Price Category: B

This house is perfect as a starter home with opportunities for later expansions.

CAD FILE AVAILABLE

Features:

- Foyer: The spacious foyer makes for an inviting entrance into a charming open floor plan. The space is complete with a coat closet and is just steps away from the formal living room.

- Master Suite: Plenty of windows, a walk-in closet, and a luxurious bath with dual sinks and a large oval tub make this suite the perfect retreat at the end of a long day.

- Living Room: This room is the perfect place for family gatherings. The open design of the space allows for the easy flow of guests while you are entertaining.

- Kitchen: This U-shaped kitchen that is open to the dining room offers modern conveniences. The open design of the space contributes to pleasurable meal prep and dining. Large sliding glass doors provide easy access to outdoor dining as well.

- Deck: The ample-size deck at the rear of the house expands the indoor living space to the beautiful outdoors through sliding glass doors.

This house is one that all your guest and family can truly see as a home.

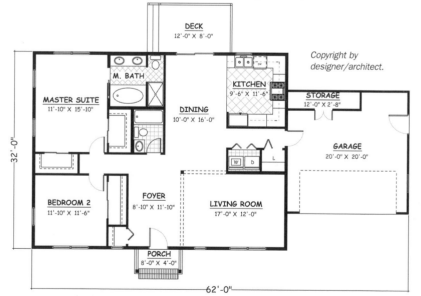

Copyright by designer/architect.

YOU CAN EXPAND THIS HOUSE!

For the ever-growing family, this home is designed to be expanded. When you're ready to "grow" the house you can purchase its second floor addition, Plan #723006. To see the finished 2-story version go to page 192.

Plan #721070

Dimensions: 71'3" W x 27'6" D

Levels: 1

Heated Square Footage: 1,345

Bedrooms: 3

Bathrooms: 2

Foundation: Crawl space, slab or basement

Material Take-off Included: Yes

Price Category: B

Images provided by designer/architect.

This lovely ranch home, with its cozy covered entry and simple yet elegant design, features spaces that are sure to please all members of the family.

Features:

- Covered Entry: This simple covered entry welcomes you home, while providing you with shelter from the elements.

- Dining Room: Open and airy, this dining room is sure to be the host to both family meals and intimate dinner parties. Sliding glass doors at the rear of the room connect the room to a large rear deck, encouraging dining outdoors.

- Kitchen: Thoughtful design makes this kitchen easy to organize. Adjacent to the dining area, it encourages interaction between the cook and diners during mealtime prep.

- Master Suite: Set apart from the secondary bedrooms in the home, this master suite offers a bit of privacy. The suite features a generously sized walk-in closet and a private bathroom that houses an oversized tub, a separate shower, and dual vanities, continuing the feeling of solitude.

Thoughtful design enables this home to not only be affordably built but also expanded upon if the family's needs change.

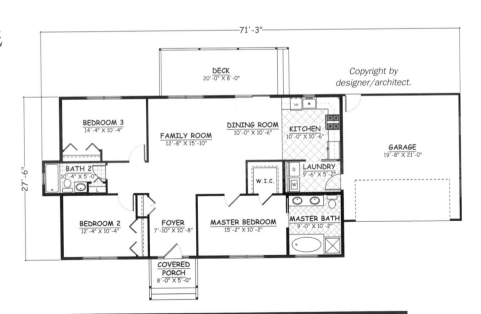

YOU CAN EXPAND THIS HOUSE!

For the ever-growing family, this home is designed to be expanded. When you're ready to "grow" the house you can purchase its second floor addition, Plan #723070. To see the finished 2-story version go to page 163.

Images provided by designer/architect.

Plan #721029

Dimensions: 45'5" W x 50' D

Levels: 1

Heated Square Footage: 1,358

Bedrooms: 3

Bathrooms: 2

Foundation: Crawl space, slab or basement

Material Take-off Included: Yes

Price Category: B

Hip roofs and large windows grace the exterior of this home, giving it a pleasant appeal.

Features:

- **Covered Porch:** This moderate covered entry porch provides an elegant entrance to the home.

- **Living Room:** This spacious area flows into the kitchen, making it the perfect room for entertaining friends and family.

- **Kitchen:** This warm and inviting kitchen is open to the living room and features French doors to the rear deck. The pantry offers plenty of storage, and the snack bar provides seating for informal meals.

- **Deck:** The large deck that is connected to both the kitchen and a bedroom is the ideal spot for enjoying a morning cup of coffee or for grilling in the summer.

- **Master Suite:** This room is bathed in natural light by a large triple window. The generous walk-in closet and en-suite bath add to the luxury of the space. The whirlpool tub, separate shower, and dual sinks complete the lavish amenities.

- **Secondary Bedrooms:** Two additional bedrooms share a full-size bath. One also features French doors to the rear deck.

Copyright by designer/architect.

YOU CAN EXPAND THIS HOUSE!

For the ever-growing family, this home is designed to be expanded. When you're ready to "grow" the house you can purchase its second floor addition, Plan #723029. To see the finished 2-story version go to page 133.

Plan #721039

Dimensions: 70' W x 39' D

Levels: 1

Heated Square Footage: 1,358

Bedrooms: 3

Bathrooms: 2

Foundation: Crawl space, slab or basement

Material Take-off Included: Yes

Price Category: B

Images provided by designer/architect.

The rooflines of this home add to its curb appeal.

Features:

- **Living Room:** Open to the dining room, kitchen, and entry hall, this gracious room welcomes friends and family alike.

- **Kitchen:** This tidy kitchen, with its thoughtful layout and large pantry, makes it easy for the family cook to prepare meals.

- **Dining Room:** Connected to both the kitchen and living room, this space will certainly be used for both intimate family dinners and formal gatherings. Sliding glass doors that lead to the extensive rear deck ensure that dining outdoors will be a common occurrence.

- **Master Suite:** Set apart from the secondary bedrooms in the home, this generously sized master suite features a private bath for added comfort. At the back of the room, French doors open to an expansive deck.

- **Secondary Bedrooms:** There are two additional bedrooms in the home. Both feature lovely twin double-hung window units that will bathe the space in natural light.

This home can easily be expanded to accommodate the needs of a growing family.

Copyright by designer/architect.

YOU CAN EXPAND THIS HOUSE!

For the ever-growing family, this home is designed to be expanded. When you're ready to "grow" the house you can purchase its second floor addition, Plan #723039. To see the finished 2-story version go to page 142.

Plan #721042

Dimensions: 62' W x 36'6" D
Levels: 1
Heated Square Footage: 1,360
Bedrooms: 3
Bathrooms: 2
Foundation: Crawl space, slab or basement
Material Take-off Included: Yes
Price Category: B

This home features a wonderfully spacious rear deck and a charming front covered porch. It is perfect for the family that enjoys outdoor living space.

CAD FILE AVAILABLE

Features:

- Covered Porch: Deep enough to fit a small seating area, this covered porch welcomes all home.

- Dining Room: This dining room is open to the kitchen and provides an easy flow between rooms. The sliding glass door to the expansive rear deck will ensure alfresco dining.

- Kitchen: This well-designed kitchen offers plenty of cabinet and counter space that will surely please the family cook.

- Master Suite: Set apart from the other bedrooms in the home, is a spacious master suite featuring a walk-in closet and a private bath. The bath features an oversize tub, a separate shower, and a dual vanity adding both comfort and privacy.

- Secondary Bedrooms: Rounding out the home are two additional moderately sized bedrooms and a full bath.

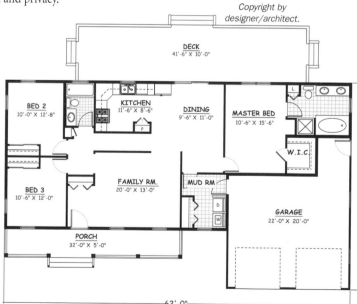

YOU CAN EXPAND THIS HOUSE!

For the ever-growing family, this home is designed to be expanded. When you're ready to "grow" the house you can purchase its second floor addition, Plan #723042. To see the finished 2-story version go to page 165.

Images provided by designer/architect.

Plan #721072

Dimensions: 78'4" W x 31' D

Levels: 1

Heated Square Footage: 1,366

Bedrooms: 3

Bathrooms: 1

Foundation: Crawl space, slab or basement

Material Take-off Included: Yes

Price Category: B

• Secondary Bedrooms: Two additional bedrooms, featuring generously sized closets, provide all the private space a family will need.

This moderately sized home has clean and simple lines that will make future expansion an affordable option as the family grows.

The large multiple window units, front porch, and covered breezeway connecting the house to the garage add curb appeal and functionality. The interior of the home is filled with amenities to please the entire family.

CAD FILE AVAILABLE

Features:

• Kitchen: This tidy kitchen features a cooktop, a wall oven, and a snack bar that is perfect for informal meals. A door leads to the expansive rear deck, extending the living space to the exterior.

• Dining Room: This dining room is just steps from the kitchen and the living room, which makes it ideal for entertaining. It also features an entry leading to the covered breezeway.

• Master Bedroom: Relax at the end of the day in this lovely master bedroom, with its large walk-in closet.

Copyright by designer/architect.

DECK
25'-6" X 8'-0"

MASTER BEDROOM
15'-0" X 12'-0"

BATH

KITCHEN
10'-0" X 12'-0"

DINING ROOM
15'-0" X 12'-0"

BREEZEWAY
10'-0" X 18'-0"

GARAGE
22'-0" X 24'-0"

31'-0"

LIVING ROOM
21'-0" X 15'-0"

BEDROOM #2
12'-0" X 15'-0"

BEDROOM #3
12'-0" X 15'-0"

COVERED PORCH
22'-0" X 3'-6"

78'-4"

YOU CAN EXPAND THIS HOUSE!

For the ever-growing family, this home is designed to be expanded. When you're ready to "grow" the house you can purchase its second floor addition, Plan #723072. To see the finished 2-story version go to page 185.

Images provided by designer/architect.

Plan #721069

Dimensions: 76'10" W x 31'4" D
Levels: 1
Heated Square Footage: 1,370
Bedrooms: 3
Bathrooms: 2
Foundation: Crawl space, slab or basement
Material Take-off Included: Yes
Price Category: B

The multiple gables, dormers, and a gracious front porch give this lovely home a country feel.

CAD FILE AVAILABLE

Features:

- Covered Porch: Many evenings of relaxation are sure to be spent sitting on this charming covered porch, which features turned columns.

- Dining Room: Bright and airy, this dining room will certainly be used for everyday family meals as well as intimate dinner parties. With the space being open to the living room, the transition from pre-dinner conversation to the sit-down meal will be easy.

- Kitchen: This U-shaped kitchen, with its plethora of cabinets and ample counter space, is a cook's dream. The moderately sized pantry provides even more storage space, making organization easy.

- Master Suit: Featuring a generously sized walk-in closet and a private bathroom, this spacious master suite is sure to please. The private bathroom with dual vanities, an over-sized tub, and a separate shower will provide you with the comfort and privacy you seek.

This home can be affordably built due to its simple and thoughtful design. The layout of the home ensures that it can be expanded quite easily as the family grows.

YOU CAN EXPAND THIS HOUSE!

For the ever-growing family, this home is designed to be expanded. When you're ready to "grow" the house you can purchase its second floor addition, Plan #723069. To see the finished 2-story version go to page 188.

Plan #721058

Dimensions: 68' W x 36' D
Levels: 1
Heated Square Footage: 1,372
Bedrooms: 3
Bathrooms: 2
Foundation: Crawl space, slab or basement
Material Take-off Included: Yes
Price Category: B

The wraparound front porch gives this ranch-style home a country cottage feel.

CAD FILE AVAILABLE

Features:

- Covered Porch: Large enough to accommodate a seating area, this charming covered wraparound porch is sure to have all gathering on a warm summer's evening.

- Foyer: This expansive entry foyer welcomes you into the home. With its ample size, this area may be just the spot to display a few pieces of treasured artwork.

- Kitchen: This U-shaped kitchen, with its plethora of cabinets and ample counter space, is sure to please the family cook. A cased opening leading to the dining/family room will keep the chef engaged while preparing meals.

- Master Suite: With a spa-like private bathroom, this master suite is hard to resist. The bathroom features a dual vanity, a separate shower, and a large soaking tub that is guaranteed to leave you feeling refreshed and renewed.

- Secondary Bedrooms: Two additional bedrooms and a full-sized bathroom help to complete the private areas of the charming home.

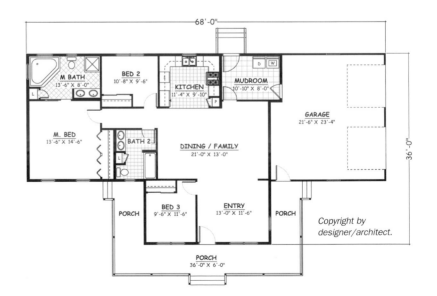

Rear Elevation

YOU CAN EXPAND THIS HOUSE!

For the ever-growing family, this home is designed to be expanded. When you're ready to "grow" the house you can purchase its second floor addition, Plan #723058. To see the finished 2-story version go to page 158.

Right Elevation

Left Elevation

SMARTtip
Practical Role of a Window

Always consider the way a window opens and closes before choosing a window treatment. Double-hung windows pose the fewest problems. However, casement windows and French doors that swing into a room require a design that will not obstruct their paths of operation.

This article was reprinted from *The New Smart Approach to Kids' Rooms* (Creative Homeowner 2005).

Bathrooms Designed for Kids

Bathing is a key part in everyone's life, and children are no exception. The bathroom, therefore, is an important environment that deserves particular attention. One that is designed around a child's smaller size enables him to move most effortlessly into taking charge of his own personal hygiene. Special safety concerns should always take precedence over other design elements. If you share a bathroom with your child, take prudent steps to accommodate his size and needs in addition to your own.

Most newer homes contain a second bath, which is often designated for the children in the family. What should be included in it depends on the ages and number of children who will use it. If your child is lucky enough to have the room all to herself, plan it for her growing and changing needs. Anticipate the storage and lighting requirements of a teenage girl's grooming habits, for example. If more than one child will share the bath, consider their genders, and whether they will use the room at the same time. How many lavatories do they need? At least two. The best designs for shared bathrooms include compartmentalized spaces—one for the toilet, one for bathing (with a separate shower, if space permits), and one for grooming. A double-bowl vanity would be most practical. At least try to set the toilet apart from the bathing area—even a half wall will help.

There are fixtures on the market that are tailored for a child's use, but you may not want to make the investment in something that will have to be replaced once your child matures or leaves home. As always, it's a matter of choice. If you want to make the room appealing to the younger set but your funds are limited, look into wallpaper

Top left: A rubber mat will prevent slipping.

Above: Avoid accidents by installing antiscalding devices on faucets.

Below: Make the room accessible for children.

patterns that have a juvenile theme and use lively, kid-friendly colors and accessories.

Sensible and Basic

There are lots of things you can do to make any bathroom practical, comfortable, and safe for family members of all ages. When you're planning to build a bath that will be used by a child, careful consideration should be given to both of you, but pay particular attention to the age-specific needs of the youngster.

Caring for Baby

The baby's bathroom should be a warm, draft-free environment. You should organize this space around your needs for bathing the baby. You'll want everything right at hand so you can keep a constant vigil. Remember: a child can drown in less than 2 inches of water in a baby tub or toilet, or even in a bucket filled with water.

Appropriate furnishings include a comfortable seating area where you can dry the baby or towel a toddler, a convenient place to house the baby bath, perhaps a changing table, and ample storage for the baby's bath toiletries and linens, diapers, bath toys, a hamper, and a diaper pail.

Consider your own comfort when positioning the baby bath. Counter height will probably be most comfortable, or you may consider a freestanding bathing unit. Install an anti-scald faucet, which contains a device that keeps water temperate. Because a child's skin is thinner and more tender than an adult's, it can be burned within 3 seconds after coming into contact with water that's over 120 degrees Fahrenheit. Fixtures equipped with a pressure-balancing feature will maintain the same degree of hotness even when cold-

water flow is reduced (when you flush the toilet, for example). Style-wise, a single-lever faucet, as opposed to two separate valves, is much easier for a child to use when regulating water flow and temperature. You can present some of them, as well.

A hand-held shower device that allows you to position the showerhead at a convenient level can be retrofitted onto a con-

Above: Special hand-painted tile looks charming in this one-of-a-kind boys' bathroom.

ventional showerhead or installed separately. Look for one that's been designed for children to handle.

Once you start to bathe the baby in the tub, you'll want to make it slip-resistant. A textured surface helps. You can easily add this with antislip decals and mats. Install soft covers over the faucet and spout so that a little one can't be bruised. Parents can protect themselves by using a mat that extends over the side of the tub to cushion their arms while holding up and bathing the baby. Part of the mat also rests on the floor to pad adult knees.

It's a good idea to install easy-care wallcovering and flooring. From the first moment a toddler learns to splash, all claims to toughness are tested. Classic selections include tiles, waterproof wallcovering that has a built-in

mildewcide, solid-surfacing material or a fiberglass tub surround, and gloss or semi-gloss paint, with a mildewcide.

A one-piece toilet hugs closer to the wall and has an elongated bowl that makes toilet training a little easier. Because it sits lower than a two-piece model, this type is better-scaled for a child yet comfortable for an adult.

Helping Preschoolers

Toilet training and the beginning of self-grooming mark this stage, necessitating a few changes in the way your child will use the bathroom. Tubs and toys seem to go together here. You'll need more room for toy storage; gear it to something your child can access himself, such as a plastic basket that can be kept inside a vanity cabinet or on the floor of the linen closet. You'll also need a place to keep a small step stool when it's not in use as a booster in front of the lav. If you're renovating or building a new bathroom for a child, consider installing a lav into a vanity or countertop that is built at a lower height.

Because the standard rule of thumb is to install a mirror 8 inches above a standard-height vanity countertop (to avoid splatters), you may want to include a standing mirror or one that extends from the wall at a proper height to suit your child. To encourage neatness, a towel rack that is within a child's reach is another good idea. A low freestanding rack works well, too.

Accommodating School-Age Kids

Socializing skills in school reinforce the needs for individual identity at home, including specific grooming styles as a child gets older. Storage niches once devoted to bathtub toys can be used for hair ribbons, special soaps and shampoos, or other toiletries. Keep electrical appliances, such as hair dryers and steam rollers, or electric shavers out of the room until your child is old enough to handle them responsibly and understand the hazards posed by electricity and water.

More About Shared Spaces. The crunch starts when kids begin toilet training and continues through the school years when everybody has to get bathed, dressed, and out of the house at the same time. To cope with the increased demands, create private areas within the room, such as the separate bathing, grooming, and toilet areas suggested earlier. Color-code towels and accessories so that everyone can clearly see what belongs to each person who uses the room.into a vanity or countertop that is built at a lower height.

Above: Hang a deep basket from a peg, and tuck bath toys or small laundry items into it.

Left: Here's a stylish way to make sure everyone has his or her own bath towel.

Bathroom Safety

Here's a list of things that you should have on hand at all times to make sure any bathroom
that is intended for a child's use is safe and comfortable.

Tub & Shower Areas

- Safety glazing on glass doors
- Doors that are hinged to swing out into the room
- Grab bars at adult and child heights
- A shower seat

Toilets & Water Closets

- No lock on the water-closet door
- Locked toilet lid
- Tip-resistant training step stool
- Toilet-paper holder installed within the child's reach

Plumbing

- Water valves within easy reach
- Single-lever controls
- Anti-scald and pressure-balanced faucets
- Adjustable child-size hand shower

Electric

- Ground-fault circuit interrupters (GFCIs) on all outlets
- Covered receptacles

- Vapor-proof light fixtures installed out of the child's reach
- Low-voltage task lighting
- Night light

Cabinet & Counter Surfaces

- Small doors that can be easily opened
- Childproof locks
- Locked medicine cabinet
- No more than 8-inch-deep cabinets installed over the toilet
- Rounded corners and edges
- Seating for drying off and dressing

Flooring

- Nonslip surface
- Water-resistant surface
- Anchors for area rugs and mats

Windows & Doors

- Doors that swing into the room
- Door locks that can be opened from the outside
- Safety bars on all windows

Finally, move certain activities to other rooms. Dressing and grooming can be done in the bedroom, for example. Whether your home has one small bathroom that is shared by all or a separate bathroom for each member of the family, there are steps you can take to make space more efficient.

Step One: Plan storage. If you don't have a linen closet or large cabinet in the room, add shelving to hold extra towels, bars of soap, and other necessities. Small storage niches created between the wall studs make handy spots for shampoo and toiletries. Mount hooks or pegged racks to the wall or behind the door for hanging extra towels or robes. New medicine cabinets come with extra deep shelves that are large enough to hold rolls of toilet paper or bulky hair dryers.

Step Two: Consider a better way to use space.
Cramped floor space? Replace the bathroom door with a pocket door to free up floor space that might allow you to create a separate shower stall or a double vanity.

Step Three: Light it properly. Besides general lighting, plan adequate task lighting at the sink and mirror for grooming. Avoid locating lights above the mirror where they create glare and shadows. Side lights are better.

Step Four: Keep the air clear. Invest in a good exhaust fan to make the room's air quality healthier and surfaces less slick. It will also deter water build up and mildew, which can damage surfaces and materials.

1. Rounded edges are gentle on kids.
2. Here's one way to keep towels neat.
3. A spacious vanity and lots of storage are important when kids share a bathroom.
4. Kids can help pick out cute accessories for their bathroom.
5. A shower seat is a safety feature that should be included in every bathroom.
6. Secure all rugs with a nonskid backing.
7. A handheld sprayer in the bath makes it easy to rinse shampoo out of hair.
8. Kids can personalize the space by painting their own designs in the room.

Design Ideas for Kids' Baths

Images provided by designer/architect.

Plan #721063

Dimensions: 50'4" W x 27'6" D
Levels: 1
Heated Square Footage: 1,381
Bedrooms: 3
Bathrooms: 2
Foundation: Crawl space, slab or basement
Material Take-off Included: Yes
Price Category: B

Optional Free Garage: If you would like an optional FREE 2-car garage plan, select one from page 8 or 9.

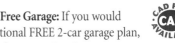

The expansive covered front porch and dormers give this wonderfully designed ranch home a bit of country charm.

Features:

• Covered Porch: This delightful covered porch spanning the length of the home will surely be a spot to sit on a warm evening.

• Great Room: Step directly into this grand great room from the covered front porch, a space that is certain to be the gathering spot for all. The room is open to both the kitchen and dining room, allowing for a seamless transition from one area to the next.

• Kitchen: The center island in this kitchen provides the chef with additional counter space, making meal preparations a joy. Open to both the great room and the great room, this allows the chef to interact with the rest of the family.

• Master Suite: Set apart from the secondary bedrooms in the home is this generously sized master suite. The suite features a large walk-in closet and a private bathroom, thus providing you with the perfect place to relax after a long day. The bathroom features a tub, a separate shower, and dual vanities, adding to the privacy and comfort of the suite.

• Secondary Bedrooms - There are two graciously sized secondary bedrooms in the home, along with an additional full bathroom.

The generous layout of this home is perfect for the young family. It is affordable to build and can easily be expanded to fit the needs of the ever-changing family dynamics.

SMARTtip

Arts and Crafts Style in Your Kitchen

The heart of this style lies in its earthy connection. The more you can bring nature into it, the more authentic it will appear. An easy way to do this is with plants. Open the space up to nature with glass doors that provide a view to a green garden.

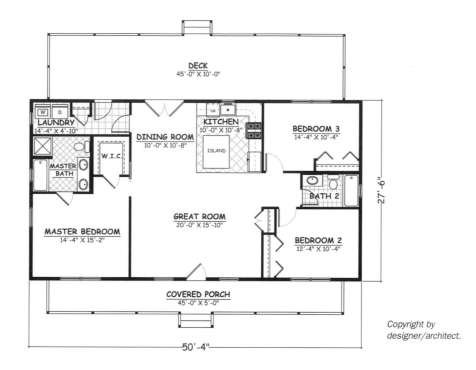

DECK
45'-0" X 10'-0"

LAUNDRY
14'-4" X 4'-10"

DINING ROOM
10'-0" X 10'-8"

KITCHEN
10'-0" X 10'-8"

ISLAND

BEDROOM 3
14'-4" X 10'-4"

MASTER BATH

W.I.C.

BATH 2

GREAT ROOM
20'-0" X 15'-10"

MASTER BEDROOM
14'-4" X 15'-2"

BEDROOM 2
12'-4" X 10'-4"

27'-6"

COVERED PORCH
45'-0" X 5'-0"

50'-4"

Rear Elevation

YOU CAN EXPAND THIS HOUSE!

For the ever-growing family, this home is designed to be expanded. When you're ready to "grow" the house you can purchase its second floor addition, Plan #723063. To see the finished 2-story version go to page 114.

Left Elevation

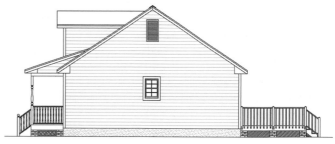

Right Elevation

Images provided by designer/architect.

Plan #721008

Dimensions: 50' W x 45'6" D

Levels: 1

Heated Square Footage: 1,375

Bedrooms: 3

Bathrooms: 2

Foundation: Crawl space, slab or basement

Material Take-off Included: Yes

Price Category: B

This traditional-style home has simple rooflines, making it easy to build.

Features:

- Covered Porch: This large covered porch is the ideal place to gather in the evenings and enjoy the outdoors while being sheltered from the elements.

- Kitchen: This spacious U-shaped kitchen features a snack bar and a breakfast area that opens onto an expansive deck. This room will become a central gathering place for family and friends.

- Master Suite: Offers a large bath with whirlpool tub, private toilet area, separate shower, and dual vanities. It's the perfect place for busy couples to get ready for the day. The room also features a large walk-in-closet, as well as French doors that open onto a large deck.

- Deck: This large deck is accessible from both the master suite and the breakfast area. You will find it to be the perfect spot for a quiet coffee in the morning or a large family event.

Copyright by designer/architect.

YOU CAN EXPAND THIS HOUSE!

For the ever-growing family, this home is designed to be expanded. When you're ready to "grow" the house you can purchase its second floor addition, Plan #723008. To see the finished 2-story version go to page 147.

Images provided by designer/architect.

Plan #721073

Dimensions: 49'2" W x 47' D
Levels: 1
Heated Square Footage: 1,380
Bedrooms: 3
Bathrooms: 1
Foundation: Crawl space, slab or basement
Material Take-off Included: Yes
Price Category: B

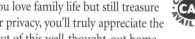

If you love family life but still treasure your privacy, you'll truly appreciate the layout of this well-thought-out home.

Features:

- Covered Porch: This covered entry porch is centered on the front of this home, adding to its curb appeal. It will offer shelter from the elements as you greet your guests.

- Living Room: This living room is part of an open floor plan that allows family and guests to flow from room to room. It is both large enough for a crowd and cozy enough for the family.

- Kitchen: Enjoy this well-designed space that features a double sink and both a range and a wall oven. Large cased openings give it a touch of elegance.

- Dining Room: This dining room adjoins the kitchen, making family meals a joy. A double French door unit leads you into the backyard.

- Secondary Bedrooms: Two additional bedrooms flanking a full bathroom complete the home.

BEDROOM #2
13'-0" X 13'-0"

DINING ROOM
10'-0" X 11'-0"

KITCHEN
11'-0" X 11'-0"

MASTER BEDROOM
15'-0" X 15'-0"

BATH

LIVING ROOM
16'-0" X 15'-0"

PANTRY

W.I.C.

BEDROOM #3
13'-0" X 13'-0"

UTILITY

MASTER BATH

COVERED PORCH
16'-0" X 4'-0"

GARAGE
20'-0" X 20'-0"

Copyright by designer/architect.

47'-0"

49'-2"

YOU CAN EXPAND THIS HOUSE!

For the ever-growing family, this home is designed to be expanded. When you're ready to "grow" the house you can purchase its second floor addition, Plan #723073. To see the finished 2-story version go to page 200.

Plan #721046

Dimensions: 58'2" W x 40'3" D

Levels: 1

Heated Square Footage: 1,384

Bedrooms: 3

Bathrooms: 2

Foundation: Crawl space, slab or basement

Material Take-off Included: Yes

Price Category: B

The multiple gables, covered porch, and large windows combine to give this home character. The well-designed floor plan provides plenty of public and private spaces.

Features:

- Covered Porch: This covered porch presents a gracious entryway into the home, complete with columns and brick accents.

- Great Room: Enter the home and step directly into this wonderfully spacious room. This great room is not only open to the kitchen but also has a sliding glass door leading to an expansive rear deck. The open floor plan that extends to the outdoors is ideal for entertaining family and friends.

- Kitchen: Located directly off of the great room, this L-shaped kitchen will surely please any cook in the family.

- Master Suite: This master bathroom is complete with a large walk-in closet, a whirlpool tub, and a patio door to the rear deck, making it a spa-like oasis to retreat to after a long day.

- Secondary Bedrooms: Two additional bedrooms, with generous closets and a full bathroom, round out the private areas of the home.

Images provided by designer/architect.

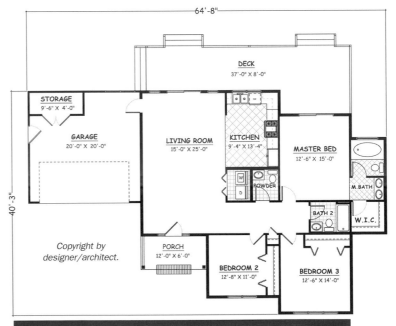

Copyright by designer/architect.

YOU CAN EXPAND THIS HOUSE!

For the ever-growing family, this home is designed to be expanded. When you're ready to "grow" the house you can purchase its second floor addition, Plan #723046. To see the finished 2-story version go to page 145.

Plan #721047

Dimensions: 26'3" W x 58' D

Levels: 1

Heated Square Footage: 1,384

Bedrooms: 3

Bathrooms: 2

Foundation: Crawl space, slab or basement

Material Take-off Included: Yes

Price Category: B

Optional Free Garage: If you would like an optional FREE 2-car garage plan, select one from page 8 or 9.

CAD FILE AVAILABLE

This attractive home is designed for a narrow lot, without sacrificing style or spaciousness.

Features:

• **Covered Porch:** This covered porch provides a roomy place to sit and enjoy the outdoors.

• **Great Room:** This generously sized great room spans the width of the home and features two sets of triple windows, allowing for an abundance of natural light. Connected to the kitchen through a snack bar, this room will surely be the main gathering place of the entire family.

Copyright by designer/architect.

• **Kitchen:** The wraparound snack bar linking this kitchen to the great room will be your favorite feature of this efficiently designed space. For evenings of alfresco dining, the kitchen has a lovely French door that leads to the side deck.

• **Master Suite:** Design elements such as a large walk-in closet, a private bathroom, and sliding doors to an expansive deck help to make this room a true oasis. The private bathroom features a sunlit whirlpool tub, a separate shower, a private toilet room, and a double vanity, ensuring privacy and comfort.

• **Secondary Bedrooms:** A full bathroom and two additional bedrooms complete the private areas of the home.

The unique design of this home makes it ideal for a lot with limited space. Its layout allows for future expansion as the family continues to grow.

YOU CAN EXPAND THIS HOUSE!

For the ever-growing family, this home is designed to be expanded. When you're ready to "grow" the house you can purchase its second floor addition, Plan #723047. To see the finished 2-story version go to page 199.

Images provided by designer/architect.

Plan #721053

Dimensions: 50' W x 49'3" D

Levels: 1

Heated Square Footage: 1,384

Bedrooms: 3

Bathrooms: 2

Foundation: Crawl space, slab or basement

Material Take-off Included: Yes

Price Category: B

This ranch-style home is given a country feel with its wraparound porch.

CAD FILE AVAILABLE

Features:

- **Living Room:** Accessed from the front entry door and a side French door, this gracious living room will offer the homeowners a wonderful place to relax and entertain.

- **Dining Room:** Adjacent to the kitchen and open to the family room, this dining room is the perfect spot for family meals or festive dinner parties. At the rear of the room are sliding glass doors leading to the generously sized rear deck, ensuring many occasions of dining outdoors.

- **Family Room:** Open to the dining room and next to the kitchen, this vast family room will surely be the spot where all gravitate.

- **Master Suite:** A large walk-in closet and private bathroom give additional appeal to this already generously sized master suite. The space will certainly offer you a bit of respite after a long day.

- **Secondary Bedrooms:** Two moderately sized bedrooms along with a full bathroom round out the private areas of this home.

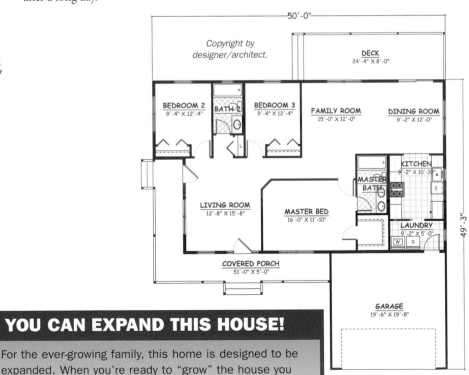

YOU CAN EXPAND THIS HOUSE!

For the ever-growing family, this home is designed to be expanded. When you're ready to "grow" the house you can purchase its second floor addition, Plan #723053. To see the finished 2-story version go to page 126.

Images provided by designer/architect.

Plan #721014

Dimensions: 56' W x 43'6" D

Levels: 1

Heated Square Footage: 1,386

Bedrooms: 3

Bathrooms: 2

Foundation: Crawl space, slab or basement

Material Take-off Included: Yes

Price Category: B

You will love the free-flowing nature of this thoughtfully designed ranch home.

Features:

- **Entry Porch:** This covered porch gives the entrance to this home an understated elegance.

- **Living Room:** This lovely room, with its open design, welcomes both friends and family into the home.

- **Dining Room:** With sliding glass doors leading to a moderately sized deck, this room makes a weeknight family dinner or a formal dinner party with friends a pleasure.

- **Kitchen:** This tidy kitchen, with its thoughtful layout and large pantry, makes it easy for the family cook to prepare meals.

- **Master Suite:** Set apart from the secondary bedrooms in the home, this generously sized master suite features a private bath for added comfort.

Copyright by designer/architect.

YOU CAN EXPAND THIS HOUSE!

For the ever-growing family, this home is designed to be expanded. When you're ready to "grow" the house you can purchase its second floor addition, Plan #723014. To see the finished 2-story version go to page 183.

Images provided by designer/architect.

Plan #721001

Dimensions: 46' W x 40' D

Levels: 1

Heated Square Footage: 1,390

Bedrooms: 3

Bathrooms: 2½

Foundation: Crawl space, slab or basement

Material Take-off Included: Yes

Price Category: B

This lovely home offers a wonderfully open kitchen and dining area, perfect for family gatherings.

CAD FILE AVAILABLE • CAD

Features:

- Covered Porch: Simple, yet stately, columns flank this covered porch, providing an inviting entry to this charming home.

- Living Room: Located off the entrance, this formal living room welcomes guests for an evening of enjoyment.

- Dining Room: With large front windows and a sliding glass door, this room is bright and inviting. The door opens onto a generously sized deck, allowing for both indoor and outdoor dining.

- Kitchen: This spacious kitchen has ample counter space for preparing meals, while the countertop seating area allows interaction between the chef and the rest of the family.

- Master Suite: Set toward the rear of the home, this spacious room has two walk-in closets and a private bath. The bath features an oversized tub and dual vanity, adding comfort as well as privacy.

Floor plan:

46'-0"

- BEDROOM 2 — 12'-6" X 11'-6"
- BATH 2
- BEDROOM 3 — 11'-0" X 8'-0"
- MASTER BATH — 10'-6" X 8'-0"
- KITCHEN — 11'-0" X 12'-6"
- POWDER RM
- REAR HALL — 9'-9" X 4'-0"
- MASTER BEDROOM — 15'-0" X 11'-0"
- DECK — 10'-0" X 10'-0"
- DINING ROOM — 11'0" X 10'-6"
- LIVING ROOM — 10'0" X 12'-6"
- GARAGE — 20'-0" X 20'-0"
- COVERED PORCH — 16'-0" X 4'-0"

40'-0"

Copyright by designer/architect.

YOU CAN EXPAND THIS HOUSE!

For the ever-growing family, this home is designed to be expanded. When you're ready to "grow" the house you can purchase its second floor addition, Plan #723001. To see the finished 2-story version go to page 197.

Plan #721031

Dimensions: 68' W x 29' D

Levels: 1

Heated Square Footage: 1,392

Bedrooms: 3

Bathrooms: 2

Foundation: Crawl space, slab or basement

Material Take-off Included: Yes

Price Category: B

Images provided by designer/architect.

This spacious traditional-style home, with its inviting front porch, is designed for comfortable family living.

CAD FILE AVAILABLE

Features:

- **Covered Porch:** This covered porch provides a place to sit while waiting for family and friends to arrive.

- **Great Room:** This generously sized room, with its open views of the kitchen, is the perfect place for family gatherings.

- **Kitchen:** Perfectly located off the family room and connected to the breakfast room by a snack bar, this kitchen is ideal for informal gatherings and family meals.

- **Rear Deck:** Accessed through patio doors from the master bedroom or the breakfast room, this rear deck is just the place for outdoor entertaining.

- **Master Suite:** This master suite is a comfortable place to relax after a long day. Its

amenities include a large walk-in closet, a spa-like master bath, and a patio door that connects to an expansive rear deck. The bath features a whirlpool tub, a separate shower, and a private toilet room.

- **Secondary Bedrooms:** Two additional bedrooms and a full bath round out the private areas of the home, providing space for all.

Copyright by designer/architect.

YOU CAN EXPAND THIS HOUSE!

For the ever-growing family, this home is designed to be expanded. When you're ready to "grow" the house you can purchase its second floor addition, Plan #723031. To see the finished 2-story version go to page 144.

Plan #721034

Dimensions: 64'5" W x 28' D

Levels: 1

Heated Square Footage: 1,392

Bedrooms: 3

Bathrooms: 2

Foundation: Crawl space, slab or basement

Material Take-off Included: Yes

Price Category: B

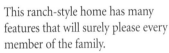

This ranch-style home has many features that will surely please every member of the family.

Features:

- Covered Porch: This covered porch is a wonderful space that will provide the perfect place for sitting on a warm summer evening.

- Living Room: When stepping through the front door, you are welcomed immediately into this living room, the heart of this home.

- Dining Room: This dining room is open to the kitchen and has sliding glass doors that open onto a large deck, perfect for dining alfresco.

- Kitchen: This spacious kitchen, with its large pantry, has a wonderful amount of storage, making it easy to organize all of your food and appliances. The kitchen also features a countertop eating area, inviting interaction between the cook and the family.

- Master Suite: Separate from the other bedrooms, this master suite features a private bath with a large tub and a double vanity.

- Secondary Bedroom: This modestly sized bedroom offers a set of sliding glass doors onto the rear deck.

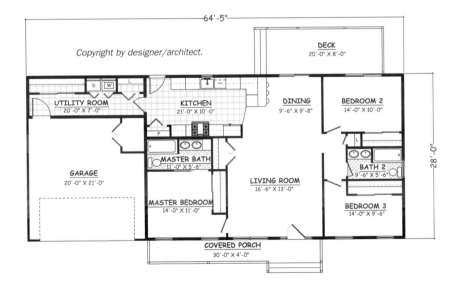

Copyright by designer/architect.

YOU CAN EXPAND THIS HOUSE!

For the ever-growing family, this home is designed to be expanded. When you're ready to "grow" the house you can purchase its second floor addition, Plan #723034. To see the finished 2-story version go to page 162.

Plan #721064

Dimensions: 89'11" W x 26'7" D
Levels: 1
Heated Square Footage: 1,400
Bedrooms: 3
Bathrooms: 2½
Foundation: Crawl space, slab or basement
Material Take-off Included: Yes
Price Category: B

Images provided by designer/architect.

You'll love the open and airy feel of this ranch style home with its variety windows, making the rooms sunny and bright.

Features:

- **Covered Porch:** With stately columns and a generous width, this covered porch area is certain to be a spot for gathering on warm evenings.

- **Great Room:** This immense great room, with its open floor plan and variety of windows, is airy and bright. It is open to the kitchen and features French doors leading to an expansive deck, making the transition between the indoor and outdoors seamless.

- **Kitchen:** This kitchen is a cook's dream. It features a 48-in.-wide range, a plethora of cabinets, and ample counter space, making time spent in the kitchen a joy. The large double window over the sink looks out on the rear yard and allows for lots of natural light, while the countertop seating area encourages interaction between the chef and family members.

- **Master Suite:** Gracious in nature, this lovely master suite houses a private bathroom that will provide you with added comfort.

- **Secondary Bedrooms:** Two moderately sized bedrooms and a full bathroom help to complete the private areas of the home.

This spacious home is affordable to build due to its simple, yet elegant, design. While this home has many lovely features, it can be easily expanded to meet the demands of a growing family.

Copyright by designer/architect.

YOU CAN EXPAND THIS HOUSE!

For the ever-growing family, this home is designed to be expanded. When you're ready to "grow" the house you can purchase its second floor addition, Plan #723064. To see the finished 2-story version go to page 148.

Images provided by designer/architect.

Plan #721068

Dimensions: 50' W x 28' D

Levels: 1

Heated Square Footage: 1,400

Bedrooms: 3

Bathrooms: 2

Foundation: Crawl space, slab or basement

Material Take-off Included: Yes

Price Category: B

Optional Free Garage: If you would like an optional FREE 2-car garage plan, select one from page 8 or 9.

A covered porch, oval windows, and sidelights combine to enhance the exterior of this home. The interior layout is just as attractive and will be a delight to any family.

Features:

- **Great Room:** This generously sized room is open to the dining room and the kitchen, making it ideal for entertaining.

- **Kitchen:** Adjoining the dining room, this kitchen offers plenty of counter space. The angled snack bar open to the great room is perfect for quick family meals.

- **Master Suite:** This master suite is situated apart the other bedrooms in the house, thus providing ultimate privacy. The suite boasts a bathroom with a sunlit whirlpool tub, a double vanity, his and her walk-in closets,

and plenty of storage space. It is the ideal place to retreat to after a long day.

- **Secondary Bedrooms** - Two additional bedrooms and a full bathroom allow ample room for the entire family.

The design of this home is ideal if you want a generously sized home now with the ability to expand in the future.

Copyright by designer/architect.

50'-0"

28'-0"

DECK
12'-0" X 8'-0"

UTILITY

BEDROOM 3
9'-8" X 12'-2"

DINING
10'-6" X 9'-0"

KITCHEN
10'-4" X 11'-6"

M. BATH
11'-6" X 11'-6"

BEDROOM 2
9'-8" X 12'-2"

BATH 2

GREAT ROOM
21'-0" X 15'-4"

MASTER BED
11'-6" X 15'-4"

PORCH
28'-0" X 6'-0"

YOU CAN EXPAND THIS HOUSE!

For the ever-growing family, this home is designed to be expanded. When you're ready to "grow" the house you can purchase its second floor addition, Plan #723068. To see the finished 2-story version go to page 160.

Images provided by designer/architect.

Plan #721002

Dimensions: 47' W x 50' D

Levels: 1

Heated Square Footage: 1,410

Bedrooms: 3

Bathrooms: 2½

Foundation: Crawl space, slab or basement

Material Take-off Included: Yes

Price Category: B

The large windows lead to light-filled rooms.

Features:

- **Foyer:** Step up onto the covered porch and enter the home through this foyer.

- **Living Room:** This generously sized room is open to the foyer, immediately welcoming your guests into the home.

- **Dining Room:** This bright room connects to the deck through sliding glass doors.

- **Kitchen:** This spacious kitchen with a pantry and center island has plenty of counter space for cooking. Because the room is open to the dining room, the family will find it easy to interact during the preparation of meals.

- **Master Suite:** This room features a private bath with large tub and dual vanity, making it a welcome respite after a long day.

With its simple and uncomplicated design elements, this home is easy to build.

Copyright by designer/architect.

47'-0"

50'-0"

DECK
10'-0" X 10'-0"

BEDROOM 2
10'-0" X 9'-6"

BEDROOM 3
10'-6" X 10'-0"

KITCHEN
12'-0" X 10'-6"
ISLAND

DINING ROOM
10'0" X 10'-6"

BATH 2

HALL

POWDER

MASTER BED
9'-0" X 14'-6"

M. BATH

UTILITY

LIVING ROOM
10'-0" X 11'-0"

FOYER
7'-0" X 11'-0"

STORAGE
7'-0" X 4'-0"

MECHANICAL RM
10'-0" X 4'-0"

COVERED PORCH
22'-0" X 4'-0"

GARAGE
25'-0" X 20'-0"

YOU CAN EXPAND THIS HOUSE!

For the ever-growing family, this home is designed to be expanded. When you're ready to "grow" the house you can purchase its second floor addition, Plan #723002. To see the finished 2-story version go to page 214.

Plan #721009

Dimensions: 51' W x 47' D
Levels: 1
Heated Square Footage: 1,419
Bedrooms: 3
Bathrooms: 2½
Foundation: Crawl space, slab or basement
Material Take-off Included: Yes
Price Category: B

This traditional-style home features multiple gables and a front porch for pleasing curb appeal.

CAD FILE AVAILABLE

Features:

- **Covered Porch:** This practical covered porch offers shelter from the elements and is perfect for greeting guests.

- **Living Room:** This is the perfect room for family and friends, whether it's to watch the game or just to sit and talk. The large opening highlights the open nature of the floor plan.

- **Kitchen:** This thoroughly modern kitchen features an angled snack bar, pantry, and plenty of counter space, making cooking a pleasure. Nearby, the dining room contains a French door that opens onto the rear deck.

- **Deck:** A modest deck directly off the dining room provides the perfect transition to the backyard. It's a place that is sure to host many summer barbecues.

- **Master Suite:** This private retreat offers a luxurious bath with a dual vanity, a whirlpool tub, and a walk-in closet. The room is also just steps away from the laundry area for added convenience.

YOU CAN EXPAND THIS HOUSE!

For the ever-growing family, this home is designed to be expanded. When you're ready to "grow" the house you can purchase its second floor addition, Plan #723009. To see the finished 2-story version go to page 138.

Copyright by designer/architect.

Plan #721051

Dimensions: 53' W x 30' D

Levels: 1

Heated Square Footage: 1,420

Bedrooms: 3

Bathrooms: 2

Foundation: Crawl space, slab or basement

Material Take-off Included: Yes

Price Category: B

Images provided by designer/architect.

Optional Free Garage: If you would like an optional FREE 2-car garage plan, select one from page 8 or 9.

CAD FILE AVAILABLE

The gracious covered porch welcomes both friends and family into this wonderfully designed ranch-style home.

Features:

• **Covered Porch:** This lovely covered entryway to the home is wide enough for a small sitting area.

• **Living Room:** Through the front entry door you step into this spacious living room. This room serves as a central gathering spot in the home for spending time together as a family as well as entertaining friends.

• **Kitchen:** This L-shaped kitchen is designed with efficiency in mind. The kitchen is open to the breakfast nook, helping to provide a continuous flow between the rooms.

• **Breakfast Nook:** A cased opening off the living room leads you into this cozy breakfast nook. Continuity is added by having the space also be completely open to the adjacent kitchen area.

• **Master Suite:** This gracious master suite, featuring a private bathroom and a large walk-in closet, will be a welcome retreat after a long day. The bathroom contains a whirlpool tub, dual vanities, and a separate shower, providing additional comfort.

• **Secondary Bedrooms:** Two moderately sized bedrooms, along with a full bathroom featuring a dual vanity, complete the home.

With its straightforward design and simple layout, this home can be affordably built.

Copyright by designer/architect.

DECK 18'-0" X 8'-0"

MASTER BATH 12'-6" X 10'-0"

BEDROOM #2 11'-0" X 10'-0"

BREAKFAST NOOK 8'-4" X 10'-0"

KITCHEN 11'-0" X 10'-0"

HALL

MASTER SUITE 12'-6" X 18'-10"

BEDROOM #3 11'-10" X 10'-0"

LIVING ROOM 19'-4" X 13'-10"

W.I.C.

PORCH 34'-0" X 5'-0"

30'-0"

53'-0"

YOU CAN EXPAND THIS HOUSE!

For the ever-growing family, this home is designed to be expanded. When you're ready to "grow" the house you can purchase its second floor addition, Plan #723051. To see the finished 2-story version go to page 201.

Images provided by designer/architect.

Plan #721022

Dimensions: 51' W x 45'2" D

Levels: 1

Heated Square Footage: 1,422

Bedrooms: 3

Bathrooms: 2

Foundation: Crawl space, slab or basement

Material Take-off Included: Yes

Price Category: B

This moderately sized home has a mix of public areas and private quarters that is sure to please every member of the family.

Features:

- **Entry Porch:** This entry porch is just the right size for sheltering guests from the elements.

- **Great Room:** This great room is a large and airy room that will make everyone feel at home. French doors leading to a covered rear porch allow for outdoor entertaining throughout the year.

- **Kitchen:** This kitchen is perfectly located between a laundry room and bright, sunny dinette. Both the kitchen and dinette open into the great room.

- **Master Suite:** You'll love this master suite, a relaxing retreat that has its own private bath and a large walk-in closet.

- **Secondary Bedrooms:** Two additional bedrooms and a full bath round out the private areas of this home. This area is sure to provide enough room for each member of the family.

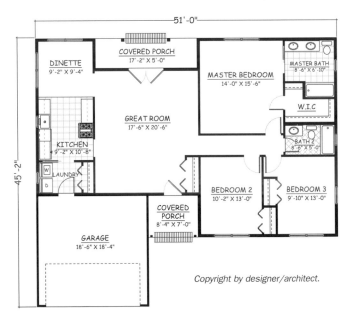

Copyright by designer/architect.

YOU CAN EXPAND THIS HOUSE!

For the ever-growing family, this home is designed to be expanded. When you're ready to "grow" the house you can purchase its second floor addition, Plan #723022. To see the finished 2-story version go to page 186.

Images provided by designer/architect.

Plan #721057

Dimensions: 30' W x 51' D
Levels: 1
Heated Square Footage: 1,422
Bedrooms: 3
Bathrooms: 2
Foundation: Crawl space, slab or basement
Material Take-off Included: Yes
Price Category: B

Optional Free Garage: If you would like an optional FREE 2-car garage plan, select one from page 8 or 9.

CAD FILE AVAILABLE — CAD

This ranch-style house, with its simple and straightforward design, is the perfect starter home.

Features:

• **Covered Porch:** This cozy covered entry to the home provides you with shelter from the elements.

• **Kitchen:** This spacious and well-designed kitchen is sure to please all. With a pantry and plenty of cabinet space, the room will be easy to organize.

• **Dining Room:** Bright and airy, this lovely dining room is directly off the kitchen and will be the main area for everyday family meals.

• **Master Suite:** Separated from the secondary bedrooms in the home is this master suite. The suite features a bathroom with a dual vanity and a separate toilet/tub area that will help to provide additional privacy and comfort.

• **Secondary Bedrooms:** Two more moderately sized bedrooms and a full bathroom help to round out the home.

This home is well-designed, affordable to build, and can also be expanded to meet the demands of a growing family.

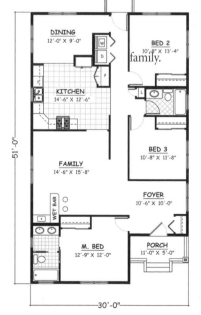

Copyright by designer/architect.

DINING 12'-0" X 9'-0"
BED 2 10'-8" X 13'-4"
KITCHEN 14'-6" X 12'-6"
BED 3 10'-8" X 11'-8"
FAMILY 14'-6" X 15'-8"
FOYER 10'-6" X 10'-0"
WET BAR
M. BED 12'-9" X 12'-0"
PORCH 11'-0" X 5'-0"
51'-0"
30'-0"

YOU CAN EXPAND THIS HOUSE!

For the ever-growing family, this home is designed to be expanded. When you're ready to "grow" the house you can purchase its second floor addition, Plan #723057. To see the finished 2-story version go to page 198.

Plan #721054

Dimensions: 59'4" W x 39'6" D
Levels: 1
Heated Square Footage: 1,424
Bedrooms: 3
Bathrooms: 2
Foundation: Crawl space, slab or basement
Material Take-off Included: Yes
Price Category: B

- **Master Suite:** Set apart from the other bedrooms in the home, this master suite will offer you a sanctuary to relax in after a long day. A private bathroom features a tub, a separate shower, and a dual vanity, which will ensure the comfort and privacy you desire.

With classically clean lines, this home is affordable to build. The design elements in this home also offer the ability for expansion if the need arises.

This three-bedroom ranch home with multiple gables and a lovely front porch has a country feel.

CAD FILE AVAILABLE

Features:

- **Covered Porch:** Welcoming all to this charming home is this attractive front porch, featuring turned columns.

- **Dining Room:** Open to both the family room and the kitchen, this dining room will not only serve for weekly family meals but is sure to be the host to many festive dinner parties. The sliding glass door provides a transition to the covered patio, extending the dining area to the outdoors.

- **Family Room:** Open to the dining room and featuring large windows, this spacious room will certainly be the gathering spot for all.

- **Kitchen:** Designed for cooks who appreciate efficient workspaces, this kitchen offers ample counter space and is sure to delight the whole family.

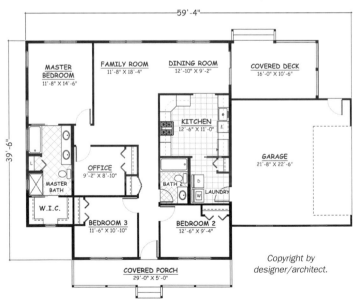

Copyright by designer/architect.

YOU CAN EXPAND THIS HOUSE!

For the ever-growing family, this home is designed to be expanded. When you're ready to "grow" the house you can purchase its second floor addition, Plan #723054. To see the finished 2-story version go to page 139.

Plan #721036

Dimensions: 68'10" W x 44' D
Levels: 1
Heated Square Footage: 1,433
Bedrooms: 3
Bathrooms: 2
Foundation: Crawl space, slab or basement
Material Take-off Included: Yes
Price Category: B

This lovely ranch home features front and rear covered patios, ensuring many afternoons and evenings spent outdoors.

Features:

- **Great Room:** Step through the entry directly into this spacious room. Open to both the kitchen and the breakfast area, this room will certainly be a gathering spot for all.

- **Kitchen/Breakfast Nook:** Counterspace is plentiful in this well designed kitchen. The sink is perfectly located in a wraparound countertop seating area, which allows for interaction with the family during the preparations of meals. The breakfast nook features sliding glass doors that lead to the rear patio.

- **Master Suite:** This gracious room, with its large walk-in closet, and private bath, will offer you a bit of peace and quiet after a long day. The bath features a full-size tub, as well as a shower area, providing you with even more comfort.

- **Bedrooms:** Two additional bedrooms, a full bathroom, and a lovely powder room help to complete this already comfortable home

The simple lines and thoughtful design of this home make it affordable to build, and leave plenty of room to expand for a growing family.

Copyright by designer/architect.

YOU CAN EXPAND THIS HOUSE!

For the ever-growing family, this home is designed to be expanded. When you're ready to "grow" the house you can purchase its second floor addition, Plan #723036. To see the finished 2-story version go to page 212.

Plan #721048

Dimensions: 47'7" W x 35'4" D
Levels: 1
Heated Square Footage: 1,438
Bedrooms: 3
Bathrooms: 2
Foundation: Crawl space, slab or basement
Material Take-off Included: Yes
Price Category: B

Images provided by designer/architect.

Optional Free Garage: If you would like an optional FREE 2-car garage plan, select one from page 8 or 9.

With its covered porch and multiple window units, this two-story house evokes the charm of a traditional home.

Features:

- Great Room: This generously sized great room is the centerpiece of a spacious and flowing design that is perfectly suited for family entertaining.

- Kitchen: The step-saving design of this U-shaped kitchen will make cooking a pleasure for everyone in the family. It is open to the dining area and is just steps away from the utility room, which adds to its convenience.

- Master Suite: This master suite is situated apart from the other bedrooms in the home to ensure privacy. The triple window and large walk-in closet enhance this elegant retreat that is served by a luxurious bathroom. The bathroom features a sunlit whirlpool tub and a private toilet room.

- Secondary Bedrooms: Two additional bedrooms and a full bathroom round out the private areas of this home.

Spaciousness and functionality characterize this home while offering the growing family the opportunity to expand.

Rear Elevation

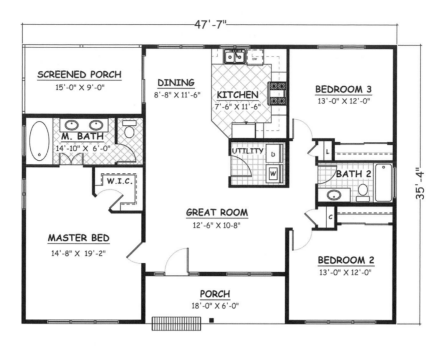

— 47'-7" —

SCREENED PORCH
15'-0" X 9'-0"

DINING
8'-8" X 11'-6"

KITCHEN
7'-6" X 11'-6"

BEDROOM 3
13'-0" X 12'-0"

M. BATH
14'-10" X 6'-0"

UTILITY

W.I.C.

BATH 2

GREAT ROOM
12'-6" X 10-8"

MASTER BED
14'-8" X 19'-2"

35'-4"

BEDROOM 2
13'-0" X 12'-0"

PORCH
18'-0" X 6'-0"

Copyright by designer/architect.

Left Elevation

Right Elevation

YOU CAN EXPAND THIS HOUSE!

For the ever-growing family, this home is designed to be expanded. When you're ready to "grow" the house you can purchase its second floor addition, Plan #723048. To see the finished 2-story version go to page 172.

Color

No other decorating component has more power and greater effect at such little cost than color. It can fill a space and make furnishings look fresh and new. Color can also show off fine architectural details or downplay a room's structural flaws. A particular color can make a cold room cozy, while another hue can cool down a sunny cooker. And color comes cheap, giving a tremendous impact for your decorating dollar: elbow grease, supplies, prep work, and paint will all cost pretty much the same if you choose a gorgeous hue over plain white.

But finding the color—the right color—isn't easy. Where do you begin to look? Like the economy, color has leading indicators. You have a market basket full of choices, and there are lots of signposts to direct you where to go.

The Lay of the Land

For the past 200 years, white has been the most popular choice for American home exteriors. And it still is, followed by tan, brown, and beige. You can play it safe and follow the leader. But you should also think about the architecture of your house and where you live when you're considering exterior color. For example, traditional Colonials have a color-combination range of about two that look appropriate: white with black or green shutters and gray with white trim. Mediterranean-style houses typically pick up the colors of terra-cotta and the tile that are indigenous to the regions that developed the architecture— France, Italy, and Spain. A ranch-style house shouldn't be overdone—it is, after all, usually a modest structure. On the other hand, a cottage can be fanciful. Whimsical colors also look charming on Victorian houses in San Francisco, but they would be out of place in conservative Scarsdale, New York, where you must

check with the local building board even when you want to change the exterior color of your house.

How's the Weather?

Like exteriors, interiors often take their color cues from their environs and local traditions. In the rainy and often chilly Pacific Northwest, cozy blanket plaids in strong reds and black abound. In the hot-and-arid climate of the West, indigo or brown ticking-stripes and faded denim look appropriately casual and cool. Subtle grays and neutrals, reflecting steel, lime-stone, and concrete, look apropos for sophisticated city life. In extremely warm southern climates, the brilliant sun tends to overpower lighter colors. That explains the popularity of strong hues in tropical, sun-drenched locales.

Natural Light. That's the one you don't pay for. Its direction and intensity greatly affects color. A room with a window that faces trees will look markedly different in summer, when warm white sunlight is filtered through the leaves, than in winter, when the trees are bare and the color of natural light takes on a cool blue cast. Time of day affects color, too. Yellow walls that are pleasant and cheerful in the early morning can be stifling and blinding in the afternoon. That's because afternoon

The yellow-colored wall, above, complements the antique painted dresser.

Warm neutral-color walls, opposite, and touches of red make this bedroom cozy.

sun is stronger than morning sun.

When you're choosing a color for an interior, always view it at different times of day, but especially during the hours in which you will inhabit the room.

Artificial Light. Because artificial light affects color rendition as much as natural light, don't judge a color in the typically chilly fluorescence of a hardware store. The very same color chip will look completely different when you bring it home, which is why it's so important to test out a paint color in your own home. Most fluorescent light is bluish and distorts colors. It depresses red and exaggerates green, for example. A romantic faded rose on your dining room walls will just wash out in the kitchen if your use a fluorescent light there. Incandescent light, the type produced by the standard bulbs you probably use in your chandelier and in most of your home's light fixtures, is warm but slightly yellow. Halogen light, which comes from another newer type of incandescent bulb, is white and the closest to natural sunlight. Of all three types of bulbs, halogen is truest in rendering color.

 # red

RED is powerful, dramatic, motivating. Red is also hospitable, and it stimulates the appetite, which makes it a favorite choice for dining rooms. Some studies have indicated that a red room actually makes people feel warmer.

 # yellow

YELLOW illuminates the colors it surrounds. It warms rooms that receive northern light but can be too bright in a sunny room. It's best for daytime rooms, not bedrooms. It has a short range, which means as white is added to yellow, it disappears. Yellow highlights and calls attention to features—think of bright taxicabs.

green

GREEN is tranquil, nurturing, rejuvenating. It is a psychological primary, and because it is mixed from yellow and blue, it can appear both warm and cool. Time seems to pass more quickly in green rooms. Perhaps that's why waiting rooms off-stage are called "green rooms."

 **neutrals**

GRAY goes with all colors—it is a good neighbor. Various tones of gray range from dark charcoal to pale oyster.

BLACK (technically the absence of color) enhances and brightens other colors, making for livelier decorating schemes when used as an accent.

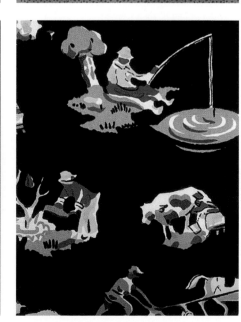

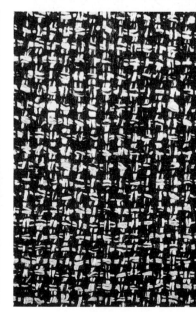

 # pink

PINK is perceived as outgoing and active. It's also a color that flatters skin tones. Hot shades are invigorating, while soft, toned-down versions can be relaxed and charming.

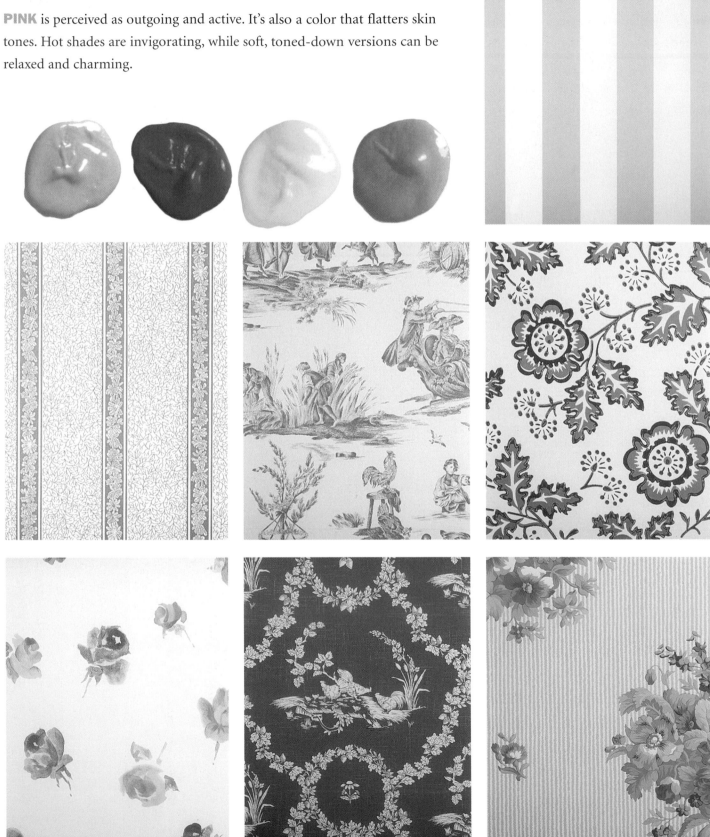

order direct: 1-800-523-6789

blue

BLUE, with its associations of sea and sky, offers serenity, which is why it is a favorite in bedrooms. Studies have shown that people think better in blue rooms. Perhaps that explains the popularity of the navy blue suit. Cooler blues show this color's melancholy side, however.

Plan #721015

Dimensions: 52'4" W x 40' D

Levels: *1*

Heated Square Footage: 1,448

Bedrooms: 3

Bathrooms: 2

Foundation: Crawl space, slab or basement

Material Take-off Included: Yes

Price Category: B

Images provided by designer/architect.

You will love the free-flowing nature of this thoughtfully designed ranch home.

CAD FILE AVAILABLE

Features:

- **Entry Porch:** This covered porch gives the entrance to this home an understated elegance.

- **Living Room:** This lovely room, with its open design, welcomes both friends and family into the home.

- **Dining Room:** With sliding glass doors leading to a moderately sized deck, this room makes a weeknight family dinner or a formal dinner party with friends a pleasure.

- **Kitchen:** This tidy kitchen, with its thoughtful layout and large pantry, makes it easy for the family cook to prepare meals.

- **Master Suite:** Set apart from the secondary bedrooms in the home, this generously sized master suite features a private bath for added comfort.

Left Elevation

Right Elevation

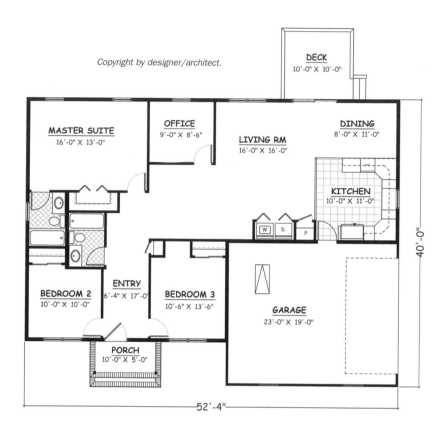

Copyright by designer/architect.

DECK
10'-0" X 10'-0"

MASTER SUITE
16'-0" X 13'-0"

OFFICE
9'-0" X 8'-6"

LIVING RM
16'-0" X 16'-0"

DINING
8'-0" X 11'-0"

KITCHEN
10'-0" X 11'-0"

W D P

BEDROOM 2
10'-0" X 10'-0"

ENTRY
6'-4" X 17'-0"

BEDROOM 3
10'-6" X 13'-6"

GARAGE
23'-0" X 19'-0"

40'-0"

PORCH
10'-0" X 5'-0"

52'-4"

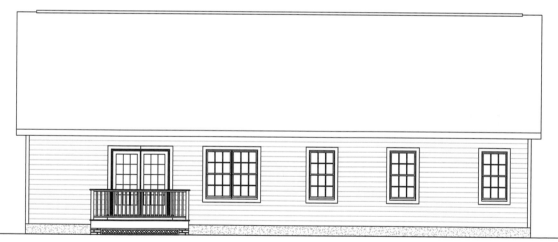

Rear Elevation

YOU CAN EXPAND THIS HOUSE!

For the ever-growing family, this home is designed to be expanded. When you're ready to "grow" the house you can purchase its second floor addition, Plan #723015. To see the finished 2-story version go to page 143.

Plan #721060

Dimensions: 59'7" W x 31'2" D

Levels: 1

Heated Square Footage: 1,453

Bedrooms: 3

Bathrooms: 2

Foundation: Crawl space, slab or basement

Material Take-off Included: Yes

Price Category: B

Images provided by designer/architect.

• Secondary Bedrooms: Generously sized bedrooms and a full bathroom help to complete the private areas of this home.

With its fluid design, this modestly sized ranch home is affordable to build and can be expanded to fit the needs of the ever-changing family dynamic.

You'll love this spacious ranch-style home with its open floor plan.

Features:

• Covered Porch: The turned columns at this entry porch add a country feel to the home.

• Living Room: From the entry porch, step directly into the central gathering spot of the home. This spacious living room that is open to the dining area will be the place that family will congregate and guests will gather.

• Kitchen: The open floor plan of this kitchen allows for the interaction between the chef, family members, and guests during the preparation of meals.

• Master Suite: This gracious master suite features an immense walk-in closet and a private bathroom and will be a welcome retreat after a long day. The private bathroom features a dual vanity, an oversized tub, a separate shower, and a private toilet room, providing additional comfort.

Copyright by designer/architect.

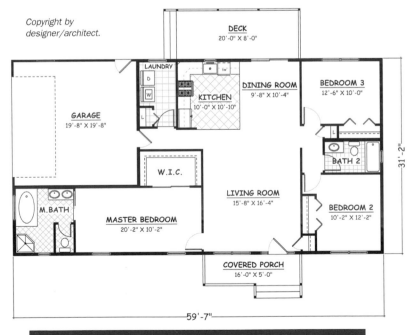

YOU CAN EXPAND THIS HOUSE!

For the ever-growing family, this home is designed to be expanded. When you're ready to "grow" the house you can purchase its second floor addition, Plan #723060. To see the finished 2-story version go to page 171.

Plan #721065

Dimensions: 42'4" W x 42'6" D
Levels: 1
Heated Square Footage: 1,454
Bedrooms: 3
Bathrooms: 2
Foundation: Crawl space, slab or basement
Material Take-off Included: Yes
Price Category: B

Images provided by designer/architect.

Optional Free Garage: If you would like an optional FREE 2-car garage plan, select one from page 8 or 9.

CAD FILE AVAILABLE

The hipped roofs and multiple windows provide distinction to this home while the interior design brings functionality.

Features:

- Great Room: This great room is a generously sized room that flows into the breakfast room and the kitchen. It features an abundance of windows to wash it in natural light and will be the main gathering place for the entire family.

- Breakfast: This breakfast area adjoins the kitchen and is open to the living room. A sliding glass door leads onto a rear deck, giving the family the opportunity to enjoy dining both indoors and outdoors.

- Master Suite: This master suite boasts a bath with a sunlit whirlpool tub, a double vanity, and a large walk-in closet. The French door to the expansive deck makes this room an ideal place to retreat to after a long day.

- Secondary Bedrooms: Two additional bedrooms and a full bathroom allow plenty of room for the entire family.

The unique blend of private and public spaces makes this home ideal for any family. It is also designed to make future expansion affordable as the family continues to grow.

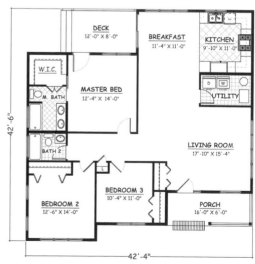

Copyright by designer/architect.

YOU CAN EXPAND THIS HOUSE!

For the ever-growing family, this home is designed to be expanded. When you're ready to "grow" the house you can purchase its second floor addition, Plan #723065. To see the finished 2-story version go to page 190.

Images provided by designer/architect.

Plan #721012

Dimensions: 51'2" W x 44'6" D

Levels: 1

Heated Square Footage: 1,465

Bedrooms: 3

Bathrooms: 2

Foundation: Crawl space, slab or basement

Material Take-off Included: Yes

Price Category: B

Brick trim and sidelights are just some of the features of this charming cottage-style home that give it unique curb appeal.

Features:

- Covered Porches: These front and rear porches are perfect for enjoying the outdoors while being protected from the elements.

- Foyer: This elegant entrance has its own closet. It invites in family and friends alike

- Living Room: This living room adjoins the dining and kitchen for an open, spacious lay out. It also features a set of sliding glass doors that opens onto the rear covered porch.

- Kitchen: This tidy U-shaped kitchen is located adjacent to the dining room for an open feel, whether you are preparing the meal or enjoying it.

- Master Suite: This retreat comes complete with a tray ceiling, a walk-in closet and a luxurious master bath. The bath is a spa-like oasis that features a large corner whirlpool tub, double dual vanities, and a large linen closet. A room you'll never want to leave.

Copyright by designer/architect.

YOU CAN EXPAND THIS HOUSE!

For the ever-growing family, this home is designed to be expanded. When you're ready to "grow" the house you can purchase its second floor addition, Plan #723012. To see the finished 2-story version go to page 112

Plan #721043

Dimensions: 65' W x 30' D

Levels: 1

Heated Square Footage: 1,480

Bedrooms: 3

Bathrooms: 2½

Foundation: Crawl space, slab
or basement

Material Take-off Included: Yes

Price Category: B

Images provided by designer/architect.

This lovely traditional-style home is sure to please every member of the family.

Features:

- **Family Room:** Connected to the dining room and featuring sliding glass doors out to the screened-in porch, this family room will certainly be the place for family and friends to gather.

- **Kitchen:** This well-designed galley kitchen offers plenty of counter space for preparing meals. A rear hallway leads to the laundry facility, which makes the multitasking that is needed for today's active family easy.

- **Master Suite:** This gracious master suite features a large walk-in closet and a private

bathroom. The private bath has a spa-like feel with such features as a large soaking tub, a separate shower, and a dual vanity.

- **Secondary Bedrooms:** The additional two bedrooms in this home are moderately sized

and just steps away from a centrally located full bath.

With wonderfully designed public and private spaces, this home still remains affordable to build.

Copyright by designer/architect.

YOU CAN EXPAND THIS HOUSE!

For the ever-growing family, this home is designed to be expanded. When you're ready to "grow" the house you can purchase its second floor addition, Plan #723043. To see the finished 2-story version go to page 189.

Plan #721055

Dimensions: 60'8" W x 36' D

Levels: 1

Heated Square Footage: 1,480

Bedrooms: 3

Bathrooms: 2

Foundation: Crawl space, slab or basement

Material Take-off Included: Yes

Price Category: B

You'll appreciate the free flowing nature of this ranch-style home.

Features:

- Covered Porch: Turned columns grace the front of this covered porch, adding to the charm of the home.

- Living Room: Step from the covered porch into this gracious living room, which is sure to be the central gathering spot for all.

- Kitchen: This L-shaped kitchen, with its large center island, is a cook's dream. The room is designed to be open to both the living and dining areas, making interaction between the cook and the rest of the family during mealtime prep easy.

- Master Suite: Featuring a private bath and a large walk-in closet, this expansive room has a bit more privacy, as it is set apart from the additional bedrooms in the home.

- Secondary Bedrooms: Located off of a small hallway are two moderately sized secondary bedrooms and a full bathroom.

YOU CAN EXPAND THIS HOUSE!

For the ever-growing family, this home is designed to be expanded. When you're ready to "grow" the house you can purchase its second floor addition, Plan #723055. To see the finished 2-story version go to page 195.

Images provided by designer/architect.

Plan #721025

Dimensions: 53'8" W x 53'4" D
Levels: 1
Heated Square Footage: 1,498
Bedrooms: 3
Bathrooms: 2
Foundation: Crawl space, slab or basement
Material Take-off Included: Yes
Price Category: B

The spa-like bath makes this lovely ranch home's master suite hard to resist.

CAD FILE AVAILABLE

Features:

- **Entry Foyer:** This entryway ushers you into the family home, with its conveniently located hall closet and close proximity to the dining room.

- **Dining Room:** Cased openings at both entries give this room a touch of elegance. Located just steps away from the foyer and the kitchen, this space will host many a dinner party.

- **Living Room:** Open to the kitchen and featuring sliding glass doors to a rear covered porch, this living room is the central gathering spot for all.

- **Master Suite:** Set on the opposite side of the home from the secondary bedrooms, this spacious suite will surely be a welcome retreat after a long day. The bath features amenities that include a dual vanity, a private toilet room, a separate shower, and a large soaking tub that will surely leave you feeling renewed.

- **Secondary Bedrooms:** The spacious secondary bedrooms in this home offer ample closet space and are located on either side of a hall bath for additional comfort.

Copyright by designer/architect.

YOU CAN EXPAND THIS HOUSE!

For the ever-growing family, this home is designed to be expanded. When you're ready to "grow" the house you can purchase its second floor addition, Plan #723025. To see the finished 2-story version go to page 187.

Plan #721045

Dimensions: 51'10" W x 54' D

Levels: 1

Heated Square Footage: 1,503

Bedrooms: 3

Bathrooms: 2

Foundation: Crawl space, slab or basement

Material Take-off Included: Yes

Price Category: C

The moderate size of this home, along with its thoughtful layout, makes it easy to build.

CAD FILE AVAILABLE

Features:

- **Covered Porch:** This large covered entry porch offers shelter from the elements and is large enough for a small seating area.

- **Dining Room:** Directly across from the kitchen, this dining room has a set of sliding glass doors leading onto the large deck.

- **Kitchen:** This tidy kitchen features a built-in banquette, perfect for the morning family breakfast.

- **Deck:** This large deck that is connected to both the master suite and dining room is perfect for quiet morning breakfasts or outdoor summer entertaining.

Images provided by designer/architect.

- **Master Suite:** This master suite offers a private bath with a large tub, a separate toilet room, and a dual vanity. The room also features a large walk-in-closet, as well as sliding glass doors that open onto a large deck.

Copyright by designer/architect.

YOU CAN EXPAND THIS HOUSE!

For the ever-growing family, this home is designed to be expanded. When you're ready to "grow" the house you can purchase its second floor addition, Plan #723045. To see the finished 2-story version go to page 221.

Plan #721049

Dimensions: 68'8" W x 29'6" D
Levels: 1
Heated Square Footage: 1,508
Bedrooms: 3
Bathrooms: 2
Foundation: Crawl space, slab or basement
Material Take-off Included: Yes
Price Category: C

The brick accents and hip roof line of this home give it a traditional feel.

Features:

- Covered Porch: Stately columns and brick accents grace this covered entry, adding charm to the home.

- Dining Room: A more formal space for meals, this dining room is open to the kitchen and the great room and features a sliding glass door leading onto a large rear deck.

- Kitchen: Thoughtfully designed, this kitchen will surely please the family cook with its open feel and abundance of counter space. The countertop seating area will be used quite often for weekday breakfasts or after noon snacks.

- Utility Room: This utility room is located directly off of the kitchen and houses the washer and dryer, making the multitasking that is often required with today's active family lifestyle much easier.

- Rear Deck/Grilling Porch: With this covered grilling porch located off the kitchen area and the expansive rear deck connected to the dining room, dining outdoors will be a common occurrence.

- Master Suite: This lovely master suite features its own bathroom, which will provide privacy. The bathroom has a tub, a separate shower, and dual vanities, continuing the comfortable feeling of an already delightful space.

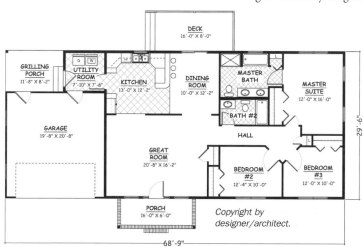

YOU CAN EXPAND THIS HOUSE!

For the ever-growing family, this home is designed to be expanded. When you're ready to "grow" the house you can purchase its second floor addition, Plan #723049. To see the finished 2-story version go to page 218.

Images provided by designer/architect.

Plan #721027

Dimensions: 65' W x 40' D
Levels: 1
Heated Square Footage: 1,554
Bedrooms: 3
Bathrooms: 2
Foundation: Crawl space, slab or basement
Material Take-off Included: Yes
Price Category: C

The flowing layout of this home is designed for entertaining, but it will also suit every member of the family. Its unique floor plan lends itself to future expansion.

CAD FILE AVAILABLE

Features:

- Great Room: This generous room's convenient location to the kitchen and sliding glass doors leading to a rear deck make it a great space for entertaining.

- Kitchen: Next door to the breakfast nook and just off the great room, this kitchen will become the family's gathering place.

- Rear Deck: This large deck, which is connected to both the master suite and great room, is perfect for quiet morning coffee or family gatherings in summer.

- Master Suite: Spacious retreat features his and her walk-in closets and a patio door that opens onto the rear deck. The attached bath offers a soaking tub, a separate shower, and a dual-sink vanity. It truly is a place to escape to after a long day.

- Secondary Bedrooms: Two additional bedrooms and a full bath complete this home.

This spacious and versatile home is ideal for any family.

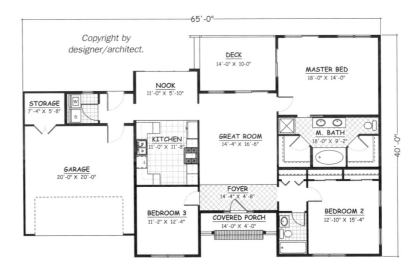

Copyright by designer/architect.

YOU CAN EXPAND THIS HOUSE!

For the ever-growing family, this home is designed to be expanded. When you're ready to "grow" the house you can purchase its second floor addition, Plan #723027. To see the finished 2-story version go to page 161.

Plan #722011

Dimensions: 56' W x 38' D
Levels: 2
Heated Square Footage: 1,566
Main Level Sq. Ft.: 1,167
Upper Level Sq. Ft.: 399
Bedrooms: 3
Bathrooms: 3
Foundation: Crawl space, slab or basement
Material Take-off Included: Yes
Price Category: C

This two-story cottage style house makes it the perfect first home for a young family.

Features:

- **Living Room:** The living room is part of an open floor plan. The rooms flow into one another, creating a space that is light and airy, making it seem larger than it is.

- **Dining Room:** This space adjoins the kitchen and has a set of sliding glass doors that open onto a large deck. It's perfect for dining inside or out.

- **Kitchen:** This large L-shaped kitchen features ample counter space and modern conveniences. The adjacent dining room is just steps away, making family dinners a snap.

- **Deck:** The large deck is perfect for quiet morning breakfasts or outdoor summer entertaining.

Images provided by designer/architect.

- **Master Suite:** This master suite has a tray ceiling and large windows, creating a bright and airy space that makes relaxing a joy. It also offers a private bath with a dual vanity and a large walk-in-closet.

- **Upper Level:** This upper level features an additional bedroom and a private office that is perfect for a home business or as a place where family members can spend some quiet time.

Main Level Floor Plan

Copyright by designer/architect.

Upper Level Floor Plan

Images provided by designer/architect.

Plan #721017

Dimensions: 52'4" W x 52' D
Levels: 1
Heated Square Footage: 1,664
Bedrooms: 3
Bathrooms: 2
Foundation: Crawl space, slab or basement
Material Take-off Included: Yes
Price Category: C

A comfortable front porch welcomes you into this lovely home, which offers a wonderful balance between public and private areas.

CAD FILE AVAILABLE

Features:

• **Dining:** Open to both the kitchen and family room, this dining area is the perfect place for both informal family dining and intimate dinner parties.

• **Family Room:** The open layout, large windows, and sliding glass doors to the rear deck will make this the central gathering place for family and friends alike.

• **Kitchen:** The ample counter space of this well designed kitchen will make preparing the family meals a snap. The room also features a French door onto a rear deck, making dining outdoors a common occurrence.

• **Rear Deck:** Nestled between the kitchen and master suite, and spanning the length of the family room, the rear deck expands the already generous family living areas.

• **Master Suite:** This spacious area offers a generously sized walk-in closet, sliding glass doors to the rear deck, and a private bath. Located apart from the secondary bedrooms in the home, this space will be a welcome retreat after a long day.

Copyright by designer/architect.

YOU CAN EXPAND THIS HOUSE!

For the ever-growing family, this home is designed to be expanded. When you're ready to "grow" the house you can purchase its second floor addition, Plan #723017. To see the finished 2-story version go to page 215.

Images provided by designer/architect.

Plan #721074

Dimensions: 62' W x 39' D
Levels: 1
Heated Square Footage: 1,704
Bedrooms: 3
Bathrooms: 2½
Foundation: Crawl space, slab or basement
Material Take-off Included: Yes
Price Category: C

Optional Free Garage: If you would like an optional FREE 2-car garage plan, select one from page 8 or 9.

CAD FILE AVAILABLE

With such features as a wraparound front porch and small gabled dormers, this home evokes the charm of an old-fashioned farmhouse.

Features:

• Covered Porch: This expansive wraparound porch adds to the charm of this home while providing a relaxing place to sit and enjoy the outdoors. It also features French doors leading to two of the bedrooms.

• Living Room: This living room features a bayed area with large windows that will fill this room with natural light. The open design

and generous size will make this room a gathering place for the entire family.

• Kitchen: The step-saving design of this kitchen will make cooking a joy for everyone in the family. It also features a snack bar, which will host many an informal meal.

• Master Suite: With a large walk-in closet and a private bathroom, this stylish master suite offers you a bit of respite from the everyday. Relax in the corner whirlpool tub, and step out feeling relaxed and renewed. A French door leading to the front porch invites you to step outside and enjoy some fresh air.

Copyright by designer/architect.

YOU CAN EXPAND THIS HOUSE!

For the ever-growing family, this home is designed to be expanded. When you're ready to "grow" the house you can purchase its second floor addition, Plan #723074. To see the finished 2-story version go to page 222.

Plan #722033

Dimensions: 51'4" W x 41'2" D
Levels: 2
Heated Square Footage: 1,773
Main Level Sq. Ft.: 1,295
Upper Level Sq. Ft.: 478
Bedrooms: 3
Bathrooms: 3
Foundation: Crawl space, slab or basement
Material Take-off Included: Yes
Price Category: C

Images provided by designer/architect.

• **Master Suite:** This master suite, which features a private bath and a large walk-in closet, lends both comfort and privacy.

• **Secondary Bedrooms:** With two additional bedrooms and bathrooms, this home offers each member of the family the privacy and comfort they deserve.

The brick facade on this lovely two-story home gives it a country feel.

Features:

• **Entry:** This simple entry ushers you directly into the home, making your guests feel welcome.

• **Great Room:** This gracious great room is enhanced with sliding glass doors leading to an expansive deck, offering you an expanded area for entertaining. This room will surely be a place that your family gravitates to.

• **Dining Room:** The easy flow between the kitchen, the great room, and this dining room makes this space perfect for entertaining. Family members and guests alike will enjoy many meals in this lovely room.

• **Kitchen:** Designed with efficiency in mind, this kitchen makes mealtime tasks simple. Busy families will find the utility room being steps away an added convenience.

Main Level Floor Plan

Copyright by designer/architect.

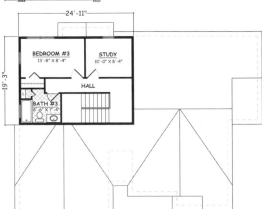

Upper Level Floor Plan

Plan #722007

Dimensions: 56' W x 32' D

Levels: 2

Heated Square Footage: 1,821

Main Level Sq. Ft.: 1,030

Upper Level Sq. Ft.: 791

Bedrooms: 4

Bathrooms: 3

Foundation: Crawl space, slab or basement

Material Take-off Included: Yes

Price Category: D

Images provided by designer/architect.

A wraparound porch, multiple gables, and a circle-topped window give this farmhouse-style home true curb appeal.

CAD FILE AVAILABLE

Features:

- **Porch:** This wraparound covered porch will become a favorite place for the family to gather during the day or in the evenings to watch outdoor activities. Just add a swing or rocker to make it complete.

- **Dining Room:** Hold dinner parties in this welcoming space. It is located near the entry for the convenience of guests.

- **Kitchen:** This large kitchen, with a snack bar that can be used for informal dining as well as after school snacks, features easy access to the utility room and the formal dining room.

- **Guest Bedroom:** This bedroom provides a place for visiting friends and family to lay their heads in privacy and comfort.

- **Master Suite:** This suite is complete with a luxurious bath that has a private toilet area, dual vanities, and a whirlpool tub. The room has its own unique sitting area that is perfect for curling up with a good book.

- **Upper Level:** This area features two additional bedrooms for the youngsters, as well as an additional full bath for them to share.

Main Level Floor Plan

Upper Level Floor Plan

Copyright by designer/architect.

Plan #721016

Dimensions: 52'4" W x 52' D

Levels: 1

Heated Square Footage: 1,840

Bedrooms: 3

Bathrooms: 2

Foundation: Crawl space, slab or basement

Material Take-off Included: Yes

Price Category: D

Images provided by designer/architect.

With its spacious layout this home is designed for the active family.

Features:

- **Covered Porch:** The turned columns and decorative rail add charm to the covered entry porch, welcoming all home.

- **Dining Room:** Open to the kitchen and featuring a set of double windows, this generously sized room will be host to both casual and formal dining.

- **Kitchen:** With its expansive countertops and numerous cabinets, this space will make meal prep a delight. Step through the French door and onto an expansive deck for outdoor dining.

- **Family Room:** All will be flocking to this wonderfully sized space that includes large windows and a set of sliding doors to the rear deck.

- **Master Suite:** Set apart from the secondary bedrooms in the home, this generously sized master suite features sliding glass doors to the outdoor deck, as well as a private bath. The bath, with its oversize tub, separate shower, and private toilet area adds to the comfort of the entire suite.

Copyright by designer/architect.

YOU CAN EXPAND THIS HOUSE!

For the ever-growing family, this home is designed to be expanded. When you're ready to "grow" the house you can purchase its second floor addition, Plan #723016. To see the finished 2-story version go to page 225.

Plan #721013

Dimensions: 54' W x 48' D

Levels: 1

Heated Square Footage: 1,870

Bedrooms: 3

Bathrooms: 2

Foundation: Crawl space, slab or basement

Material Take-off Included: Yes

Price Category: D

Images provided by designer/architect.

This house is ideal for any family due to its spacious design and versatility.

Features:

- **Great Room:** This expansive room invites you into the heart of the home. It flows to the rear of the house and takes you straight through to sliding glass doors that welcome you to the backyard.

- **Kitchen:** This kitchen features a center island that adds convenience to this L-shaped kitchen. The adjacent breakfast nook is sure to be occupied day and night.

- **Rear porch:** The rear porch is perfect for outdoor entertaining because of its easy access from the great room.

- **Master Suite:** This master bedroom offers a tray ceiling, his and her walk-in closets, and private bath with large tub, separate shower and dual vanities. The space is a genuine oasis that will be difficult to leave.

- **Secondary Bedrooms:** Two additional bedrooms provide lots of space for the younger members of the family.

Copyright by designer/architect.

YOU CAN EXPAND THIS HOUSE!

For the ever-growing family, this home is designed to be expanded. When you're ready to "grow" the house you can purchase its second floor addition, Plan #723013. To see the finished 2-story version go to page 168.

Images provided by designer/architect.

Plan #721026

Dimensions: 60' W x 49'2" D
Levels: 1
Heated Square Footage: 1,878
Bedrooms: 3
Bathrooms: 2
Foundation: Crawl space, slab or basement
Material Take-off Included: Yes
Price Category: D

Because of its spaciousness and versatility, this home is ideal for any family.

Features:

- Covered Porch: Centered at the front of the home is a covered entry porch. The porch not only provides a place to enjoy the outdoors but also adds curb appeal.

- Great Room: With its large picture window, sliding patio doors, and easy access to the kitchen, this expansive great room will be a favorite gathering place of the entire family.

- Kitchen: An island with snack bar is the highlight of this eat-in kitchen. Double windows and double French pocket doors provide plenty of light. This kitchen is an ideal place for all your family dinners.

- Master Suite: A private retreat, located apart from the rest of the house. It features a sitting area, large walk-in closet, a luxurious bath and a French door to a rear deck. The bath includes a corner whirlpool tub, a separate shower, dual vanities and a private toilet room. It will wash all your troubles away.

- Secondary Bedrooms: Two additional bedrooms and a full bath complete this spectacular home.

Copyright by designer/architect.

YOU CAN EXPAND THIS HOUSE!

For the ever-growing family, this home is designed to be expanded. When you're ready to "grow" the house you can purchase its second floor addition, Plan #723026. To see the finished 2-story version go to page 219.

Plan #721005

Dimensions: 60' W x 47' D
Levels: 1
Heated Square Footage: 1,880
Bedrooms: 3
Bathrooms: 2½
Foundation: Crawl space, slab or basement
Material Take-off Included: Yes
Price Category: D

Images provided by designer/architect.

• **Kitchen:** This spacious kitchen with large prep areas also features a countertop seating area, connecting the kitchen to the dining room. This encourages extra family time while dinner is being prepared.

• **Master Suite:** Upon entering this master suite through dual pocket doors, you feel immediate comfort. The room also features such luxuries as a private bath, a large walk-in closet, and French doors that open onto a private deck. Such amenities will surely recharge you after a long day.

The large front porch welcomes family and friends to this home.

CAD FILE AVAILABLE

Features:

• **Foyer:** This open foyer connects to both the living and dining rooms, taking you directly into the heart of the home.

• **Living Room:** With its tray ceiling and large picture window, this area is a wonderful space for entertaining guests. The room also features sliding glass doors that lead to a generously sized deck, a great place to enjoy warm summer evenings.

YOU CAN EXPAND THIS HOUSE!

For the ever-growing family, this home is designed to be expanded. When you're ready to "grow" the house you can purchase its second floor addition, Plan #723005. To see the finished 2-story version go to page 226.

Copyright by designer/architect.

Images provided by designer/architect.

Plan #721019

Dimensions: 60'6" W x 48' D

Levels: 1

Heated Square Footage: 1,885

Bedrooms: 3

Bathrooms: 2

Foundation: Crawl space, slab or basement

Material Take-off Included: Yes

Price Category: D

This expansive home features a smart mix of open public areas and private quarters that is sure to please every member of the family.

Features:

- Covered Porch: This centrally located covered entry porch provides an elegant entrance into the home.

- Dining Room: The cased openings to this room give it a formal feel. It is also located near the kitchen and entry for the convenience of guests.

- Kitchen: This modern kitchen is equipped with a center island and spacious counters. It adjoins the breakfast nook, which features sliding glass doors leading to a rear covered porch. This unique design is perfect for indoor and outdoor dining.

- Master Suite: This bright and spacious room is served by a private bath. The corner whirlpool tub invites one to rejuvenate after a long day. There's also a separate shower, a private toilet room, a dual vanity, and a walk-in closet.

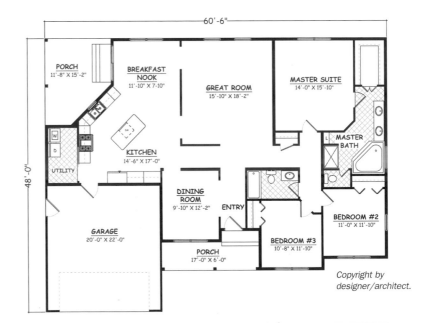

Copyright by designer/architect.

YOU CAN EXPAND THIS HOUSE!

For the ever-growing family, this home is designed to be expanded. When you're ready to "grow" the house you can purchase its second floor addition, Plan #723019. To see the finished 2-story version go to page 216.

Plan #722052

Dimensions: 70' W x 25' D
Levels: 2
Heated Square Footage: 1,900
Main Level Sq. Ft.: 1,150
Upper Level Sq. Ft.: 750
Bedrooms: 4
Bathrooms: 3
Foundation: Crawl space, slab or basement
Material Take-off Included: Yes
Price Category: D

You will love the features in this traditional-style two-story home.

Images provided by designer/architect.

Features:

- **Entry Foyer:** Step from the covered porch into this spacious entry foyer. With an ample coat closet and views through to the dining room, this foyer welcomes all into the home.

- **Kitchen:** This kitchen is designed with efficiency in mind. Just steps away is a utility room housing the washer and dryer, ensuring that the multitasking that is often required with today's active lifestyles is made much simpler.

- **Office:** Placed at the rear of the home is this moderately sized office. This room is a perfect spot for completing homework or managing the household finances.

- **Master Suite:** This lovely master suite provides a quiet area to relax after a long day. This room is set apart from the secondary bedrooms in the home and houses a private bathroom for additional comfort.

- **Upper Level:** In addition to two of the secondary bedrooms and a full bathroom, this level houses a generously sized family room.

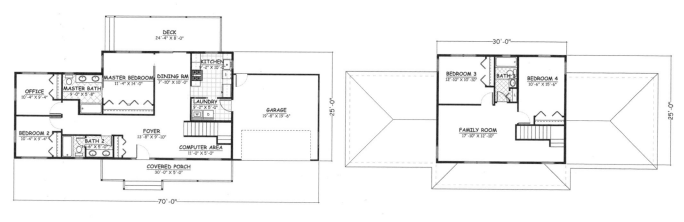

Main Level Floor Plan

Upper Level Floor Plan

Copyright by designer/architect.

Plan #722012

Dimensions: 51'2" W x 44'6" D

Levels: 2

Heated Square Footage: 1,910

Main Level Sq. Ft.: 1,465

Upper Level Sq. Ft.: 445

Bedrooms: 3

Bathrooms: 3

Foundation: Crawl space, slab or basement

Material Take-off Included: Yes

Price Category: D

Features:

- **Covered Porches:** These front and rear porches are perfect for enjoying the outdoors while being protected from the weather.

- **Foyer:** This elegant entrance has its own closet. It invites in family and friends alike.

- **Kitchen:** This modern U-shaped kitchen is located adjacent to the dining room for an open feel. It has plenty of counter space and a double sink.

- **Master Suite:** This retreat comes complete with a tray ceiling, a walk-in closet, and a luxurious spa-like master bath. The bath features a large whirlpool tub, double dual vanities, and a large linen closet.

- **Upper Level:** This upper level features an additional bedroom and bath. It also has a playroom that is sure to become a favorite location of young and old alike.

Brick trim and sidelights are just some of the features of this charming two-story cottage-style home that give it unique curb appeal.

CAD FILE AVAILABLE

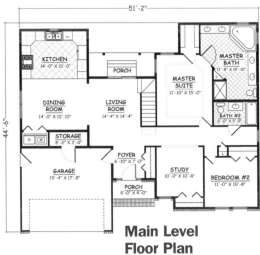

Main Level Floor Plan

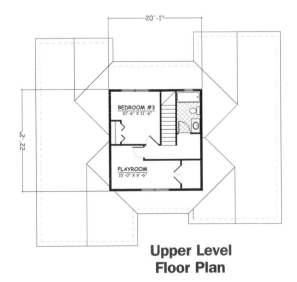

Upper Level Floor Plan

Copyright by designer/architect.

Plan #722061

Dimensions: 65'6" W x 35'4" D
Levels: 2
Heated Square Footage: 1,917
Main Level Sq. Ft.: 1,294
Upper Level Sq. Ft.: 623
Bedrooms: 4
Bathrooms: 3
Foundation: Crawl space, slab or basement
Material Take-off Included: Yes
Price Category: D

You'll love the open layout and excellent design of this spacious-feeling home.

 CAD FILE AVAILABLE

Images provided by designer/architect.

Features:

- Covered Porch: The facade of this home is graced with a charming covered porch. This porch is wide enough for the placement of a small seating area, sure to used on many a summer's evening.

- Living Room : A central gathering spot for all and the primary area for entertaining, this living room can be reached directly from the covered entry porch and is open to the dining room at the rear.

- Office: This private office, set apart from the public spaces in the house, is a perfect area for completing homework or working on the household finances.

- Master Suite: This lovely master suite, with its large walk-in closet and private bathroom, is sure to provide you a quiet place to relax after a long day. The private bathroom features a dual vanity, an oversize tub, and a separate shower, which add comfort to already lovely space.

- Upper Level: Along with the additional secondary bedrooms, this floor features a family room and full-size bathroom.

Expanded to allow for the family's growth, this home, with its simple and fluid lines, remains affordable to build.

Main Level Floor Plan

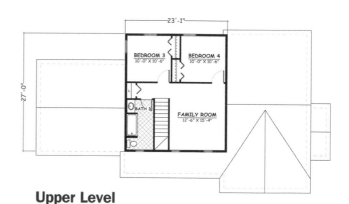

Upper Level Floor Plan

Copyright by designer/architect.

Plan #722063

Dimensions: 50'4" W x 27'6" D
Levels: 2
Heated Square Footage: 1,955
Main Level Sq. Ft.: 1,381
Upper Level Sq. Ft.: 574
Bedrooms: 4
Bathrooms: 3
Foundation: Crawl space, slab or basement
Material Take-off Included: Yes
Price Category: D

Optional Free Garage: If you would like an optional FREE 2-car garage plan, select one from page 8 or 9.

CAD FILE AVAILABLE

Images provided by designer/architect.

The expansive covered front porch and dormers give this wonderfully designed ranch home a bit of country charm.

Features:

• Great Room: From the covered porch, step directly into this grand great room. The generous size and central location of this room make it an area that is certain to be the gathering spot for all. The great room is open to both the kitchen and the dining room, allowing for a seamless transition from one area to the next.

• Kitchen: The family chef will certainly find this kitchen a delight. With its center island, the already ample counter space in this well-designed kitchen is expanded, making meal preparations a joy. The kitchen is open to both the great room and the kitchen, allowing the chef to interact with the rest of the family.

• Master Suite: A generously sized space that is set apart from the secondary bedrooms in this home, this master suite will be the perfect spot to relax after a long day. It features a large walk-in closet and a private bathroom, providing additional comfort. The bathroom houses a tub, a separate shower, and dual vanities.

• Upper Level: In addition to two secondary bedrooms and a full bathroom, this floor boasts a generously sized playroom.

Main Level Floor Plan

DECK
45'-0" X 10'-0"

LAUNDRY
14'-4" X 4'-10"

KITCHEN
10'-0" X 10'-8"
ISLAND

DINING ROOM
10'-0" X 10'-8"

BEDROOM 2
14'-4" X 10'-4"

MASTER BATH

W.I.C

BATH 2

MASTER BEDROOM
14'-4" X 15'-2"

GREAT ROOM
16'-8" X 15'-10"

OFFICE
12'-4" X 10'-4"

COVERED PORCH
45'-0" X 5'-0"

50'-4"

27'-6"

Upper Level Floor Plan

20'-11"

BEDROOM 3
9'-10" X 10'-10"

BEDROOM 4
9'-10" X 10'-10"

27'-6"

BATH 3

PLAYROOM
8'-2" X 11'-4"

Copyright by designer/architect.

Plan #721023

Dimensions: 67'10" W x 58'2" D
Levels: 1
Heated Square Footage: 1,975
Bedrooms: 3
Bathrooms: 2½
Foundation: Crawl space, slab or basement
Material Take-off Included: Yes
Price Category: D

Images provided by designer/architect.

• **Master Suite:** Set apart from the secondary bedrooms in the home is a spacious master suite. The suite features two walk-in closets as well as a private bath. The private bath includes a separate shower, a private toilet room, a dual vanity, and a luxurious soaking tub, which will make this space a haven from the everyday.

• **Office:** Located steps from the foyer and a good distance from the heart of family activity, this room offers enough privacy for doing household finances or homework. For additional comfort, a powder room is nearby.

This thoughtfully designed ranch home, with a country-style front porch, welcomes friends and family.

Features:

• **Entry Foyer:** This spacious foyer ushers you in, immediately making you feel comfortable.

• **Formal Dining Room:** Located conveniently off the foyer and across from the kitchen, this room will surely be the host to many gatherings.

• **Kitchen:** With its center island that adds both additional counter-space and an informal eating area, this kitchen will be a delight for any chef.

Copyright by designer/architect.

YOU CAN EXPAND THIS HOUSE!

For the ever-growing family, this home is designed to be expanded. When you're ready to "grow" the house you can purchase its second floor addition, Plan #723023. To see the finished 2-story version go to page 203.

Plan #722030

Dimensions: 72'7" W x 26' D

Levels: 2

Heated Square Footage: 1,978

Main Level Sq. Ft.: 1,200

Upper Level Sq. Ft.: 778

Bedrooms: 4

Bathrooms: 3

Foundation: Crawl space, slab or basement

Material Take-off Included: Yes

Price Category: D

Images provided by designer/architect.

- **Master Suite:** Privacy is assured in this master suite, as it is separated from the main part of the house. A separate bath and his and her walk-in closets add convenience as well as luxury.

- **Master Bath:** This space features a sunlit whirlpool tub, separate shower, private toilet room, and dual sink vanity. These amenities will soothe you at the end of a busy day.

- **Upper Level:** This space contains three additional bedrooms and a full bath. The second bedroom has a private entrance to the bath with a separate tub and toilet area. The third bedroom features a built-in desk. This is a layout that is perfect for the older children in the family.

A feeling of spaciousness is generated in this home by its generous rooms and excellent design.

CAD FILE AVAILABLE

Features:

- **Living Room:** This large room is open to the kitchen and offers sliding glass doors to the rear deck. The open floor plan will ensure that it becomes the central gathering place for the entire family.

- **Kitchen:** The large pantry and plenty of extra storage space will keep the cook organized. The rest of the family will enjoy the companionship that the snack bar encourages.

Rear Elevation

Main Level Floor Plan

Upper Level Floor Plan

Copyright by designer/architect.

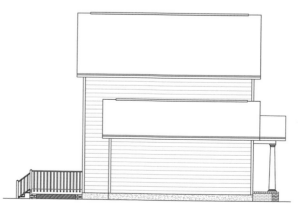

Left Elevation

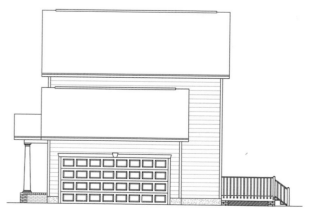

Right Elevation

Kitchen Cabinets

Of all the rooms in a house, kitchens present unique decorating challenges because so much tends to happen in these spaces. In addition to preparing meals, most families use kitchens as gathering and entertaining areas. Kitchens need to be functional, comfortable, and inviting.

Who can't relate to this scenario: you turn on the oven to preheat it, but wait, did you take out the large roasting pan first?

How about the lasagna dish, muffin tins, pizza stone, and cookie sheets that are in there, too? Now where can you put everything that was in the oven while the casserole is baking and the countertop is laden with the rest of tonight's dinner ingredients? Good cabinetry outfitted with an assortment of organizing options can help you there. It can make your kitchen more efficient and a whole lot neater while establishing a style, or "look," for the room.

Cabinet Construction

Basically, cabinets are constructed in one of two ways: framed or frameless. Framed cabinets have a traditional look, with a full frame across the face of the cabinet box that may show between closed doors. This secures adjacent cabinets and strengthens wider cabinet boxes with a center rail. Hinges on framed cabinets may or may not be visible around doors when they are closed. The door's face may be ornamented with raised or recessed panels, trimmed or framed panels, or a framed-glass panel with or without muntins (the narrow vertical and horizontal strips of wood that divide panes of glass).

Frameless Cabinets. Also known as European-style cabinets, although American manufacturers also make them, frameless cabinets are built without a face frame and sport a clean, contemporary look, often not befitting a Southern or Country style. There's no trim or molding with this simple design. Close-fitting doors cover the entire front of the box, no ornamentation appears on the face of the doors, and hinges are typically hidden inside the cabinet box.

Selecting Cabinets

Choosing one type over another is generally a matter of taste, although framed units offer slightly less interior space. But the quality of construction is a factor that should always be taken into consideration. How do you judge it? Solid wood is too expensive for most of today's budgets, but it might be used on just the doors and frames. More typical is plywood box construction, which offers good structural support and solid wood on the doors and frames. To save money, cabinetmakers sometimes use strong plywood for support elements, such as the box and frame, and medium-density fiberboard for other parts, such as doors and drawer fronts. In

yet another alternative, good-quality laminate cabinets can be made with high-quality, thick particleboard underneath the laminate finish.

Quality Points. There are other things to look for in cabinet construction. They include dovetail or mortise-and-tenon joinery and solidly mortised hinges. Also, make sure that the interior of every cabinet is well finished, with adjustable shelves that are a minimum ⅜ inch thick to prevent bowing.

Bead-board paneled doors, opposite, are at home in Southern-style kitchens.

Framed cabinets, above, offer a traditional look to an otherwise modern kitchen.

Country-style designs have many attributes of Cottage decor, right.

Unless you have the time and skill to build the cabinets yourself or can hire someone else to do it, you'll have to purchase them in one of four ways. **Knockdown cabinetry** (also known as RTA, ready to assemble) is shipped flat and, sometimes, unfinished because you put the pieces together. **Stock cabinetry** comes in standard sizes but limited styles and colors; it is often available on the spot or can be delivered quickly. Like stock, **semicustom cabinetry** comes in standard styles, but it is manufactured to fit a home-owner's specific size and finish needs. **Custom cabinetry** is not limited in terms of style or size because it is built to the designer's specifications.

The Decorative Role of Cabinets

The look you create in your kitchen will be largely influenced by the cabinetry you select. Finding a style that suits you and how you will use your new kitchen is similar to shopping for furniture. In fact, don't be surprised to see many furniture details dressing up the cabinets on view in show-rooms and home centers today.

Details That Stand Out. Besides architectural elements such as fluted pilasters, corbels, moldings, and bull's-eye panels, look for details such as fretwork, rope motifs, gingerbread trim, balusters, composition ornamentation (it looks like carving), even footed cabinets that mimic separate furniture pieces. If your taste runs toward less fussy design, you'll also find handsome door and drawer styles that feature minimal decoration, if any. Woods and finishes are just as varied, and range from informal looks in birch, oak, ash, and maple to rich mahogany and cherry. Laminate finishes, though less popular than they were a decade ago, haven't completely disappeared from the marketplace, but an array of colors has replaced the once-ubiquitous almond and white finishes.

Color

Color is coming on strong on wood cabinetry, too. Accents in one, two, or more hues are pairing with natural wood tones. White-painted cabinets take on a warmer glow with tinted shades of this always popular neutral. Special "vintage" finishes, such as translucent color glazes, continue to grow in popularity, as do distressed finishing techniques such as wire brushing and rubbed-through color that add both another dimension and the appeal of handcraftmanship, even on mass-produced items.

If you're shy about using color on such a high-ticket item as cabinetry, try it as an accent on molding, door trim, or island cabinetry. Just as matched furniture suites have become passé in other rooms of the house, the same is true for the kitchen, where mixing several looks can add sophistication and visual interest.

Cabinet Hardware

Another way to emphasize your kitchen's style is with hardware. From exquisite reproductions in brass, pewter, wrought iron, or ceramic to handsome bronze, chrome, nickel, glass, steel, plastic, rubber, wood, or stone creations, a smorgasbord of shapes and designs is available. Some pieces are highly polished; others are matte-finished, smooth, or hammered. Some are abstract or geometrical; others are simple,

elegant shapes. Whimsical designs take on the forms of animals or teapots, vegetables or flowers. Even just one or two great-looking door or drawer pulls can be showstoppers in a kitchen that may otherwise be devoid of much personality. Like mixing cabinet finishes, a combination of two hardware styles—perhaps picked up from other materials in the room— makes a big design statement. As the famed architect Mies Van der Rohe once stated, "God is in the details," and the most perfect detail in your new kitchen may be the artistic hardware that you select.

Cabinet style will set the tone for the design of the entire kitchen. The simple door styles keeps the room at left airy and casual.

The rustic look of the cabinets above is tailor-made for any Country style kitchen.

Color accents, such as the splash of color on the kitchen island shown right, can customize any simple cabinet design.

Cabinet hardware should complement the cabinet door and drawer designs, but it should also be easy for everyone in the household to grasp, above.

Kitchen storage comes in a variety of forms, including cabinets, drawers, pullout extensions, and the glass-front bins shown to the right.

Besides looks, consider the function of a pull or knob. You have to be able to grip it easily and comfortably. If your fingers or hands get stiff easily, or if you have arthritis, select C- or U-shaped pulls. If you like a knob, try it out in the showroom to make sure it isn't slippery or awkward when you grab it. Knobs and pulls can be inexpensive if you can stick to unfinished ones that you can paint in an accent color picked up from the tile or wallpaper. If you don't plan to buy new cabinets, changing the hardware on old ones can redefine their style. The right knob or pull can suggest any one of a number of vintage looks or decorative styles, from Colonial to Victorian, and reinforce your decor.

Types of Storage
Storage facilities can make or break a kitchen, so choose the places you'll put things with care. Here's a look at a few alternatives:

Pantries. How often you shop and how many groceries you typically bring home determine the amount of food storage space your family needs. If you like to stock up or take advantage of sales, add a pantry to your kitchen. To maximize a pantry's convenience, plan shallow, 6-inch-deep shelves so that cans and packages will never be stored more than two deep. This way, you'll easily be able to see what you've got on hand. Pantries range in size from floor-to-ceiling models to narrow units designed to fit between two standard-size cabinets.

Appliance Garages. Appliance garages make use of dead space in a corner, but they can be installed anywhere in the vertical space between wall-mounted cabinets and the countertop. A tambour (rolltop) door hides small appliances like a food processor or anything else you want within reach but hidden from view.

Lazy Susans and Carousel Shelves. Rotating shelves like lazy Susans and carousels maximize dead corner storage and put items like dishes or pots and pans within easy reach. A lazy Susan rotates 360 degrees, so just spin it to find what you're looking for. Carousel shelves, which attach to two right-angled doors, rotate 270 degrees; open the doors, and the shelves swing out allowing you to reach items easily.

Pivoting Shelves. Door-mounted shelves and in-cabinet swiveling shelf units offer easy access to kitchen supplies. Taller units serve as pantries that hold a great deal in minimal space.

Pullout Tables and Trays. In tight kitchens, pullout tables and trays are excellent ways to gain eating space or an extra work surface. Pullout cutting boards come in handy near cooktops, microwaves, and food prep areas. Pullout tea carts are also available.

Customized Organizers. If you decide to use value-priced cabinets or choose to forego the storage accessories offered by manufacturers, consider refitting their interiors with cabinet organizers you purchase yourself. These plastic, plastic-coated wire, or enameled-steel racks and hangers are widely available at department stores, hardware stores, and home centers.

Some of these units slide in and out of base cabinets, similar to the racks in a dishwasher. Others let you mount shallow drawers to the undersides of wall cabinets. Still others consist of stackable plastic bins with plenty of room to hold kitchen sundries.

Beware of the temptation to over-specialize your kitchen storage facilities. Sizes and needs for certain items change, so be sure to allot at least 50 percent of your kitchen's storage to standard cabinets with one or more movable shelves. And don't forget to allow for storing recyclable items.

Today's cabinets can be customized with storage accessories, right.

Full-height pantries, above, provide a number of different types of storage near where you need the items. This pantry is next to the food-prep area.

Base cabinets can be outfitted with accessories for kitchen storage or for wet bar storage as shown in the cabinet below.

Storage Checklist

Here's a guide to help you get your storage needs in order.

■ **Do you like kitchen gadgets?**
Plan drawer space, countertop sorters, wall magnets, or hooks to keep these items handy near where you often use them.

■ **Do you own a food processor, blender, mixer, toaster oven, electric can opener, knife sharpener, juicer, coffee maker, or coffee mill?**
If you're particularly tidy, you may want small appliances like these tucked away in an appliance garage or cupboard to be taken out only when needed. If you pre-fer to have frequently used machines sitting on the counter, ready to go, plan enough space, along with conveniently located electrical outlets.

■ **Do you plan to store large quantities of food?**
Be sure to allow plenty of freezer, bin, and shelf space for the kind of food shopping you do.

■ **Do you intend to do a lot of freezing or canning?**
Allow a work space and place to stow equipment. Also plan adequate storage for the fruits of your labor—an extra stand-alone freezer, a good-sized food safe in the kitchen, or a separate pantry or cellar.

■ **Do you bake often?**
Consider a baking center that can house your equipment and serve as a separate baking-ingredients pantry.

■ **Do you collect pottery, tinware, or anything else that might be displayed in the kitchen?**
Soffits provide an obvious place to hang small objects like collectible plates. Eliminating soffits provides a shelf on top of the wall cabinets for larger lightweight objects like baskets. Open shelving, glass-front cupboards, and display cabinets are other options.

■ **Do you collect cookbooks?**
If so, you'll need expandable shelf space and perhaps a bookstand.

Personal Profile of You and Your Family

■ **How tall are you and everyone else who will use your kitchen?**
Adjust your counter and wall-cabinet heights to suit. Multilevel work surfaces for special tasks are a necessity for good kitchen design.

■ **Do you or any of your family members use a walker, leg braces, or a wheelchair?**
Plan a good work height, knee space, grab bars, secure seating, slide-out work

boards, and other convenience features to make your kitchen comfortable for all who will use it.

■ **Are you left- or right-handed?**
Think about your natural motion when you choose whether to open cupboards or refrigerator doors from the left or right side, whether to locate your dishwasher to the left or right of the sink, and so on.

■ **How high can you comfortably reach?**
If you're tall, hang your wall cabinets high. If you're petite, you may want to hang the cabinets lower and plan a spot to keep a step stool handy.

■ **Can you comfortably bend and reach for something in a base cabinet? Can you lift heavy objects easily and without strain or pain?**
If your range is limited in these areas, be sure to plan roll-out shelving on both upper and lower tiers of your base cabinets. Also, look into spring-up shelves designed to lift mixer bases or other heavy appliances to counter height.

■ **Do you frequently share cooking tasks with another family member?**
If so, you may each prefer to have your own work area.

Fold-down ironing boards, above left, are a true luxury. If you have the space, install one near the kitchen or laundry room.

Corner cabinets often contain storage space you can't reach. Make it accessible by installing swing-out shelves, above right, or a lazy Susan.

Glass doors put your kitchen items on display. The owners of the kitchen below chose distinctive pottery and glassware for their glass-door cabinets.

Images provided by designer/architect.

Plan #722053

Dimensions: 50' W x 49'3" D

Levels: 2

Heated Square Footage: 2,032

Main Level Sq. Ft.: 1,384

Upper Level Sq. Ft.: 648

Bedrooms: 4

Bathrooms: 3

Foundation: Crawl space, slab or basement

Material Take-off Included: Yes

Price Category: D

The wraparound porch, with its turned columns, gives additional curb appeal toan already pleasing traditional-style home.

CAD FILE AVAILABLE

Features:

• Living Room: Accessed from the front entry door and a side French door, this gracious living room will offer the homeowners a wonderful place to relax and entertain.

• Kitchen: The efficient layout and ample counter space this galley-style kitchen provides will surely please the family cook.

• Family Room: Open to the dining room and next to the kitchen, this spacious family room is certain to be the main gathering spot for all.

• Master Suite: Featuring a private bathroom and a large walk-in closet, this generously sized master suite will offer you the comfort and privacy you seek.

• Upper Level: In addition to a secondary bedroom and full bathroom, this level is home to a spacious office area that offers privacy for the completion of homework or for working on the household finances. There is also a storage room for keeping seasonal items in a location that is easily accessible.

Left Elevation

Right Elevation

**Main Level
Floor Plan**

BEDROOM 2
9'-4" X 12'-4"

BATH 2

BEDROOM 3
9'-4" X 12'-4"

FAMILY ROOM
11'-4" X 12'-0"

DINING ROOM
9'-2" X 12'-0"

DECK
24'-4" X 8'-0"

KITCHEN
9'-2" X 10'-10"

LIVING ROOM
12'-8" X 15'-8"

MASTER BED
16'-0" X 11'-10"

MASTER BATH

LAUNDRY
9'-2" X 5'-0"

COVERED PORCH
51'-0" X 5'-0"

GARAGE
19'-6" X 19'-8"

50'-0"

49'-3"

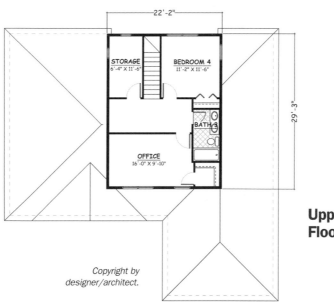

**Upper Level
Floor Plan**

STORAGE
6'-4" X 11'-6"

BEDROOM 4
11'-2" X 11'-6"

BATH 3

OFFICE
16'-0" X 9'-10"

22'-2"

29'-3"

*Copyright by
designer/architect.*

Rear
Elevation

Images provided by designer/architect.

Plan #721004

Dimensions: 59'9" W x 50'5" D

Levels: 1

Heated Square Footage: 1,981

Bedrooms: 3

Bathrooms: 2½

Foundation: Crawl space, slab or basement

Material Take-off Included: Yes

Price Category: D

The wraparound porch gives this home a farmhouse country appeal.

CAD FILE AVAILABLE

Features:

- **Porch:** Wrapping around the entire house, this wonderfully designed porch invites you to sit and relax.

- **Living Room:** With large windows at the front and side, this room is warm and inviting. It is the perfect place for entertaining guests.

- **Dining Room:** With windows mirroring those found in the formal living room, this wonderfully open space is the perfect place for large family meals or festive gatherings with friends. The room also features sliding glass doors that open out to a screened-in porch, allowing for dining alfresco in comfort.

- **Kitchen:** This spacious kitchen features a center island, large countertops, numerous cabinets, and a large pantry, making this kitchen a chef's dream. The space is also open to the dining room allowing for interaction while the chef is preparing the feast.

- **Master Suite:** Large windows and French doors that open onto the porch enhance the view from this wonderfully private space. The room also features such luxuries as a private bath, and two walk-in closets.

Copyright by designer/architect.

[Floor plan]
- COVERED PORCH
- BEDROOM 2 — 14'-0" X 12'-0"
- MASTER BEDROOM — 20'-0" X 12'-0"
- GARAGE — 20'-0" X 25'-0"
- BATH 2 — 9'-6" X 5'
- MASTER BATH — 14'-0" X 10'-0"
- POWDER RM.
- BEDROOM 3 — 14'-0" X 11'-6"
- PANTRY
- KITCHEN — 14'-0" X 12'-6"
- ISLAND
- LIVING ROOM — 14'-0" X 14'-0"
- FOYER — 8'-0" X 13'-6"
- DINING ROOM — 14'-0" X 11'-0"
- SCREEN PORCH — 6'-0" X 10'-0"
- COVERED PORCH
- 59'-9"
- 50'-5"

YOU CAN EXPAND THIS HOUSE!

For the ever-growing family, this home is designed to be expanded. When you're ready to "grow" the house you can purchase its second floor addition, Plan #723004. To see the finished 2-story version go to page 227.

Plan #721003

Dimensions: 72'6" W x 35' D
Levels: 1
Heated Square Footage: 1,996
Bedrooms: 3
Bathrooms: 2½
Foundation: Crawl space, slab or basement
Material Take-off Included: Yes
Price Category: D

This beautiful ranch-style home features clean and simple lines.

CAD FILE AVAILABLE

Images provided by designer/architect.

Features:

- Foyer: This wide and open foyer welcomes you home. With a coat closet and mudroom to the right for convenience, the foyer leads you to the large dining room and great room.

- The Great Room: This elaborate room will surely be your main gathering space. Large openings provide easy transitions from room to room, while the tray ceiling adds an elegant touch.

- Kitchen: This roomy kitchen features large countertop workspaces and numerous cabinets, making this kitchen easy to organize and an ideal place to cook. A convenient pass through to the dining room makes it easy to get dinner on the table.

- Master Suite: Double doors grant you entrance to this wonderfully private space. Separate from the other bedrooms in the home, this suite houses many additional luxuries. With a private bath, a walk-in closet, and a single French door that leads to the rear deck, you will surely look forward to the comfort that this private space offers. The bathroom houses a dual vanity, a large tub, a separate shower, and private toilet room, adding to the comfort of the entire suite.

While this home already abounds with wonderful amenities, its unique designs allows for additional expansion to fit the needs of a growing family.

YOU CAN EXPAND THIS HOUSE!

For the ever-growing family, this home is designed to be expanded. When you're ready to "grow" the house you can purchase its second floor addition, Plan #723003. To see the finished 2-story version go to page 224.

Plan #722071

Dimensions: 51'8" W x 60' D
Levels: 2
Heated Square Footage: 2,032
Main Level Sq. Ft.: 1,260
Upper Level Sq. Ft.: 772
Bedrooms: 5
Bathrooms: 3½
Foundation: Crawl space, slab or basement
Material Take-off Included: Yes
Price Category: D

This wonderfully designed traditional-style two-story home has both private and public spaces that will be sure to please all members of the family.

Features:

• Foyer: Enter into this welcoming foyer from the lovely deck. For convenience, this space features tiled flooring and a moderately sized coat closet.

• Family Room: Step from the foyer into this gracious family room, certain to be a gathering spot for all. The ample size of the room is perfect for entertaining, or just spending time together as a family.

• Master Suite: This master suite will be a welcome retreat after a long day. This gracious space is sure to delight, with its expansive

walk-in closet and private bathroom, which features an oversized tub, a separate shower, and dual vanities, providing additional comfort to the room. A French door leading to the rear deck continues the relaxation to the outdoors.

• Upper Level: This upper level provides additional public and private spaces for the family, including two additional bedrooms, a full bathroom, a craft room, and a sitting room.

• Sitting Room: While the main-level family room is a great spot for entertaining, this sitting area upstairs provides a more private area for the family to gather and perhaps curl up with a good book.

With its thoughtful design, this home has features that will please all members of the family, while remaining affordable to build.

Main Level Floor Plan

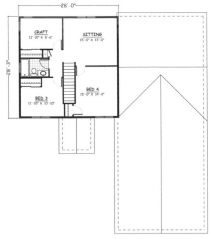

Upper Level Floor Plan

Copyright by designer/architect.

Plan #721010

Dimensions: 85' W x 35' D
Levels: 1
Heated Square Footage: 2,028
Bedrooms: 3
Bathrooms: 2
Foundation: Crawl space, slab or basement
Material Take-off Included: Yes
Price Category: D

This moderate traditional home has clean and simple lines, making it easy to build.

Features:

• Covered Porch: This large covered porch makes a great first impression on your visiting friends and family.

• Living Room: The large picture window makes this room a bright and inviting space to entertain friends or just relax with the family.

Images provided by designer/architect.

• Kitchen: The island, which features a snack bar, makes for an inviting work area in this kitchen. The windows over the corner sink provide excellent views to the backyard. The pantry and adjoining dining room complete the space.

• Mudroom/Utility Room: Located near the kitchen with direct access to the garage, this room features a washer and dryer, a storage cabinet, a hanging closet, and a bench that provides a spot to take off your muddy shoes.

• Master Suite: This is a bright, spacious room that has a luxurious bath that includes a corner whirlpool tub, a separate shower, and a dual vanity. It's the perfect place for busy workday mornings or relaxing on the weekend. The room also features a large walk-in-closet.

• Deck: The large deck is the perfect transition from house to yard, while providing a place for the grill for outdoor summer entertaining.

Copyright by designer/architect.

YOU CAN EXPAND THIS HOUSE!

For the ever-growing family, this home is designed to be expanded. When you're ready to "grow" the house you can purchase its second floor addition, Plan #723010. To see the finished 2-story version go to page 220.

Plan #722067

Dimensions: 49'7" W x 29'5" D

Levels: 2

Heated Square Footage: 2,077

Main Level Sq. Ft.: 1,293

Upper Level Sq. Ft.: 784

Bedrooms: 4

Bathrooms: 3

Foundation: Crawl space, slab or basement

Material Take-off Included: Yes

Price Category: D

Optional Free Garage: If you would like an optional FREE 2-car garage plan, select one from page 8 or 9.

CAD FILE AVAILABLE CAD

If you like the look of a traditional-style home this one is sure to please the entire family.

Features:

- Covered Entry: This cozy covered entry porch provides you with some shelter from the elements.

- Dining Room: This gracious space will surely be the spot for festive dinner parties as well as the everyday family meal. At the rear of the room is a set of sliding glass doors leading to an expansive deck that will continue the already generous living area.

- Master Suite: This master suite's private bathroom with dual vanities, an oversized tub, and a separate shower will provide you a bit

of comfort. The spacious suite is separated from the other bedrooms in the home, ensuring you the privacy you seek.

- Upper Level: In addition to two secondary bedrooms, a full bathroom, and a storage closet, this floor also has a wonderfully spacious family room.

- Office: This bright and airy office will make studying more enjoyable. The room is located away from the main gathering areas in the home, giving you the privacy you need to complete your tasks.

With its well thought out design, this two-story home remains affordable to build.

Main Level Floor Plan

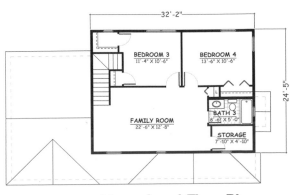

Upper Level Floor Plan

Copyright by designer/architect.

Plan #722029

Dimensions: 45'5" W x 50' D

Levels: 2

Heated Square Footage: 2,089

Main Level Sq. Ft.: 1,358

Upper Level Sq. Ft.: 731

Bedrooms: 4

Bathrooms: 3

Foundation: Crawl space, slab or basement

Material Take-off Included: Yes

Price Category: D

Images provided by designer/architect.

A classic hip roof design and large windows grace the exterior of this two-story home.

Features:

- Covered Porch: This moderate covered entry porch provides an elegant entrance to the home.

- Dining Room: This room, which is adjacent to the kitchen and has a entrance to the rear deck through French doors, is ideal for both elegant dinner parties and casual summer gatherings.

- Kitchen: This warm and inviting kitchen is open to the living room and features French doors to the rear deck. The pantry offers plenty of storage, and the snack bar provides seating for informal meals.

- Master Suite: This first floor master suite is located away from the other bedrooms for maximum privacy. The generous walk-in

closet and en-suite bath add to the luxury of the space. The whirlpool tub, separate shower, and dual sinks complete the lavish amenities.

- Upper Level: Two additional bedrooms, a full bath with dual sinks, and a laundry room allow the younger members of the family a measure of privacy.

- Computer Room: A loft-style room with a built-in desk and large storage closet is just the place for the family computer.

Main Level Floor Plan

Copyright by designer/architect.

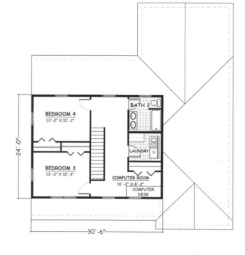

Upper Level Floor Plan

Plan #721075

Dimensions: 98' W x 31' D
Levels: 1
Heated Square Footage: 2,114
Bedrooms: 3
Bathrooms: 2½
Foundation: Crawl space, slab or basement
Material Take-off Included: Yes
Price Category: D

A grand front porch creates an inviting entry to this spacious ranch home.

CAD FILE AVAILABLE

Features:

- Covered Porch: Across the length of the main portion of the home is this delightfully designed covered porch. Turned columns add charm, while the width of the porch allows for the placement of chairs and planters, creating a welcoming entry to the home.

- Kitchen: Organization will be made easy in this spacious kitchen featuring a large pantry, ample counter space, and lots of cabinet space. Large cased openings leading to both the dining room and the central hallway, along with a window above the sink, make this space feel bright and airy.

- Master Suite: This relaxing master suite features a large walk-in closet and a private bathroom. The private bathroom features an oversize tub and a dual vanity adding comfort and privacy.

- Secondary Rooms: Rounding out the home are an additional two bedrooms that have private entrances to the hall bathroom. The home also features a powder room, providing additional comfort for family and guests alike.

This home remains affordable to build while including amenities sure to please all members of the family. Thoughtful design also ensures that the home can be easily expanded to fit the needs of a growing family.

DECK
35'-0" X 10'-0"

DINING ROOM
20'-0" X 14'-6"

KITCHEN
15'-6" X 14'-6"

W.I.C.

PANTRY

MASTER SUITE
17'-0" X 14'-6"

MASTER BATH
10'-0" X 9'-6"

GARAGE
28'-0" X 24'-0"

LAUNDRY
10'-0" X 8'-0"

GREAT ROOM
20'-0" X 15'-6"

BATH 2

BEDROOM 3
11'-6" X 15'-0"

BEDROOM 2
15'-0" X 12'-0"

COVERED PORCH
60'-0" X 8'-0"

31'-0"

98'-0"

Copyright by designer/architect.

YOU CAN EXPAND THIS HOUSE!

For the ever-growing family, this home is designed to be expanded. When you're ready to "grow" the house you can purchase its second floor addition, Plan #723075. To see the finished 2-story version go to page 227.

Images provided by designer/architect.

Plan #721020

Dimensions: 70' W x 48' D
Levels: 1
Heated Square Footage: 2,121
Bedrooms: 3
Bathrooms: 2½
Foundation: Crawl space, slab or basement
Material Take-off Included: Yes
Price Category: B

The open design of this traditional house gives the home a spacious feel, while the clean lines keep it affordable to build.

Features:

• Covered Porch: This large centrally located covered entry porch is just the place to greet guests.

• Dining Room: Adjacent to the kitchen, this dining room features a set of French doors that open onto the large covered rear porch.

• Kitchen: A work island in this L-shaped kitchen makes this room a delight for any cook.

• Master Suite: A tray ceiling and French doors leading to the bath give this suite understated elegance. The luxurious bath features a corner whirlpool tub, a separate shower, a private toilet room, and a double vanity.

Secondary Bedrooms: Two additional bedrooms share a bath that is complete with a tub, a separate shower, and a dual vanity.

This well-designed house is just the place for the busy family to call home.

CAD FILE AVAILABLE

Copyright by designer/architect.

YOU CAN EXPAND THIS HOUSE!

For the ever-growing family, this home is designed to be expanded. When you're ready to "grow" the house you can purchase its second floor addition, Plan #723020. To see the finished 2-story version go to page 217.

Plan #722028

Dimensions: 66' W x 26' D

Levels: 2

Heated Square Footage: 2,125

Main Level Sq. Ft.: 1,085

Upper Level Sq. Ft.: 1,040

Bedrooms: 4

Bathrooms: 3

Foundation: Crawl space, slab or basement

Material Take-off Included: Yes

Price Category: D

The covered porch and large windows add to this two-story traditional home's curb appeal.

CAD FILE AVAILABLE

Features:

- Covered Porch: This large covered entry porch, with its elegant columns, offers shelter from the elements and has enough room for a small seating area.

- Living Room: This room opens from the foyer and is connected to the kitchen through a cased opening. It features sliding glass doors that open onto a rear deck and French doors that lead to a covered porch. This living room truly invites indoor and outdoor entertaining.

- Kitchen: This eat-in kitchen is just steps away from the utility room and a full bath. It also opens up to the living room, which allows for easy traffic flow when entertaining guests.

- Master Suite: This master suite enjoys a private bath that includes a tub, a separate shower, and a dual vanity. The room also features a large walk-in-closet and is situated away from the other bedroom to ensure privacy.

**Main Level
Floor Plan**

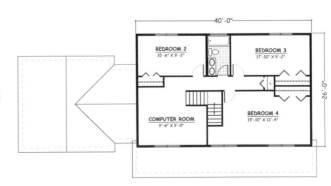

**Upper Level
Floor Plan**

Copyright by designer/architect.

Images provided by designer/architect.

Plan #722032

Dimensions: 40'2" W x 51'6" D

Levels: 2

Heated Square Footage: 2,126

Main Level Sq. Ft.: 1,224

Upper Level Sq. Ft.: 902

Bedrooms: 3

Bathrooms: 3

Foundation: Crawl space, slab or basement

Material Take-off Included: Yes

Price Category: D

This lovely two-story home is perfect for the expanding family.

Features:

• Great Room: Centrally located and generous in size, this great room will be a gathering place for all. Sliding glass doors grace the rear of this room, allowing for added natural light as well as entrance to expansive covered patio area.

• Kitchen: Spacious with a plethora of countertops, this kitchen will make mealtime prep more enjoyable. Keeping up with today's active lifestyle is made easier as this kitchen also features a small utility area housing a washer and dryer.

• Master Suite: This master suite's gracious size, along with its private bath, will bring you the comfort and privacy you seek.

• Office: Located on the main floor, this office space will provide just the right amount of privacy for the completion of homework or keeping the household finances in order.

• Upper Floor: In addition to housing a third bedroom, this floor contains a large full bathroom, a game room, and a study. The game room can be easily changed to an additional secondary bedroom by adding a closet.

Main Level Floor Plan

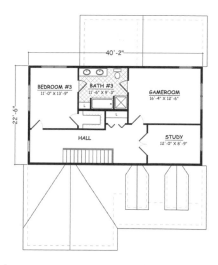

Upper Level Floor Plan

Copyright by designer/architect.

Plan #722009

Dimensions: 51' W x 47' D
Levels: 2
Heated Square Footage: 2,128
Main Level Sq. Ft.: 1,419
Upper Level Sq. Ft.: 709
Bedrooms: 4
Bathrooms: 3
Foundation: Crawl space, slab or basement
Material Take-off Included: Yes
Price Category: D

A two-story traditional design has multiple gables and a front porch for pleasing curb appeal. Its design makes it an affordable larger home.

Images provided by designer/architect.

Features:

- Covered Porch: This practical covered porch provides shelter and is perfect for greeting guests.

- Living Room: This room is inviting to family and friends, whether it's to watch the game or just sit and talk. It has a large cased opening and built-in media storage.

- Kitchen: This thoroughly modern kitchen features an angled snack bar, pantry, and plenty of counter space to make cooking a pleasure. The nearby dining room offers access to the rear deck through a French door.

- Master Suite: This private retreat offers a bathroom that includes a whirlpool tub, a dual vanity, and a walk-in closet. The room is just steps away from the laundry area for convenience.

- Upper Level: This level features two additional bedrooms. The shared bath has a separate dual vanity area. A family room and computer room complete the space, making it a place for kids to be kids without disturbing the adults of the family.

This house is just the place for the established family.

Main Level Floor Plan

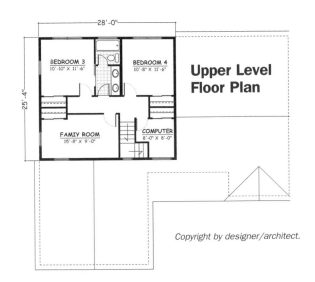

Upper Level Floor Plan

Copyright by designer/architect.

Plan #722054

Dimensions: 59'4" W x 39'6" D
Levels: 2
Heated Square Footage: 2,133
Main Level Sq. Ft.: 1,424
Upper Level Sq. Ft.: 709
Bedrooms: 4
Bathrooms: 3
Foundation: Crawl space, slab or basement
Material Take-off Included: Yes
Price Category: D

This expanded ranch home with multiple gables and lovely front porch has a country feel.

CAD FILE AVAILABLE

Images provided by designer/architect.

Features:

- Dining Room: Open to both the family room and the kitchen, this room will not only serve for weekly family meals but is sure to be the host to many festive dinner parties. The sliding glass door leads to the covered patio extending the dining area to the outdoors.

- Family Room: A central spot for all to gather, this family room is open to the dining room and features large windows sure to bathe the room in natural light, thus enhancing its open and airy feel.

- Kitchen: Designed with efficiency in mind, this wonderful kitchen features a multitude of cabinets and ample counter space sure to delight the family chef.

- Master Suite: Set apart from the other bedrooms and featuring a private bathroom, this master suite offers a quiet place to relax after a long day. The bathroom features a tub, a separate shower, and a dual vanity, which will ensure the comfort and privacy one desires.

- Upper Floor: Along with the secondary bedrooms, this floor has large linen and storage closets. The storage area is the perfect place for keeping seasonal items in a location that is easily accessible.

Copyright by designer/architect.

Main Level Floor Plan

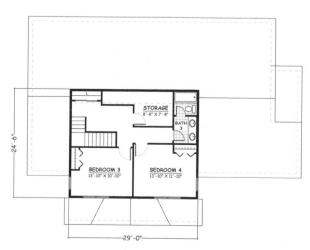

Upper Level Floor Plan

Images provided by designer/architect.

Plan #722040

Dimensions: 56'6" W x 50' D

Levels: 2

Heated Square Footage: 2,142

Main Level Sq. Ft.: 1,226

Upper Level Sq. Ft.: 916

Bedrooms: 4

Bathrooms: 3

Foundation: Crawl space, slab or basement

Material Take-off Included: Yes

Price Category: D

This delightful two-story home features amenities that will surely please each member of the family.

CAD FILE AVAILABLE

Features:

- **Entry:** Step through the front door and be welcomed immediately into the heart of the home. The area is spacious and has a free-flowing nature, allowing for easy passage between rooms.

- **Mud Room:** This tiled entry area, which includes the laundry facilities, provides a transition between the exterior breezeway and the family room.

- **Kitchen:** This spacious kitchen is open to the dining room and located close to the expansive family room. Its layout makes organization and meal preparation simple.

- **Master Suite:** Located at the rear of the home, this master suite features a private bath with a double vanity. The suite also has French doors that lead to a generously sized deck. This outdoor space offers you a place of respite for morning coffee or for sitting on a warm summer evening.

- **Secondary Bedrooms:** Three moderately sized bedrooms and two additional full bathrooms allow each member of the family the privacy they desire.

With room for all and lovely features, this home still remains affordable to build.

Main Level Floor Plan

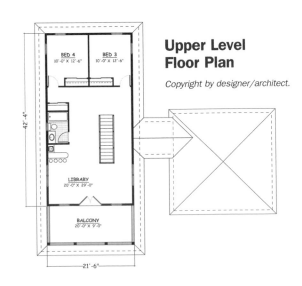

Upper Level Floor Plan

Copyright by designer/architect.

Plan #722037

Dimensions: 49' W x 50'3" D

Levels: 2

Heated Square Footage: 2,148

Main Level Sq. Ft.: 1,328

Upper Level Sq. Ft.: 820

Bedrooms: 4

Bathrooms: 3

Foundation: Crawl space, slab or basement

Material Take-off Included: Yes

Price Category: E

This charming, traditional-style two-story home is perfect for the established family.

CAD FILE AVAILABLE

Images provided by designer/architect.

Features:

- **Living/Dining Room:** Step through the entry and directly into this lovely living/dining room combination. The openness of the space allows for an easy transition between rooms and makes this the heart of the home.

- **Kitchen:** With plenty of counter and cabinet space in this U-shaped kitchen, the family chef will surely find this space easy to organize.

- **Master Suite:** This room will provide you with the comfort and solace you seek. The en-suite bath features a vanity with dual sinks

and an oversize tub that's perfect for soaking in after a long day.

- **Upper Floor:** In addition to a second floor bedroom, this floor includes a playroom, an office, a game room, and a full bathroom.

Designed with the needs of each family member in mind, this home still remains affordable to build.

Main Level Floor Plan

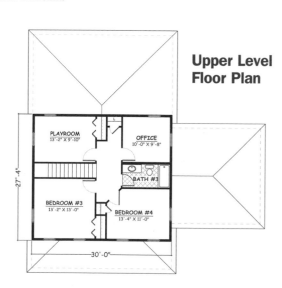

Upper Level Floor Plan

Copyright by designer/architect.

Images provided by designer/architect.

Plan #722039

Dimensions: 70' W x 39' D
Levels: 2
Heated Square Footage: 2,172
Main Level Sq. Ft.: 1,358
Upper Level Sq. Ft.: 814
Bedrooms: 5
Bathrooms: 3
Foundation: Crawl space, slab or basement
Material Take-off Included: Yes
Price Category: D

The rooflines of this charming two-story home add to its curb appeal.

CAD FILE AVAILABLE

Features:

• Living Room: Open to the dining room, kitchen, and entry hall, this gracious room welcomes friends and family alike.

• Kitchen: This tidy kitchen, with its thoughtful layout and large pantry, makes it easy for the family cook to prepare meals.

• Dining Room: Connected to both the kitchen and living room, this space will certainly be used for both intimate family dinners and formal gatherings. Sliding glass doors that

lead to the extensive rear deck ensure that dining outdoors will be a common occurrence.

• Master Suite: Set apart from the secondary bedrooms in the home, this generously sized master suite features a private bath for added comfort. At the back of the room, French doors open to an expansive deck.

• Upper Level: In addition to the bedrooms, this level includes a game room, a full bath room, and a wonderfully open loft space. The loft is an ideal spot for the family's computer-or perhaps it can be used as a small den.

Main Level Floor Plan

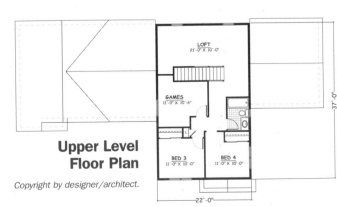

Upper Level Floor Plan

Copyright by designer/architect.

Plan #722015

Dimensions: 52'4" W x 40' D

Levels: 2

Heated Square Footage: 2,202

Main Level Sq. Ft.: 1,448

Upper Level Sq. Ft.: 754

Bedrooms: 5

Bathrooms: 3

Foundation: Crawl space, slab or basement

Material Take-off Included: Yes

Price Category: E

This traditionally styled two-story home contains an open floor plan in the main living area.

Images provided by designer/architect.

Features:

- Entry: The width of this entry allows for a gentle and easy flow towards the heart of the home.

- Living Room: Open to both the kitchen and the dining room, this room will certainly be the gathering spot for all.

- Kitchen: With today's active lifestyle, the efficient layout of this kitchen will make meal prep easy and enjoyable.

- Home Office: Located directly off the living/dining area, this room is the perfect place for the children to complete their homework.

- Library: When additional study space is needed, this is the room for the job. Located apart from the main gathering areas, this wonderful library will allow privacy for studying or just a quiet place to relax with a good book.

- Master Suite: Located at the rear of the home and housing a full en-suite bath, this room offers both privacy and comfort.

Main Level Floor Plan

Copyright by designer/architect.

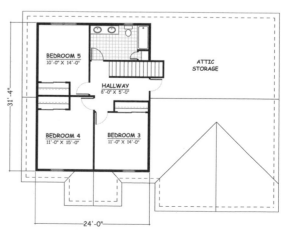

Upper Level Floor Plan

Plan #722031

Dimensions: 68' W x 29' D

Levels: 2

Heated Square Footage: 2,204

Main Level Sq. Ft.: 1,392

Upper Level Sq. Ft.: 812

Bedrooms: 4

Bathrooms: 3

Foundation: Crawl space, slab or basement

Material Take-off Included: Yes

Price Category: E

- Master Suite: After a long day relax in the comfort of this master suite, which is complete with a large walk-in closet, a spa-like master bath, and a patio door that connects to the expansive rear deck. The bath features a whirlpool tub, a separate shower, and a private toilet room.

- Secondary Bedrooms - A guest bedroom on the first floor and two large rooms and a bathroom on the second floor provide privacy and plenty of room for guests or kids.

CAD FILE AVAILABLE

This spacious two-story traditional-style home, with its inviting front porch, is designed for comfortable family living.

Features:

- Covered Porch: This covered porch provides a place to sit while waiting for family and friends to arrive.

- Dining Room: The cased openings of this dining room lend elegance for formal dinners.

- Kitchen: Perfectly located off the family room and connected to the breakfast room by a snack bar, this kitchen is ideal for informal gatherings and family meals.

- Rear Deck: This rear deck is accessed through patio doors from the master bedroom or the breakfast room, and is just the place for outdoor entertaining.

Main Level Floor Plan

Copyright by designer/architect.

Upper Level Floor Plan

Plan #722046

Dimensions: 58'2" W x 40'3" D
Levels: 2
Heated Square Footage: 2,214
Main Level Sq. Ft.: 1,310
Upper Level Sq. Ft.: 830
Bedrooms: 5
Bathrooms: 4½
Foundation: Crawl space, slab or basement
Material Take-off Included: Yes
Price Category: E

Images provided by designer/architect.

The multiple gables and the large inviting windows of this two-story farmhouse-style home give it character. The well-designed floor plan provides plenty of public and private spaces for every member of the family.

Features:

- **Covered Porch:** This covered porch presents a gracious entryway into the home.

- **Great Room:** This great room is open to both the kitchen and the dining room, providing continuous flow throughout the open floor plan. It also offers sliding glass doors that lead to the expansive rear deck, which extends the space for indoor and outdoor entertaining.

- **Master Suite:** This master suite's location makes it a private spa-like oasis to retreat to after a long day. Complete with a large walk-in closet, a master bathroom with a whirlpool tub, and a patio door to the rear deck.

- **Upper Level:** Upstairs, you will find three additional bedrooms and two full bathrooms. Two of the bedrooms have private entrances to the bathrooms, making it the perfect space for raising teenagers.

- **Family Room:** This upper-level family room is ideal for family fun away from the day-to-day living spaces on the first floor.

The layout of this gracious home is designed for the family. It allows family members to both gather together or to retreat to their own space.

Copyright by designer/architect.

Main Level Floor Plan

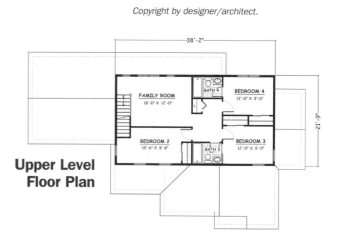

Upper Level Floor Plan

Plan #722044

Dimensions: 26' W x 50' D

Levels: 2

Heated Square Footage: 2,224

Main Level Sq. Ft.: 1,300

Upper Level Sq. Ft.: 924

Bedrooms: 5

Bathrooms: 3

Foundation: Crawl space, slab or basement

Material Take-off Included: Yes

Price Category: E

Optional Free Garage: If you would like an optional FREE 2-car garage plan, select one from page 8 or 9.

This two-story single family home has design elements similar to those of colonial row homes.

Features:

• Foyer: Generous in size, this foyer offers just the right amount of space to welcome guests into your home.

• Family Room: This graciously sized family room is located directly off the foyer. With a lovely set of double windows, this room will surely be the place where all will congregate.

• Kitchen: The L-shaped layout of this kitchen provides you with an abundant amount of counter space, making meal prep more enjoyable. It also features a large pantry that will make storage and organization much easier.

• Master Suite: Graciously sized, this master suite is enhanced by its private bath and large walk-in closets.

• Secondary Bedrooms: This home features three additional bedrooms and two full bathrooms. Two of the bedrooms and one of the bathrooms are on the upper floor.

While this home has many amenities, its straightforward design helps to keep it affordable to build.

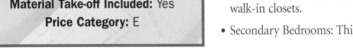

Copyright by designer/architect.

Upper Level Floor Plan

Main Level Floor Plan

Plan #722008

Dimensions: 50' W x 45'6" D

Levels: 2

Heated Square Footage: 2,227

Main Level Sq. Ft.: 1,375

Upper Level Sq. Ft.: 852

Bedrooms: 5

Bathrooms: 3

Foundation: Crawl space, slab or basement

Material Take-off Included: Yes

Price Category: E

The two-story traditional home has simple rooflines, making it easy to build.

CAD FILE AVAILABLE

Images provided by designer/architect.

Features:

- Covered Porch: This large covered porch is the ideal place to gather in the evenings and enjoy the outdoors while being sheltered from the elements.

- Kitchen: This spacious kitchen features a snack bar and a breakfast area that opens onto an expansive deck. It is a space that will become a central gathering place for family and friends.

- Master Suite: This private retreat offers a large bath that includes a whirlpool tub, a private toilet area, separate shower, and dual vanities.

The room also features a large walk-in-closet, as well as French doors that open onto a large deck.

- Upper Level: This area features three additional bedrooms and a bathroom that has a separate dual vanity area. A computer room is the perfect place for homework, but it is open enough so that mom and dad can keep an eye on things.

This home is ideal for people that love to gather with family and friends.

Main Level Floor Plan

Upper Level Floor Plan

Copyright by designer/architect.

Plan #722064

Dimensions: 89'11" W x 26'7" D

Levels: 2

Heated Square Footage: 2,227

Main Level Sq. Ft.: 1,400

Upper Level Sq. Ft.: 827

Bedrooms: 5

Bathrooms: 4½

Foundation: Crawl space, slab or basement

Material Take-off Included: Yes

Price Category: E

Images provided by designer/architect.

You'll love the open and airy feel of this traditional-style two-story home with its variety of windows, which make the rooms sunny and bright.

CAD FILE AVAILABLE

Features:

- **Great Room:** This great room, with its variety of windows and open floor plan, will be the central gathering spot for all. Open to the kitchen, it also features French doors leading to an expansive rear deck, making the transition between the indoors and outdoors seamless.

- **Kitchen:** This kitchen is a cook's dream. It features a 48-in.-wide range, a plethora of cabinets, and ample counter space, making time spent in the kitchen a joy. The large double window over the sink looks out on the rear yard and allows for lots of natural light, while the countertop seating area encourages interaction between the chef and family members.

- **Covered Breezeway/Rear Entry Hall:** Connecting the garage to the home is an open, yet covered, breezeway area. From this area you step into a large tiled rear entry that houses the utility room, the powder room, and spacious coat closet.

- **Master Suite:** Gracious in nature, this lovely master suite houses a private bathroom that will provide you with added comfort.

- **Upper Floor:** Housing the secondary bedrooms and two full bathrooms, this floor also features a lovely and open loft area that is a perfect spot for the family's computer.

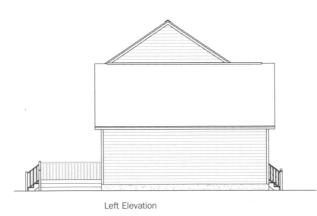

Left Elevation

Right Elevation

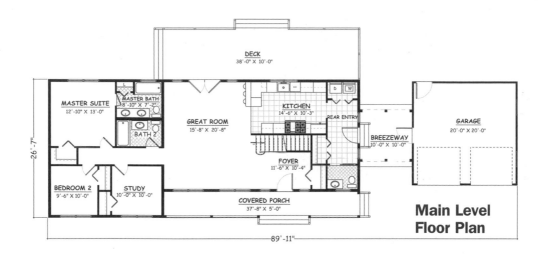

Main Level Floor Plan

Copyright by designer/architect.

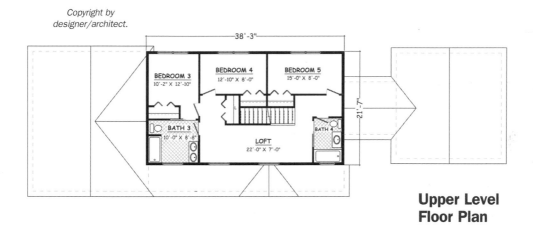

Upper Level Floor Plan

Rear Elevation

SMARTtip

Contemporary Style in Your Bathroom

Incorporate elements of Arts and Crafts, Art Deco, or other designs associated with the modern movement of the twentieth century (International Style, Bauhaus, Memphis, and the influence of Scandinavian design). Their clean geometric lines are quite compatible with this environment. This eclectic approach can be very sophisticated. Look for framed art prints, a vintage-inspired wallpaper, or reproduction hardware, faucets, or light fixtures to underscore your theme. Fortunately, manufacturers are reproducing art tiles from original molds or designs that can be used as accents.

Picking a Site for Your Outdoor Kitchen

If your house plans don't include an outdoor kitchen and you want to add one, even after the house is built, take a few moments to examine all suitable sites. Walk around your property and take note of locations that feel good to you. If a possible site is high off the ground, bring along a stepladder so you can view the site from the level at which you would be cooking and dining. Revisit candidate sites at the time of day you'd likely be using them and check for things like sun and shade, whether the neighbors can see the outdoor kitchen (should that matter to you), and the direction of prevailing winds. Try to anticipate how all of these variables will change with the seasons. Also consider your options for any electrical, water, or gas hookups that you may need.

If you're thinking about building an outdoor kitchen on your new home's patio or deck, ask yourself the following questions: Is it big enough to accommodate the grill and appliances you hope to install? Will additional footings need to be dug to support the grill island of your dreams? And is it really the best location? There's no sense in investing hundreds or thousands of dollars in a spot where you're not going to be happy. You may want to discuss some of your options with a landscape architect.

Near or Far?

There is an even more fundamental question to consider before choosing a site for an outdoor kitchen: should you build it as close as possible to your indoor kitchen, or well away from the house near a yard attraction, such as a garden or pool? There can be good reasons for each choice, and your decision will largely affect many of the design decisions that follow, not to mention the cost of the project.

The closer you build your outdoor kitchen to your indoor kitchen, the simpler it can be. After all, carrying a tray laden with dishes, napkins, and utensils a dozen or so steps is no big deal. Running back inside for the frozen dessert at the end of the meal is no big deal either. Being close to the indoor kitchen will also allow you to prepare parts of meals that require the finesse and control of your cooktop. It also makes it a lot easier when you want to cook outdoors but eat indoors. Just as important, guests will have convenient access to your home's bathrooms.

There are other big benefits as well. The biggest is what you build upon. A deck or patio can be used as the foundation of your outdoor kitchen. If you don't want to use up that space, it's likely that the yard near your back door will be flat and ready to be built upon. In addition, it will be far easier and less costly to hook up to utilities, such as water, gas, and electricity, if you select a site that's close to the house.

A grill counter under trees offers respite from the sun and wind, but it's likely to mean some extra cleanup.

SMARTtip

Dock the Barge

Try to avoid plunking your outdoor kitchen in the middle of your backyard, where it's likely to look like a barge that's broken its moorings and will get in the way of other yard activities. The best sites for outdoor kitchens are often partially enclosed. Porches, for example, offer some obvious benefits. The lee of a tall wall that surrounds the yard is another traditional site. House and outbuilding walls, fences, and areas protected by the natural terrain all offer opportunities.

Remote Outdoor Kitchens

On the other hand, a remote kitchen and dining area may take better advantage of a view, beautiful backyard landscaping, or the ideal exposure to sun and wind. Remote locations often allow greater privacy and can enhance the enjoyment of recreational home features, such as a pool or tennis court. And if it's the feeling of camping out you seek, outdoor dining and cooking areas that are at your back door just don't cut it.

Remote outdoor kitchens are more likely to be full featured, with built-in grills, multiple burners, a fridge, counter space, and lots of storage. You're far more likely to have to build a detached deck or a patio— and run electrical, water, and gas lines. And a roof is often desirable to keep surfaces from becoming messy due to tree and bird droppings.

But such a kitchen really does feel like a getaway … and keeps most of the mess well away from the house. This would be especially important if you plan to do some real barbecuing, using a smoker, for instance. The trade-off, of course, is the hefty price tag that comes with such a space. And where do you stop? Once you have duplicated your cooking and dining capability in the back corner of your property, can a cottage with an outdoor bathroom and bedroom be far behind?

Remote kitchens, however, do not have to be elaborate or expensive. You just need to be resourceful. Yes, you will need to build a level, firm surface, but consider ice chests in place of refrigerators, a freestanding grill instead of one that is built-in, and a countertop and hose-fed sink on a cart in place of permanent cabinets. To shelter your dinner guests, there are plenty of modestly priced tents and gazebos made with screens or durable outdoor fabric. The frames are corrosion resistant and many feature washable coverings that can be removed during the winter and replaced if necessary. Add a fire pit and gas or candle lanterns for light, heat, and

Before You Dig

Check out the location of everything on your property that is near the planned outdoor kitchen. Chances are, a deck or patio will limit access to, or interfere with, at least one of them. It's common, for example, to have exterior spigots end up below deck level. You should plan to have them extended to where you need them. Also, do not plan to build a deck or concrete patio over or even near a septic tank. Setbacks of 15 to 20 feet are usually required. Other in-ground obstacles may include buried well-water piping, electrical lines to the garage or pool, planned gas lines to the barbecue, sump pump and rainwater drains, basement doors,

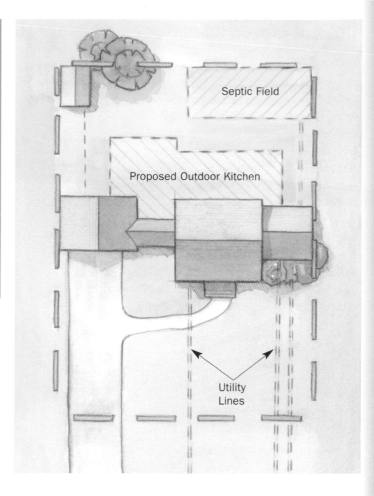

Septic Field

Proposed Outdoor Kitchen

Utility Lines

Under the yard there is more going on than most of us think. Be sure to check before you dig, right.

When viewed from the house, left, this outdoor kitchen is a focal point in the landscape. Up close, below, it offers shade and sustenance.

Get the Exposure Right

If you forget to consider exposure to the sun when choosing a site for your outdoor kitchen, you may end up broiling sooner than the burgers. Assuming you have more than one option for where to build your kitchen, exposure to the sun may be the deciding factor. Sun exposure is determined by a candidate site's orientation to the sun's daily path. A south-facing outdoor kitchen, even if built close to the house, will receive sun almost all day. Outdoor kitchens built on east- and west-facing decks or patios get sun in the morning and afternoon, respectively. Southeast- or southwest-facing kitchens will receive the sun for longer periods than those that face due east or west. North-facing sites, unless you extend them beyond the shadow of your house, will receive little or no sun for much of the day.

To decide what's best for you, think about when you are most likely to be doing your outdoor cooking and dining. If it's for morning breakfasts and brunches, southeast- or east-facing may be acceptable. Afternoon and evening users would probably prefer a southwest- or west-facing deck. If you live in a climate where summers are cool, perhaps south-facing is the ideal orientation. Conversely, if you live where it's warm most of the time, a shaded northern exposure may suit you.

Pick the Perfect Sun Exposure

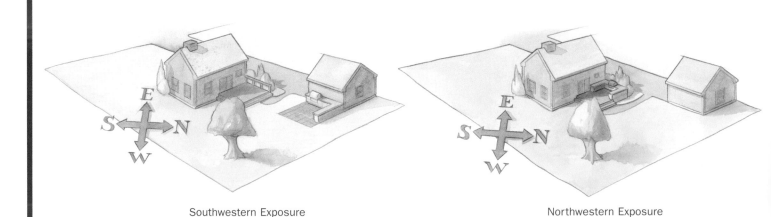

Southwestern Exposure

Northwestern Exposure

Of course, you will need to take into account the shade thrown by nearby trees, walls, and buildings. Keep in mind that you can always create shade by planting trees or adding an overhead shade structure, such as a pergola or gazebo.

A southern exposure, left, helps keep mold and mildew at bay. Deep eaves and a large tree cool the cook on a hot day.

A site with a roof, below, offers protection but requires a range hood to avoid a smoky dining area.

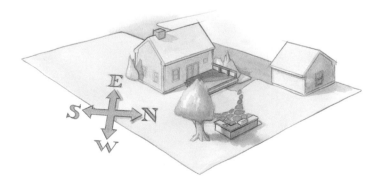

Northeastern Exposure

A southwestern exposure, far left, allows this outdoor kitchen to dry quickly after a rain. The shed offers protection from northeasterly winds.

A northwestern exposure, center, means this kitchen next to the house gets sun most of the afternoon and evening, the time when most people use an outdoor kitchen.

A northeastern exposure, near left, helps keep the afternoon crowd cool in the summer and lets the sun through once the leaves fall in autumn in this outdoor kitchen situated near a tree.

Wind Control

In many locations, wind is another factor to consider. If you live in a cool climate where the prevailing wind is frequently gusty, opt for the protected side of your house to increase the time you can enjoy your outdoor kitchen. Take advantage of natural windbreaks whenever possible. If neither works for your situation, you can build a windscreen or plant a windbreak. (See the illustration below.) If you live in a hot climate, the breeze may bring welcome relief from the heat. Prevailing winds are also a factor when it comes to placing cooking appliances, fire pits, and fireplaces because they will affect where the smoke drifts while cooking.

The lee of a house, garage, barn, or other structure provides shelter from the wind. The massive fireplace, right, performs the same function.

The Value of a Windbreak

A windbreak, typically a row of dense trees planted perpendicular to the prevailing wind, can greatly improve the comfort level of your outdoor culinary experience. The general rule is that a windbreak is effective for a distance of 30 times its height. For example, a 20-ft.-high row of conifers will reduce winds for a distance of about 600 ft.

If you live in an area where winds blow regularly, opt for a partially enclosed kitchen and dining area, such as the one above.

With all but the fridge on casters, this kitchen, right, can be rearranged as the sun moves and winds change.

When You Can't Decide

A portable outdoor kitchen may be the answer if you can't decide where to build. It's also a good solution if you want to be able to take advantage of several good sites around your yard. For example, you may prefer a spot by the pool in the summer but want to be on your deck in the fall. There are many commercially available mobile-kitchen components from which to choose, including bars, refrigerators, and

Images provided by designer/architect.

Plan #722058

Dimensions: 68' W x 36' D
Levels: 2
Heated Square Footage: 2,236
Main Level Sq. Ft.: 1,372
Upper Level Sq. Ft.: 864
Bedrooms: 5
Bathrooms: 3
Foundation: Crawl space, slab or basement
Material Take-off Included: Yes
Price Category: E

The rooflines at the front of this home give it a unique appeal.

CAD FILE AVAILABLE

Features:

- Dining/Family Room: Step from the foyer into this combination dining and family room. Its generous size will not only make it the spot for family to congregate but will also be the perfect spot for entertaining guests.

- Kitchen: This U-shaped kitchen provides the cook in the family with a vast amount of counter and cabinet space, making mealtime preparation much easier. Featuring a cased opening leading to the dining/family room, the chef will remain engaged in the activity of family life while preparing meals.

- Mudroom: Enter from the garage or the backyard into this tiled mudroom. The room houses the washer and dryer, and with the tiled flooring, cleaning up after muddy shoes or paw prints will be a breeze.

- Master Suite: This expansive master suite featuring a spa-like private bathroom is hard to resist. The bathroom houses a dual vanity, a separate shower, and a large soaking tub that is certain to help you relax after a long day.

- Upper Floor: In addition to two secondary bedrooms and a full bathroom, this upper floor houses a craft room and a generously sized sitting area.

Left Elevation

Right Elevation

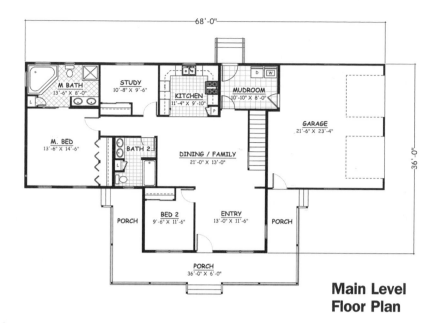

**Main Level
Floor Plan**

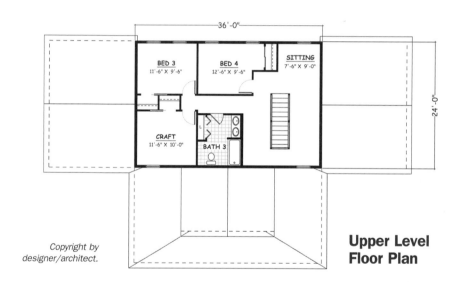

*Copyright by
designer/architect.*

**Upper Level
Floor Plan**

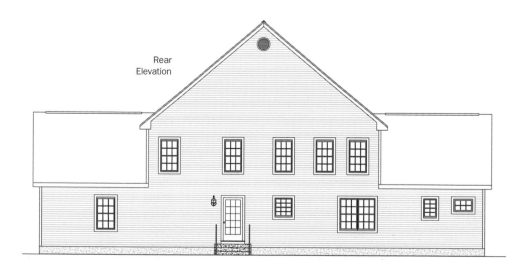

Rear
Elevation

Plan #722068

Dimensions: 50' W x 28' D

Levels: 2

Heated Square Footage: 2,240

Main Level Sq. Ft.: 1,400

Upper Level Sq. Ft.: 840

Bedrooms: 4

Bathrooms: 3

Foundation: Crawl space, slab or basement

Material Take-off Included: Yes

Price Category: E

Optional Free Garage: If you would like an optional FREE 2-car garage plan, select one from page 8 or 9.

CAD FILE AVAILABLE

Images provided by designer/architect.

A covered porch, oval windows, and sidelights combine to enhance the exterior of this two-story traditional style home. The interior layout is just as attractive and will be a delight to any family.

Features:

- Covered Porch: Add a glider or a rocking chair to take full advantage of this covered porch's comfort.

- Kitchen: The angled breakfast bar that is open to the great room will be used at any time of the day. The layout of this kitchen guarantees ample workspace that will please any cook.

- Master Suite: This master suite is situated apart from the other bedrooms in the house, thus providing ultimate privacy. The suite boasts a bathroom with a sunlit whirlpool tub, a double vanity, his and her walk-in closets, and plenty of storage space. It is the ideal place to retreat to after a long day.

- Upper Level: This upper level features a family room that is reached through French door and has a large closet that is ideal for media and game storage. Large windows will wash this room in plenty of natural light. The upper level also features a large storage room that is perfect for keeping seasonal items in a place that is out of the way, yet convenient to all.

The design of this house is ideal if you want a generously sized home with a unique blend of private and public areas.

Main Level Floor Plan

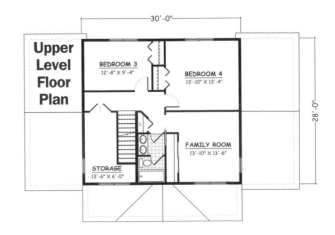

Upper Level Floor Plan

Plan #722027

Dimensions: 65' W x 40' D

Levels: 2

Heated Square Footage: 2,243

Main Level Sq. Ft.: 1,554

Upper Level Sq. Ft.: 689

Bedrooms: 4

Bathrooms: 3

Foundation: Crawl space, slab or basement

Material Take-off Included: Yes

Price Category: E

The flowing layout of this two-story farmhouse-style home is designed for entertaining.

Features:

- Great Room: This generous room's convenient location to the kitchen and sliding glass doors leading to a rear deck make it a great space for entertaining.

- Kitchen: Nestled between the breakfast nook and the dining room, this kitchen is ideal for both informal family meals and formal dinner parties. Also located just off the great room, this kitchen is truly the heart of the home.

- Guest Bedroom: A private bath and ample closet space will surely make your guests feel welcome.

- Master Suite: This spacious retreat features his and her walk-in closets and a patio door that opens onto the rear deck. The attached bath offers a soaking tub, a separate shower, and a dual-sink vanity.

- Upper Level: Two additional bedrooms, a full bath, a second laundry area, and a computer loft allow the younger members of the family a measure of privacy.

**Main Level
Floor Plan**

Copyright by designer/architect.

**Upper Level
Floor Plan**

Plan #722034

Dimensions: 64'5" W x 28' D

Levels: 2

Heated Square Footage: 2,259

Main Level Sq. Ft.: 1,392

Upper Level Sq. Ft.: 867

Bedrooms: 4

Bathrooms: 3

Foundation: Crawl space, slab or basement

Material Take-off Included: Yes

Price Category: E

This expanded two-story traditional-style home is the perfect place for the family with teens.

Features:

- Covered Porch: This covered front porch at the entrance to this charming home provides shelter and a wonderful seating area for warm summer evenings.

- Living Room: When stepping through the front door, you are welcomed immediately into this living room, the heart of this home.

- Dining Room: This room is open to the kitchen and invites the diners to interact with the cook. The room also features sliding glass doors to a large deck, perfect for summer gatherings.

- Kitchen: This kitchen is a cook's dream. With plenty of cabinets and generous counter space, this room will be easy to organize and will make mealtime preparations simple. The room also features a countertop eating area for morning breakfasts and after-school snacks.

- Master Suite: This master suite is separate from the other bedrooms in the home and houses a private bath, which provides comfort and privacy.

- Secondary Bedrooms: The secondary bedrooms, perfect for the teens in your home, share a bathroom that provides a private single vanity for each of the adjoining bedrooms.

While the home is full of amenities, its simple and thoughtful layout makes it easy to build.

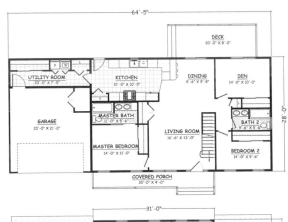

Main Level Floor Plan

Copyright by designer/architect.

Upper Level Floor Plan

Images provided by designer/architect.

Plan #722070

Dimensions: 71'3" W x 27'6" D
Levels: 2
Heated Square Footage: 2,264
Main Level Sq. Ft.: 1,345
Upper Level Sq. Ft.: 919
Bedrooms: 4
Bathrooms: 3
Foundation: Crawl space, slab or basement
Material Take-off Included: Yes
Price Category: E

This traditional-style two-story home, with its simple yet elegant design, features spaces that will certainly please each and every member of the family.

CAD FILE AVAILABLE

Features:

- Foyer: From the entry porch, step into this ample foyer with its grand staircase. The foyer gently ushers you back to the central gathering areas of the home.

- Living Room: This lovely living room is certain to be a gathering spot for all. The room is open to the dining room, allowing passage between the two rooms to be seamless.

- Kitchen: The family chef is sure to be pleased with this thoughtfully designed kitchen that is easy to organize. Adjacent to

the dining area, it encourages interaction between the cook and diners during meal-time prep.

- Master Suite: Privacy is ensured in this generously sized master suite that is set apart from the secondary bedrooms in the home. The suite features a large walk-in closet and a private bathroom with an oversize tub, a separate shower, and dual vanities, continuing the feeling of solitude.

- Upper Floor: Two of the secondary bedrooms, along with a full bathroom and a family room complete the upper floor in the home.

This expanded two-story home, while full of amenities, is designed to be affordably built.

Main Level Floor Plan

Upper Level Floor Plan

Copyright by designer/architect.

Plan #721018

Dimensions: 74' W x 44' D
Levels: 1
Heated Square Footage: 2,268
Bedrooms: 3
Bathrooms: 2
Foundation: Crawl space, slab or basement
Material Take-off Included: Yes
Price Category: E

Images provided by designer/architect.

• Master Suite: Featuring an oversize walk-in closet and private bath, this suite will be a welcome retreat after a long day.

• Upper Floor: Features an additional four bedrooms, a full bath, and a wonderfully open area that can be used as a game room and a library. The upper floor will surely be a

gathering place for the younger generation in the home. It is an area they can call their own, but will still be enjoyed by the entire family.

This home, with its spacious layout and grand outdoor amenities, is the perfect home for entertaining, as well as everyday family living.

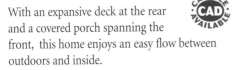

With an expansive deck at the rear and a covered porch spanning the front, this home enjoys an easy flow between outdoors and inside.

Features:

• Foyer: This entry foyer, with its grand staircase, welcomes both friends and family into the home.

• Family Room: Everyone will gather in this spacious room located directly off the foyer. The large cased opening at the rear of the room leads you toward the kitchen and dining room, allowing for an easy transition between rooms.

• Kitchen: The expansive cabinets, large pantry, and generous counter space make preparing family meals enjoyable. The area is open to the dining room, allowing for interaction between the chef, family members, and guests.

Copyright by designer/architect.

YOU CAN EXPAND THIS HOUSE!

For the ever-growing family, this home is designed to be expanded. When you're ready to "grow" the house you can purchase its second floor addition, Plan #723018. To see the finished 2-story version go to page 230.

Plan #722042

Dimensions: 62' W x 36'6" D

Levels: 2

Heated Square Footage: 2,276

Main Level Sq. Ft.: 1,360

Upper Level Sq. Ft.: 916

Bedrooms: 4

Bathrooms: 3

Foundation: Crawl space, slab or basement

Material Take-off Included: Yes

Price Category: E

Images provided by designer/architect.

This two-story home features wonderfully designed indoor and outdoor spaces, which will be sure to please every member of the family.

Features:

• Covered Porch: Deep enough to fit a small seating area, this charming covered porch welcomes everyone to your home.

• Kitchen: Thoughtfully designed with plenty of counter space, cabinets, and a large pantry, this room will be sure to please the family cook.

• Master Suite: Set apart from the other bedrooms in the home is this spacious master suite. The suite not only houses a large walk-in closet, but also a private bath. The bath features dual vanities, an oversize tub, and a separate shower, ensuring both comfort and privacy.

• Secondary Bedrooms: There are three additional bedrooms and two full bathrooms in this home, ensuring comfort for all members of the family.

With a thoughtful layout and a good balance of public and private spaces, this home remains affordable to build.

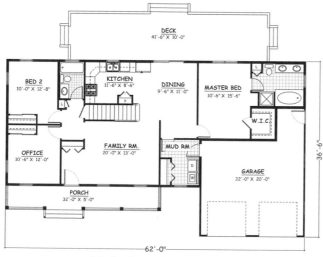

Main Level Floor Plan

Copyright by designer/architect.

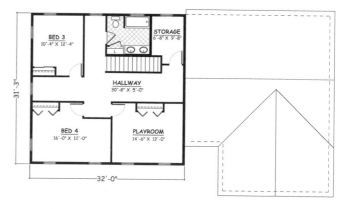

Upper Level Floor Plan

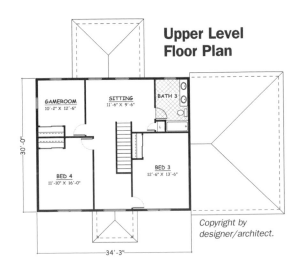

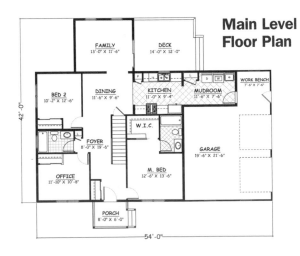

Plan #722059

Dimensions: 54' W x 42' D
Levels: 2
Heated Square Footage: 2,280
Main Level Sq. Ft.: 1,260
Upper Level Sq. Ft.: 1,020
Bedrooms: 5
Bathrooms: 3
Foundation: Crawl space, slab or basement
Material Take-off Included: Yes
Price Category: E

You'll love the design of this traditionally styled two-story home, with its balance between public and private spaces.

Images provided by designer/architect.

Features:

- Covered Porch: This charming covered entry helps to shelter you from the elements.

- Dining Room: Everyday family meals will be enjoyed in this lovely room that is open to the kitchen and the foyer, and connected to the family room through a cased opening.

- Kitchen: This galley-style kitchen provides plenty of counter and cabinet space, making it easy to organize. The kitchen is also connected to the utility room, which houses the washer and dryer, helping to make the multi tasking that is often required with today's active families much easier.

- Master Suite: Set apart from the secondary bedrooms, this master suite features a large walk-in closet and a private bathroom, and will provide you with the comfort and privacy you seek.

- Upper Floor: In addition to the secondary bedrooms and a full sized bathroom, this floor features a sitting room and game room.

This expanded two-story home is thoughtfully designed and offers many amenities while still remaining affordable to build.

CAD FILE AVAILABLE

Main Level Floor Plan

Upper Level Floor Plan

Copyright by designer/architect.

Plan #722062

Dimensions: 52' W x 42' D

Levels: 2

Heated Square Footage: 2,304

Main Level Sq. Ft.: 1,305

Upper Level Sq. Ft.: 999

Bedrooms: 4

Bathrooms: 3

Foundation: Crawl space, slab or basement

Material Take-off Included: Yes

Price Category: E

If you are looking for a home that will make the whole family comfortable, this is the one for you.

CAD FILE AVAILABLE

Images provided by designer/architect.

Features:

- Covered Porch: This expansive front porch is wide enough for a few small seating areas and is a wonderful place to enjoy warm summer evenings.

- Dining Room: Connected to both the living room and the kitchen and featuring large windows, this room has a bright and airy feel, making mealtime a pleasant experience.

- Kitchen: This galley style kitchen features a pantry and a utility closet, making storage as well as multitasking much simpler.

- Office: Whether it is to complete homework or manage the household finances, this

moderately sized room offers you enough privacy to complete each task.

- Master Suite: Featuring a large walk-in closet and a private bathroom, this generously sized master suite is certain to leave you feeling relaxed and renewed. The bathroom features an oversize tub, a separate shower, and dual vanities, providing comfort and privacy to the suite.

- Upper Level: With a full bathroom, two additional bedrooms, an exercise room, and an intimate family room, this upper level has enough amenities to please every member of the family.

Main Level Floor Plan

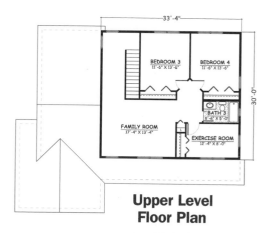

Upper Level Floor Plan

Copyright by designer/architect.

Images provided by designer/architect.

Plan #722013

Dimensions: 54' W x 48' D

Levels: 2

Heated Square Footage: 2,341

Main Level Sq. Ft.: 1,870

Upper Level Sq. Ft.: 471

Bedrooms: 3

Bathrooms: 3

Foundation: Crawl space, slab or basement

Material Take-off Included: Yes

Price Category: E

This two-story house is ideal for any family due to its spacious design and versatility.

CAD FILE AVAILABLE

Features:

- **Great Room:** This expansive room is part of an open floor plan. It flows into the kitchen and breakfast area, making it perfect for formal or informal entertaining. Sliding glass doors offer access to the rear porch.

- **Kitchen:** This kitchen features a center island that adds convenience to this L-shaped space. The adjacent breakfast nook is sure to be occupied day and night.

- **Master Suite:** This master bedroom offers a tray ceiling and his and her walk-in closets. The private bath features a large tub, a separate shower, and dual vanities. It is truly a genuine oasis that will be difficult to leave.

- **Upper Level:** This level provides a perfect getaway for the younger generation. It's complete with a bedroom, a full bath, and a playroom.

This spacious home provides the needed expansion for the ever-growing family.

**Main Level
Floor Plan**

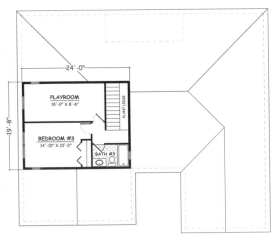

**Upper Level
Floor Plan**

Copyright by designer/architect.

Plan #722041

Dimensions: 50' W x 47'10" D

Levels: 2

Heated Square Footage: 2,342

Main Level Sq. Ft.: 1,310

Upper Level Sq. Ft.: 1,032

Bedrooms: 4

Bathrooms: 3

Foundation: Crawl space, slab or basement

Material Take-off Included: Yes

Price Category: E

This charming two-story home features generously sized rooms, providing comfort for all members of the family.

Images provided by designer/architect.

Features:

- Entry: The spacious entry foyer ushers you into the home.

- Family Room: A gracious space that is located close to the kitchen and open to the dining room, this family room will surely be the central gathering spot for all.

- Kitchen: Organization and mealtime prep will be simple in this kitchen that features a large pantry and a plethora of counter space. A computer desk, along with the thoughtfully located mudroom that houses a washer and a dryer, helps to make the multitasking that is necessary with today's active lifestyle much easier.

- Mudroom: This tiled area, featuring the laundry facilities and a large coat closet, provides the perfect transition into the home from the garage.

- Master Suite: Located at the rear of the home, this master suite features a private bath with a double vanity for comfort. A large walk-in closet and a linen closet provide generous storage space.

- Secondary Bedrooms: Three additional bedrooms and two full bathrooms provide every member of the family with the comfort and privacy they seek.

Images provided by designer/architect.

Plan #722056

Dimensions: 59' W x 39'1" D

Levels: 2

Heated Square Footage: 2,344

Main Level Sq. Ft.: 1,244

Upper Level Sq. Ft.: 1,100

Bedrooms: 5

Bathrooms: 4

Foundation: Crawl space, slab or basement

Material Take-off Included: Yes

Price Category: E

If you love the comfort of a traditional-style home, this is the one or you.

CAD FILE AVAILABLE

Features:

- Front Deck: A lovely space for sitting on a warm summer evening, this front entry deck welcomes all home.

- Living Room: This delightfully spacious living room, located in the central part of the home, will surely be the area where the family will gather.

- Kitchen: This galley-style kitchen provides plenty of counter and cabinet space, making this space easy to organize. The kitchen is also

connected to the utility room, which houses the washer and dryer, helping to make the multitasking that is often required with today' active families much easier to complete.

- Master Suite: This master suite features a large walk-in closet and a private bathroom, ensuring privacy and comfort.

- Upper Floor: Featuring two additional bedrooms, an in-law suite, an office, and a game room, this upper floor is sure to please the discerning tastes of all family members.

Main Level Floor Plan

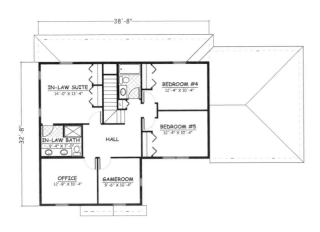

Upper Level Floor Plan

Copyright by designer/architect.

Plan #722060

Dimensions: 59'7" W x 31'2" D
Levels: 2
Heated Square Footage: 2,369
Main Level Sq. Ft.: 1,453
Upper Level Sq. Ft.: 916
Bedrooms: 4
Bathrooms: 3
Foundation: Crawl space, slab or basement
Material Take-off Included: Yes
Price Category: E

You'll love the free-flowing nature of this two-story home.

CAD FILE AVAILABLE

Images provided by designer/architect.

Features:

• Covered Porch: This covered entryway takes on a country feel, thanks to its turned columns.

• Dining Room: Open to both the living room and the kitchen, this dining room will certainly host many a dinner party, as well as the weekday family meals. Sliding glass doors at the rear of the room lead out to a generously sized deck, making outdoor dining a common occurrence.

• Kitchen: The open floor plan of this kitchen allows for the interaction between the chef, family members, and guests during the preparation of meals.

• Master Suite: This graciously sized master suite, with its immense walk-in closet and private bathroom, will be a welcome retreat after a long day. The private bathroom features a dual vanity, an oversize tub, a separate shower, and a private toilet room, providing additional comfort.

• Upper Floor: In addition to two secondary bedrooms and a full bathroom, this floor features both a family room and a playroom.

Expanded to fit the needs of the ever-changing family dynamic, this home continues to be affordable to build.

Main Level Floor Plan

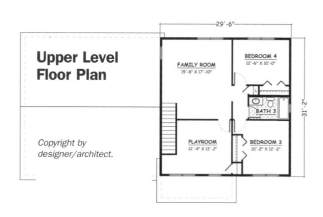

Upper Level Floor Plan

Copyright by designer/architect.

Plan #722048

Dimensions: 47'7" W x 35'4" D

Levels: 2

Heated Square Footage: 2,392

Main Level Sq. Ft.: 1,438

Upper Level Sq. Ft.: 954

Bedrooms: 4

Bathrooms: 4

Foundation: Crawl space, slab or basement

Material Take-off Included: Yes

Price Category: E

Images provided by designer/architect.

Optional Free Garage: If you would like an optional FREE 2-car garage plan, select one from page 8 or 9

CAD FILE AVAILABLE

With its covered porch and multiple window units, this home evokes the charm of a traditional home.

Features:

- Kitchen: The step-saving design of this U-shaped kitchen will make cooking a pleasure for everyone in the family. It is open to the dining area, adding to its convenience.

- Screened-In Porch: Accessed through a patio door leading from the dining room, this generously sized porch is just the place to gather on warm summer evenings to dine alfresco or to just enjoy a breeze in the screened-in area.

- Master Suite: This master suite is situated on the first floor apart from the other bedrooms in the home to ensure privacy. The triple window and large walk-in closet enhance this elegant retreat, which is served by a luxurious bathroom. The bathroom features a sunlit whirlpool tub and a private toilet room.

- Library: Double French doors open into this versatile library that features built-in bookcases.

Spaciousness and functionality characterize this home. It is designed to provide the convenience demanded by a busy family life.

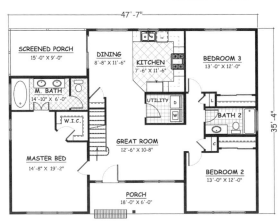

Main Level Floor Plan

Copyright by designer/architect.

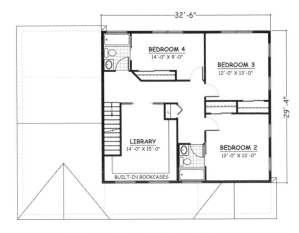

Upper Level Floor Plan

Images provided by designer/architect.

Plan #722072

Dimensions: 78'4" W x 31' D
Levels: 2
Heated Square Footage: 2,446
Main Level Sq. Ft.: 1,366
Upper Level Sq. Ft.: 1,080
Bedrooms: 4
Bathrooms: 2
Foundation: Crawl space, slab or basement
Material Take-off Included: Yes
Price Category: E

This house's multiple window units, front porch, and covered breezeway connecting the house to the garage add curb appeal.

CAD FILE AVAILABLE

Features:

- **Breezeway:** This breezeway allows you and your guests to be sheltered from the elements while traveling from the home to the garage.

- **Kitchen:** This tidy kitchen features a cooktop, a wall oven and a snack bar that is perfect for informal meals. A door leads to the expansive rear deck to allow for dining outdoors.

- **Living Room:** This living room is a generously sized room featuring a large picture window to fill the space with natural light. The room has a large cased opening that provides an elegant entrance into the dining room.

- **Master Bedroom:** Relax at the end of the day in this spacious master bedroom, which features a large walk-in closet and multiple window units making the area bright and airy.

- **Secondary Bedrooms:** Upstairs, three additional bedrooms with generous closets and a full-size bathroom with a separate tub and shower provide all the private space a family will need.

Main Level Floor Plan

Copyright by designer/architect.

Upper Level Floor Plan

Images provided by designer/architect.

Plan #722035

Dimensions: 40' W x 50' D

Levels: 2

Heated Square Footage: 2,400

Main Level Sq. Ft.: 1,200

Upper Level Sq. Ft.: 1,200

Bedrooms: 3

Bathrooms: 3

Foundation: Crawl space, slab or basement

Material Take-off Included: Yes

Price Category: E

- Master Suite: Through an elegant French door you enter this positively wonderful retreat. Featuring large closets, a private bath, and its own sitting area, this master suite provides comfort and privacy. It also includes a set of sliding glass doors onto the wonderful rear deck, allowing a relaxing connection with nature.

- Secondary Bedrooms: The secondary bedrooms, perfect for the young ones in your home, share a bath that provides a separate entrance from each of the bedrooms and a private single vanity.

This expanded home has many elegant touches with clean lines, making it simple to build.

This wonderful traditional-style home, with its large windows and patio doors, certainly invites the outdoors in.

CAD FILE AVAILABLE

Features:

- Covered Porch: Covered Porch - With its understated columns and brick accents, this porch welcomes you into this charming home.

- Kitchen: This tidy kitchen offers a large countertop eating area and is open to the dining room, allowing for interaction between the cook and the rest of the family.

- Rear Deck: Spanning the length of the house, this wonderful outdoor space connects the homeowners with nature. The dining room, den, and master suite all feature sliding glass doors leading out to this expansive deck.

Rear Elevation

Main Level Floor Plan

Upper Level Floor Plan

Copyright by designer/architect.

Left Elevation

Right Elevation

This article was reprinted from *Ultimate Guide to Basements, Attics, and Garages* (Creative Homeowner 2006).

The Ultimate Garage

For years, most homeowners have used their garages for parking cars and storing stuff that doesn't fit anywhere else or is overflow from other parts of the house. Or they have taken that valuable floor space and turned it into another master suite or family room.

Rather than using your garage as a scaled-down storage unit or new living space that looks like the rest of the house, consider making it into a high-end recreational space that is improved but at the same time more garage-like. If you like working on cars, why not create a state-of-the-art car-restoration studio? Maybe you'd prefer a furniture-making shop that will be the envy of every craftsman in town, or a big home gym.

Part of what's driving this change is the availability of new storage products designed specifically for the garage. But simple common sense plays a bigger role. Most two-car garages occupy about 500 square feet of space, and

that's space that already has a foundation under it, a floor in it, walls around it, a roof over it, and very easy access for big and heavy items through the overhead doors. In these times of high

real estate costs, you can't find 500 nearly habitable square feet for less money anywhere.

A total garage makeover, above, costs some money, especially if you choose high-end cabinets and flooring. But the results look great, create accessible storage for all the essentials, and even leave room for the cars, at least for the time being.

Modular storage systems, below, that include both cabinets and wall-hung options can accommodate just about everything that most people need to store.

Storage Systems

If you want to make the most out of the garage space you have, then you have to figure out how much space is actually available. It's no good to create a plan that calls for your expensive garden tractor to be banished suddenly to the elements, when you know you want to keep it inside.

Start by waiting for a few days of good weather. Then place everything you want to keep in the garage in the drive-way. Start putting things into the garage, starting with the biggest (your cars, if you plan to keep them inside) and moving down in size. You'll quickly see this as the zero-sum game that it is. For every box of old lawn ornaments you keep, that's one less piece of exercise equipment for your new home gym or power tool for your workshop. In this case, being ruthless is a virtue. Either get rid of nonessentials or find a new place to store them.

Once the essentials are back in place, you have defined the true available space with which you have to work. Now is the time to start looking for storage systems. You'll find two basic options: a cabinet-based system and a wall-hung system. Both are designed to make the most out of vertical storage.

The main difference between the two is the amount of floor space each occupies. For example, the typical base cabinet will measure about 24 inches deep, which makes it hard to fit alongside a car and still have room to open the cabinet or the car door. On the other hand, the average perforated hardboard wall system projects only a few inches into the room.

Because of their different virtues, a combination of the two basic systems makes sense for filling the needs of most people.

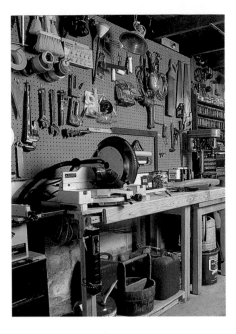

Perforated hardboard, above, is the granddaddy of all wall storage systems. The material contains holes into which you put metal hooks. It works as well today as it did 50 years ago.

Some storage systems, above, blend cabinets with traditional open shelving. This shelving is very versatile and avoids the expense of cabinet doors.

Modular cabinet systems, like those shown above, make for very flexible storage, particularly when mounted on casters. The layout can change easily when your needs change.

Many ceiling-mounted storage units, above, are available. Some have doors like this one, others are open. Large specialty units can even fit above overhead garage doors.

Cabinet Systems

A good cabinet system is best defined by how it works, not by how it looks. If you have specialty items that are difficult to store, like some sporting goods, make sure that you find a cabinet that will handle the job. Probably the best—and the most expensive—way to get a good cabinet system is to have a cabinet dealer outfit your garage for you. However, you can do the same thing by figuring out what cabinet sizes you need and then buying knockdown units at a home center.

Another option is to buy one of the new modular garage storage systems. These systems have a big selection of different base and wall cabinets, often with a caster-mounting option so you can easily reposition the units when your needs change. Some of these manufacturers also offer wall-hung storage systems that complement their cabinets.

When looking at different cabinet lines, be sure to check for specialty units that hang from the ceiling. Some are just simple boxes with clever hanging hardware.

SMARTtip

Increasing Your Mobility

Not everything in a garage is best stored permanently against a wall. Woodworking equipment and exercise machines are just two kinds of hardware that come to mind. These things need more space when they're being used and need much less when they're not. The logical solution is to mount them on casters so they're easy to move.

Sometimes the base of heavy-duty tools comes with holes for installing casters, but usually you'll have to create some way to mount them. This can take some time and often a lot of creativity. But once things are rolling you'll be happy you made the effort.

Casters come in different sizes and with different mounting hardware. Some simply swivel while others swivel and can be locked in place. Because you'll almost always need four casters for anything you want to move, it's a good idea to put a combination of two swivel and two locking casters on each item. This yields good maneuverability and locking capability, and at less cost than putting locking casters on each corner.

But others are designed to make use of the entire space above your garage doors.

Wall Systems

Traditional perforated hardboard is still going strong today because it's inexpensive, easy to install, and works well. But now consumers have a lot of other choices.

The most basic alternative is a shelving system that hangs from standards attached to the wall. One popular version of this is the steel-wire systems originally designed for organizing closets. With a wide variety of shelves, drawers, and compartments, you should be able to store most of what you need.

Another alternative is a slat-wall storage system. These slotted plastic panels are screwed directly to the garage wall, and then hooks are placed in the slots to support just about whatever you have. The system is very flexible and can easily change as your storage requirements change.

Steel-grid systems are also available. The open-grid panels are attached to the wall, and hooks and brackets are clipped onto the grid. The grids themselves are pretty inexpensive. But as with most of the wall storage systems, the cost of the hooks and brackets can add up quickly.

Easy-to-install and inexpensive, above, steel-wire storage systems, originally de-signed for closets and kitchens, work just as well in the garage.

Wall-hung metal shelving, below, is a quick and clean way to get stuff off the floor. Most systems have wall-mounted standards and adjustable shelf brackets.

Flooring Options

Most garage floors are made of concrete, which is a wonderful building material. It's hard and durable, and it can carry a tremendous amount of weight without breaking. In other words, it's perfect for garage floors. When properly installed, the only problems concrete will give you are cosmetic: it stains easily, and it's uncomfortable—standing on concrete for a long time hurts your feet and legs. Even when concrete is clean, though, some people find its appearance boring. In recent years, these people have been drawn to a number of different flooring treatments that make concrete look as good as it works.

Upgrading Concrete

The most common way to improve your concrete floor is to paint it. Until the last few years, this choice was often disappointing. The paint didn't bond well to the concrete and was damaged when hot tires were parked on it. But new garage floor paints, available at home centers, are designed to work much better. One good system has two parts. First you apply an epoxy paint; then you sprinkle colored paint chips over the fresh surface. When the floor dries, the chips provide extra traction to make the concrete much less slippery.

The high-end garage-conversion people tend to favor floor coverings rather than coatings. One popular option is floor pads. These come in rolls, often 6 feet wide, that are installed in much the same way as

Garage floors, right, have requirements that differ from other floors in your home. Standard paints won't hold up, but speciality finishes can provide an attractive, durable floor.

Specialty floor paint, far right, creates a clean, attractive surface for any garage floor. Proper preparation is essential for the paint to bond successfully to the concrete.

sheet acrylic flooring, though no adhesive is used. The material floats on the floor, and any seams are taped together. Many colors and textures are available.

Plastic floor tiles are another high-end option. They usually come in 12-inch interlocking squares and require no adhesive or tape. You lay out, measure, and cut these tiles much as you would vinyl tiles for the bathroom or kitchen. The tiles will take longer to install than the roll pads, but the work is easier and the tiles are thicker than the pads, so you'll get more cushioning if that's important to you.

Neither the pads nor the tiles are cheap, especially if you cover the entire floor of a two-car garage. Expect to pay at least $1,000 to do the job yourself. But then, nothing can change the look of your garage as dramatically as a bright red or yellow floor.

Garage Mechanicals

If you plan to use your garage a lot during cold weather, you will want some heat; and if you want heat, you're going to want insulation unless you've got money to burn. Some newer garages are built with insulation in place and finished with dry-

Brightly colored floor tiles, above, laid in a clever pattern make a strong design statement. No one could confuse this floor with a boring concrete slab.

wall, but many garages aren't. Make the space more livable by adding insulation and weather stripping the door.

Choosing your heat source can be complicated because so many different

options are available. If your garage is attached to your house and your furnace has the extra capacity, a heating contractor can often run a heat duct from your house to the garage.

SMARTtip

Keeping Your Floor Clean

Your new floor may look great when you're done installing it, but a short trip on a muddy road or a day spent driving on salty winter highways can make it look pretty bad once you get home. If you are fortunate enough to have a floor

drain, you can just wait until your cars drip dry and then hose down the floor and let the drain take the dirty water away.

On a coated or uncoated floor without a drain, a 3-foot-wide floor squeegee is a great help. Hose down the floor; then use the squeegee to

push the water out through the garage door openings. The squeegee also works for grooved floor pads, but not as well on modular floor tiles. Traditional tools, a floor mop and bucket, are required for those.

You also have space-heating options. Probably the most practical choice is an electric-resistance heater, either a standard model or a convection unit that includes a fan to circulate the warmed air quicker. These heaters have no open flame, so they can't ignite flammable fumes that might be present in your garage. And they put no combustion by-products (carbon monoxide and water vapor) into the air. But in most areas, electricity is more expensive than natural gas or heating oil. Space heaters using other fuels are available in many different designs—most are vented; some are ventless. A local heating equipment supplier can explain your options.

Ventilation

Your garage ventilation needs are directly proportional to how much your activities foul the air. In warm climates, opening the overhead doors and using a floor fan to keep fresh air moving through should do the trick. But if

Ventilation and lighting, left, can help make what was once a dank, uninviting space livable and inviting.

you keep your garage heated, you'll need active ventilation.

You'll probably find more ventilation options than heating options if you really need to clean a lot of air. The most common solution is to install an electric exhaust fan in the garage wall or on the roof. These units are rated by how much air they can move per minute (abbreviated as cfm, cubic feet of air per minute). The air they remove is replaced by fresh air coming into the building from air leaks.

If your garage is tightly constructed, you'll need to supply fresh air in another way. Some people just open a window when the fan is on. But air-to-air heat exchangers are a high-end alternative. These electric units draw warm, dusty air from the garage and dump it outside. At the same time, they pull cool, fresh air from outside into the garage. When these air streams pass each other (confined to separate tubes), the outgoing air preheats the incoming air.

Lighting

It may require work to pick a good heater and ventilator, but lighting for

Concrete floors, above, are durable, but they require much maintenance to keep them looking good.

Fluorescent fixtures, above, are inexpensive. Newer models offer truer color renderings than older types.

Hanging pendant lights, opposite, are a good way to provide task lighting for counters and worktables.

Garage Safety

The following safety checklist is worth reviewing for those who plan to spend a lot of time in their garages. It was compiled by the Home Safety Council (homesafetycouncil.org), a nonprofit, industry-supported group created to help prevent injuries in the home.

1 Organize all items in designated, easy-to-reach places so that large piles don't accumulate.

2 Store shovels, rakes, lawn chairs, bikes, and other sharp and large objects on the wall to prevent trips and falls.

3 Clear floors and steps of clutter, grease, and spills.

4 Keep children's playthings in one area and within their reach to prevent kids from exploring potentially dangerous areas.

5 Light your garage brightly with maximum safe wattage as designated by light fixtures.

6 Protect light bulbs near work areas with substantial guards to reduce risk of breakage and fire.

7 Light stairs brightly, and install on both sides secure handrails or banisters that extend the entire length of the stairs.

8 Make sure poisonous products, such as pesticides, automotive fluids, lighter fluid, paint thinner, antifreeze, and turpentine, have child-resistant caps, are clearly labeled, and are stored either on a high shelf or in a locked cabinet.

9 Do not use barbecue grills and electric generators inside the garage, as they emit carbon monoxide (CO) and pose a fire hazard.

10 Install a smoke alarm and CO detector in the garage.

11 Never leave cars running inside a closed or open garage to prevent CO poisoning.

12 Store gasoline in small quantities only and in a proper, tightly sealed container labeled "gasoline."

13 Do not keep gasoline in a garage with an appliance that contains a pilot light.

14 Mount a fire extinguisher and stocked first-aid kit in the garage, and make sure every family member knows where they are and how to use them.

15 Store pool chemicals according to the manufacturers' directions to prevent combustion and potential poisoning exposures.

16 Do not overload outlets, and make sure the electrical ratings on extension cords have been checked to ensure they are carrying no more than their proper loads.

17 Lock electrical supply boxes to prevent children from opening them.

18 Clean the garage of dust, cobwebs, and trash, which can interfere with the electrical system.

19 Properly secure shelving units to the wall; make sure they are not overloaded; and store heavier items closest to the ground.

20 Keep a sturdy step stool within easy reach to aid in reaching items stored high off the ground.

the garage is much easier. Simply put, it's hard to beat overhead fluorescent lighting for general room illumination. These units provide good light, are easy to install, and are cheap to run. Higher-end models are often sold without bulbs. Of course buying the bulbs lets you choose the bulb wattage (typically from 20 to 40 watts) and color temperature to match your needs.

Task lighting can be accomplished the old fashioned way, with small shop lights installed just where you need them. Some wall storage systems also have light fixtures that mount in the panel slots.

Images provided by designer/architect.

Plan #722014

Dimensions: 56' W x 43'6" D

Levels: 2

Heated Square Footage: 2,438

Main Level Sq. Ft.: 1,386

Upper Level Sq. Ft.: 1,052

Bedrooms: 6

Bathrooms: 3

Foundation: Crawl space, slab or basement

Material Take-off Included: Yes

Price Category: E

Features:

- Entry Porch: Sheltering you from the elements, this covered porch gives the entrance to this home an understated elegance.

- Dining Room: With sliding glass doors leading to a moderately sized deck, this room allows for both intimate and formal dining.

- Kitchen: This tidy kitchen, with its thoughtful layout and large pantry, makes it easy for the family cook to prepare meals.

- Home Office: Located on the first floor, this room will serve a multitude of purposes. Whether or not a member of the family works from the home, this space can be used for the completion of homework or the everyday running of the household.

- Master Suite: Set apart from the secondary bedrooms in the home, this generously sized master suite features a private bath for added comfort.

You will love the free flowing nature of this thoughtfully designed ranch home.

Rear Elevation

Main Level Floor Plan

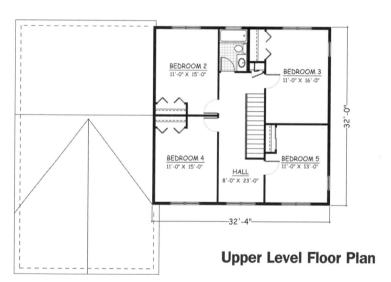

Upper Level Floor Plan

Copyright by designer/architect.

Left Elevation

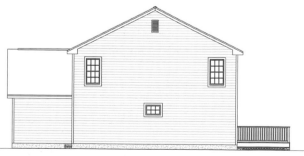

Right Elevation

Plan #722022

Dimensions: 51' W x 45'2" D

Levels: 2

Heated Square Footage: 2,510

Main Level Sq. Ft.: 1,422

Upper Level Sq. Ft.: 1,088

Bedrooms: 4

Bathrooms: 3

Foundation: Crawl space, slab or basement

Material Take-off Included: Yes

Price Category: E

Images provided by designer/architect.

This moderately sized two-story home has a unique mix of public areas and private quarters that is sure to please every member of the family.

CAD FILE AVAILABLE

Features:

- **Entry Porch:** This entry porch is just the right size for sheltering guests from the elements.

- **Great Room:** A large and airy room that will make everyone feel at home, this great room also has French doors leading to a covered rear porch to allow for outdoor entertaining throughout the year.

- **Kitchen:** This kitchen is perfectly located between a laundry room and bright, sunny dinette. Both the kitchen and dinette open into the great room.

- **Master Suite:** This master suite is a relaxing retreat that has its own private bath with dual vanities and a large walk-in closet.

- **Additional Bedrooms:** Upstairs are two generous bedrooms with ample closet space and a shared full bath. An additional bedroom on the first floor makes an ideal guest room.

Main Level Floor Plan

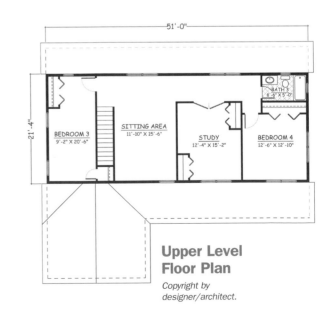

Upper Level Floor Plan

Copyright by designer/architect.

Plan #722025

Dimensions: 53'8" W x 53'4" D

Levels: 2

Heated Square Footage: 2,517

Main Level Sq. Ft.: 1,498

Upper Level Sq. Ft.: 1,019

Bedrooms: 4

Bathrooms: 3

Foundation: Crawl space, slab or basement

Material Take-off Included: Yes

Price Category: E

This traditionally styled two-story home features a main-floor master suite that will be difficult to resist.

CAD FILE AVAILABLE

Images provided by designer/architect.

Features:

- **Entry Foyer:** With its grand staircase, this elegant entry foyer welcomes you home.

- **Dining Room:** This room is conveniently located just steps away from the kitchen, allowing for interaction between the chef and the family. The dining room also features sliding glass doors to a rear covered porch that will surely have the family dining outdoors on many occasions.

- **Kitchen:** A thoughtfully designed kitchen, featuring a center island for additional prep space, will make getting dinner on the table seem effortless.

- **Master Suite:** Located on the main floor apart from the secondary bedrooms in the home, this master suite offers refuge from daily life. The bath features amenities including a dual vanity, a private toilet room, a separate shower, and a large soaking tub that will surely leave you feeling refreshed.

- **Secondary Bedrooms:** With a single secondary bedroom on the first floor and two additional bedrooms on the second, this home is certainly set for the larger family. The main-floor bedroom is the perfect spot for guests. Set apart from the other bedrooms, it will offer privacy to those who visit.

Main Level Floor Plan

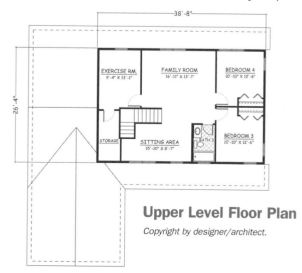

Upper Level Floor Plan

Copyright by designer/architect.

Images provided by designer/architect.

Plan #722069

Dimensions: 76'10" W x 31'4" D
Levels: 2
Heated Square Footage: 2,525
Main Level Sq. Ft.: 1,370
Upper Level Sq. Ft.: 1,155
Bedrooms: 5
Bathrooms: 4
Foundation: Crawl space, slab or basement
Material Take-off Included: Yes
Price Category: E

This traditional-style home is sure to please all members of the family with its thoughtful design.

CAD FILE AVAILABLE

Features:

- **Covered Porch:** Spanning the full length of the home, this lovely covered porch, featuring turned columns, will surely be the place to relax in the evenings.

- **Kitchen:** This U-shaped kitchen, with its plethora of cabinets and ample counter space, is a cook's dream. The moderately sized pantry provides additional storage space, making organization easy.

- **Master Suite:** Located away from the secondary bedrooms in the home is this master suite, featuring a generously sized walk-in closet and a private bathroom. The private

bathroom with dual vanities, an oversized tub, and a separate shower, will provide you with the comfort and privacy you seek.

- **Upper Floor:** Along with three additional bedrooms and two full bathrooms, this upper floor also houses a playroom, a study, and a game room.

- **Game Room:** Sure to be a hit with the tweens and teens of the family, this game room offers the younger generation a spot of their own for spending time with their friends.

With wonderful amenities and a straightforward design, this house is a home that is affordable to build.

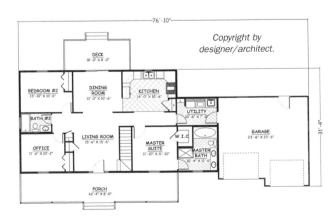

Main Level Floor Plan

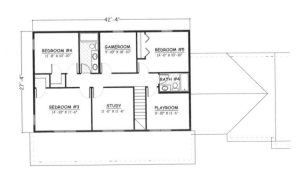

Upper Level Floor Plan

Plan #722043

Dimensions: 65' W x 30' D

Levels: 2

Heated Square Footage: 2,530

Main Level Sq. Ft.: 1,480

Upper Level Sq. Ft.: 1,050

Bedrooms: 5

Bathrooms: 3½

Foundation: Crawl space, slab or basement

Material Take-off Included: Yes

Price Category: E

Images provided by designer/architect.

This thoughtfully designed two-story traditional style home has many amenities that will please the entire family.

CAD FILE AVAILABLE

Features:

- **Covered Porch:** This charming covered front porch is deep enough to allow for a small seating area.

- **Dining Room:** This lovely dining room features large twin windows that let in lots of natural light. It is also open to both the kitchen and family room, allowing for an easy transition between the rooms.

- **Kitchen:** With a thoughtful layout and a large pantry, this kitchen will be easy to organize. Just down the hall is the laundry facility, which will enable the multitasking that is required with today's active families.

- **Master Suite:** After a long day, this gracious master suite will offer you a bit of respite. The room features a large walk-in closet and a private bath. The bath has a spa-like feel, with its large soaking tub, separate shower, and dual vanity.

- **Secondary Bedrooms:** The additional three bedrooms in the home are moderately sized and are steps away from one of two centrally located full baths.

Main Level Floor Plan

Upper Level Floor Plan

Copyright by designer/architect.

Plan #722065

Dimensions: 42'4" W x 42'6" D

Levels: 2

Heated Square Footage: 2,534

Main Level Sq. Ft.: 1,454

Upper Level Sq. Ft.: 1,080

Bedrooms: 4

Bathrooms: 4

Foundation: Crawl space, slab or basement

Material Take-off Included: Yes

Price Category: E

Optional Free Garage: If you would like an optional FREE 2-car garage plan, select one from page 8 or 9.

CAD FILE AVAILABLE

The hipped roofs and multiple windows bring distinction to this two-story home, while the interior design brings functionality.

Images provided by designer/architect.

Features:

- **Kitchen:** The U-shaped design and plentiful counter space of this kitchen will make cooking a pleasure. The pantry is an added bonus, as is the large adjoining breakfast area.

- **Formal Dining:** This formal dining room features a large cased opening and built-in storage. It will host many dinner parties within its quiet elegance.

- **Side Deck:** Reachable through patio doors from the breakfast room and a French door from the master bedroom is this generously sized deck. It is just the place for grilling in the summer or for enjoying your morning coffee.

- **Master Suite:** This master suite is truly a private space, as it is situated away from the remainder of the bedrooms in the home. This suite boasts a bathroom with a sunlit whirlpool tub, a double vanity, and a large walk-in closet. The French door to the expansive deck makes this room an ideal place to retreat to after a long day.

- **Secondary Bedrooms:** Three additional bedrooms and two full bathrooms located on the second floor provide all the space an expanded family will require. Two of the bedrooms share private entrances into the vanity area of one of the bathrooms.

Main Level Floor Plan

Upper Level Floor Plan

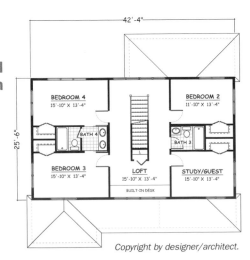

Copyright by designer/architect.

Plan #722024

Dimensions: 61'3" W x 31' D

Levels: 2

Heated Square Footage: 2,536

Main Level Sq. Ft.: 1,268

Upper Level Sq. Ft.: 1,268

Bedrooms: 4

Bathrooms: 3

Foundation: Crawl space, slab or basement

Material Take-off Included: Yes

Price Category: E

If you delight in the outdoors, you will love this traditionally styled two-story home that features front and rear porches that span the length of the home.

Images provided by designer/architect.

Features:

- **Living Room:** Stepping through the front door, you are immediately welcomed into the heart of the home. This generously sized room, open to both the kitchen and dining room, will be the gathering place for all.

- **Kitchen:** With today's active lifestyle, this tidy kitchen has a utility room located just steps away to make multitasking much easier.

- **Family Room:** While the main floor features a living room for formal entertaining, this wonderful family room on the upper floor can be used for more private family time. It also may be the perfect space for the youth in the family to entertain their friends.

- **Master Suite:** Located on the main floor, apart from the secondary bedrooms in the home, this lovely room will be a place of peace and quiet after a long day. This master suite features a large walk-in closet and a private bath to help add both privacy and comfort.

- **Upper Floor:** The upper floor of this home houses three additional bedrooms, a full bath, an exercise room, and a generously sized family room.

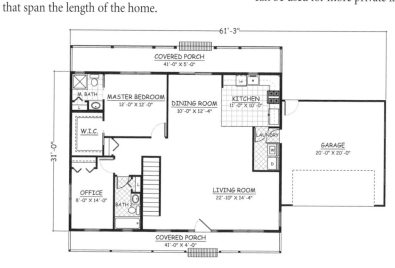

Main Level Floor Plan

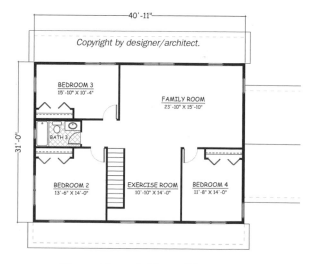

Upper Level Floor Plan

Plan #722006

Dimensions: 62' W x 32' D
Levels: 2
Heated Square Footage: 2,556
Main Level Sq. Ft.: 1,334
Upper Level Sq. Ft.: 1,212
Bedrooms: 4
Bathrooms: 4
Foundation: Crawl space, slab or basement
Material Take-off Included: Yes
Price Category: E

This Colonial-style house is perfect for the expanded family. It also has clean lines that make it a builder's dream.

CAD FILE AVAILABLE

Features:

- Foyer: The spacious two-story foyer makes for an inviting entrance with a balcony overlooking it from above. It is just steps away from an open floor plan that includes the living room, dining room, and kitchen.

- Living Room: This room is the perfect place for family gatherings. The open design of the space allows for the easy flow of guests while you are entertaining.

- Kitchen: This U-shaped kitchen that is open to the dining room offers modern conveniences. The open design of the space comntributes to pleasurable meal prep and dining. Large sliding glass doors provide easy access to outdoor dining as well.

- Office: This office is the perfect spot for one to work from home or simply a place for the family to do homework and pay bills.

- Master Suite: This private retreat is separate from the other bedrooms, which are all located on the second floor, making it the perfect getaway. It features plenty of windows, walk-in closet, and a luxurious bath with dual sinks and a large oval tub.

- Upper Level: The balcony hall leads to three bedrooms with large walk-in closets, two baths, and a large family recreation room. It's a place where younger members of the family will live and play in a style all their own.

Copyright by designer/architect.

Main Level Floor Plan

Upper Level Floor Plan

Plan #722066

Dimensions: 40' W x 44' D

Levels: 2

Heated Square Footage: 2,558

Main Level Sq. Ft.: 1,198

Upper Level Sq. Ft.: 1,360

Bedrooms: 4

Bathrooms: 3

Foundation: Crawl space, slab or basement

Material Take-off Included: Yes

Price Category: E

This convenient and comfortable two-story home is filled with many amenities to fit the lifestyle of a busy family.

Images provided by designer/architect.

Features:

- **Living Room:** This living room is part of an open floor plan that allows family and guests to flow from room to room. With double windows and a sliding glass doors, the result is a light and airy space that will accommodate all.

- **Kitchen:** This well-designed kitchen has a double sink and plenty of counter space to please any cook. It also features a snack island that opens into the generously sized dining room.

- **Home Office:** Whether one works from home or just needs a place to go over the family finances, this room is sure to fit the bill.

- **Master Suite:** Relax at the end of the day in this private master suite that is situated away from the remainder of the bedrooms in this home. Luxuriate in the private bathroom's whirlpool tub or prepare for the day at the dual-sink vanity.

- **Upper Level:** A generously sized game room, complete with its own kitchenette, will surely be host to many a game night.

This moderately sized traditional home has clean and simple lines, making it affordable to build.

Main Level Floor Plan

Upper Level Floor Plan

Copyright by designer/architect.

Images provided by designer/architect.

Plan #722050

Dimensions: 31' W x 42'5" D
Levels: 2
Heated Square Footage: 2,630
Main Level Sq. Ft.: 1,315
Upper Level Sq. Ft.: 1,315
Bedrooms: 5
Bathrooms: 4
Foundation: Crawl space, slab or basement
Material Take-off Included: Yes
Price Category: F

Optional Free Garage: If you would like an optional FREE 2-car garage plan, select one from page 8 or 9.

CAD FILE AVAILABLE CAD

Features:

- **Covered Porch:** Enjoy many warm summer evenings sitting on this lovely covered porch. Its brick accents and stately columns add to its grace and charm.

- **Living Room:** Step in from the covered porch area into this warm and inviting living room. Connected to the center hallway and open to the kitchen at the rear of the home, this room will certainly be a place where family and friends will gather.

- **Kitchen:** With its ample counter space and multitude of cabinets, this wonderfully designed kitchen will be sure to please the family cook. A utility closet housing the washer and dryer makes the multitasking that is often required for today's active family much easier.

- **Breakfast Nook:** Located directly off the kitchen, this cozy breakfast nook has many windows, bathing the space in natural light. The rear of the room features a French door leading out to a generously sized rear deck, a perfect spot for summer meals.

- **Master Suite:** Set at the rear of the home with its own hallway, this master suite features a large walk-in closet, a private bathroom, and a French door leading to the rear deck. The bathroom is sure to add to the comfort and privacy of an already lovely space.

The expansive front entry porch welcomes you into this traditional two-story home, designed to fit on a narrow lot.

Main Level Floor Plan

Upper Level Floor Plan

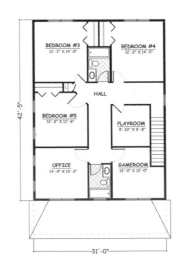

Copyright by designer/architect.

Plan #722055

Dimensions: 60'8" W x 36' D

Levels: 2

Heated Square Footage: 2,642

Main Level Sq. Ft.: 1,480

Upper Level Sq. Ft.: 1,162

Bedrooms: 4

Bathrooms: 3

Foundation: Crawl space, slab or basement

Material Take-off Included: Yes

Price Category: F

You'll appreciate the free flowing nature of this two-story traditional-style home.

CAD FILE AVAILABLE

Features:

- **Dining Room:** The casual layout of this dining room makes family dining, as well as formal dinner parties more enjoyable. The sliding glass door leading to the expansive rear deck makes the decision to dine indoors or outdoors a difficult one.

- **Kitchen:** This L-shaped kitchen, with its large center island, is a cook's dream. The room is designed to be open to both the living and dining areas, making interaction between the cook and the rest of the family during meal-time prep easy.

- **Master Suite:** Set apart from the additional bedrooms in the home, this master suite also houses a private bathroom, making it a welcoming place of respite after a long day.

- **Upper Floor:** Along with two of the secondary bedrooms, this floor houses an exercise room, a family room, and a playroom, providing a more intimate space for the family to gather.

The amenities in this home are sure to please all, while the thoughtful design elements will allow this expanded home to remain affordable to build.

Main Level Floor Plan

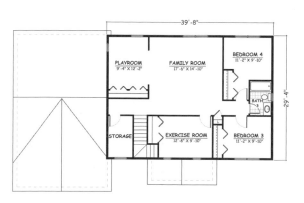

Upper Level Floor Plan

Images provided by designer/architect.

Plan #722038

Dimensions: 70'6" W x 27'4" D
Levels: 2
Heated Square Footage: 2,648
Main Level Sq. Ft.: 1,324
Upper Level Sq. Ft.: 1,324
Bedrooms: 5
Bathrooms: 4
Foundation: Crawl space, slab or basement
Material Take-off Included: Yes
Price Category: F

This expanded two-story home features wonderfully designed public and private spaces to please one and all.

CAD FILE AVAILABLE

Features:

- **Great Room:** Enter immediately into the heart of this home. This expansive space is open to both the dining room and the kitchen, making it the gathering spot for all.

- **Kitchen:** The family cook will surely be pleased with the layout of this kitchen. Open to the dining room, it features a stand-alone island with countertop seating, which enables the cook to interact with others while preparing meals.

- **Master Suite:** Situated apart from the secondary bedrooms for privacy, this lovely room also features an attached bath for added comfort.

- **Secondary Bedrooms:** Moderately sized secondary bedrooms are located on both the first and second floors. All rooms are just steps away from a full bath.

- **Game Room:** While the adults in the family will find the main floor great room the place to entertain, this second-floor game room will certainly be the spot where the teens in the family will gather with their friends.

This well-designed home provides wonderful spaces for all members of the family while keeping the expense of building low.

Copyright by designer/architect.

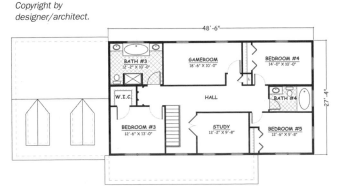

Main Level Floor Plan

Upper Level Floor Plan

Images provided by designer/architect.

Plan #722001

Dimensions: 46' W x 40' D
Levels: 2
Heated Square Footage: 2,650
Main Level Sq. Ft.: 1,390
Upper Level Sq. Ft.: 1,260
Bedrooms: 4
Bathrooms: 4½
Foundation: Crawl space, slab or basement
Material Take-off Included: Yes
Price Category: F

The simple, but classic, layout makes this house easy to build.

CAD FILE AVAILABLE

Features:

- Dining Room: The large front windows make this room bright and inviting. Step through the sliding glass door and out onto a well-proportioned deck.

- Kitchen: This spacious kitchen has ample counter space for preparing meals, while the countertop seating area allows interaction between the chef and the rest of the family.

- Playroom: Located on the upper level, this room features a bank of windows at the front that will bring lots of light and warmth to the room. It also has a large closet that is perfect for storing games and toys.

- Guest Suite: Separated from the other bedrooms in this home, this guest suite includes a private bath featuring a dual vanity and large tub. The suite will surely make your guests feel at home.

- Master Suite: Stepping through the double doors of this master suite you will immediately feel a sense of comfort. Featuring a private sitting room, a large walk-in closet, as well as a luxurious bathroom, this suite is the perfect retreat. The bath features a large tub, a separate shower, a dual vanity, and separate toilet room. While this area offers much privacy, it is also close to the other bedrooms on the upper floor, making it perfect for the young family.

Main Level Floor Plan

Upper Level Floor Plan

Copyright by designer/architect.

Images provided by designer/architect.

Plan #722057

Dimensions: 30' W x 51' D

Levels: 2

Heated Square Footage: 2,682

Main Level Sq. Ft.: 1,422

Upper Level Sq. Ft.: 1,260

Bedrooms: 5

Bathrooms: 3

Foundation: Crawl space, slab or basement

Material Take-off Included: Yes

Price Category: F

Optional Free Garage: If you would like an optional FREE 2-car garage plan, select one from page 8 or 9.

CAD FILE AVAILABLE

Features:

- Foyer: This understated entry foyer gently ushers family and friends into the heart of the home.

- Family Room: Step from the foyer directly into this central gathering spot. This generously sized room, featuring a wet bar and countertop seating, is perfect for entertaining.

- Dining Room: Bright and airy, this lovely dining room is directly off the kitchen and will be the main area for everyday family meals.

- Kitchen: This well-designed kitchen, with its spacious feel and array of cabinets, is sure to please all family members.

- Master Suite: This lovely master suite is located off the foyer and separate from the secondary bedrooms in the home. The suite features a private bathroom that houses a dual vanity and a separate toilet/tub area that will add comfort and privacy to the space.

- Upper Level: This upper level features three secondary bedrooms, a full bathroom, a play room, and a library.

The multiple gables at the front of this traditional-style home add character and curb appeal.

Main Level Floor Plan

DINING 12'-0" X 9'-0"

BED 2 10'-8" X 13'-4"

KITCHEN 14'-6" X 12'-6"

CRAFT RM. 10'-8" X 11'-8"

FAMILY 14'-6" X 15'-8"

WET BAR

FOYER 10'-6" X 10'-0"

M. BED 12'-9" X 12'-0"

PORCH 11'-0" X 5'-0"

51'-0"

30'-0"

Upper Level Floor Plan

30'-0"

BED 4 14'-6" X 13'-6"

BED 3 14'-6" X 13'-6"

BED 5 10'-0" X 11'-6"

BATH 2

42'-0"

LIBRARY 14'-6" X 15'-8"

PLAYROOM 14'-0" X 21'-10"

Copyright by designer/architect.

Plan #722047

Dimensions: 26'3" W x 54' D
Levels: 2
Heated Square Footage: 2,696
Main Level Sq. Ft.: 1,384
Upper Level Sq. Ft.: 1,312
Bedrooms: 5
Bathrooms: 4
Foundation: Crawl space, slab or basement
Material Take-off Included: Yes
Price Category: F

Images provided by designer/architect.

Optional Free Garage: If you would like an optional FREE 2-car garage plan, select one from page 8 or 9.

CAD FILE AVAILABLE

This attractive two-story home is designed for a narrow lot, without sacrificing style or spaciousness.

Features:

• Covered Porch: This covered porch provides a roomy place to sit and enjoy the outdoors.

• Kitchen: The wraparound snack bar connecting this kitchen to the great room will be the main attraction in this space. A cased opening leads you into the dining room, or for evenings of alfresco dining, there is also a lovely French door that leads to the side deck.

• Master Suite: This private first-floor master suite is situated away from the other bedrooms. It boasts a walk-in closet and a bathroom with a sunlit whirlpool tub, a separate shower, a private toilet room, and a double vanity. The sliding glass doors leading to the expansive deck make this room a getaway.

• Secondary Bedrooms: Four bedrooms and two full bathrooms are featured on the second level of this home. Two of the bedrooms offer private entrances into one of the bathrooms, ensuring privacy for each member of the family.

• Upper Level: In addition to the bedrooms, this floor also houses an exercise room, a private office, and a loft with built-in bookcases.

The unique design of this home makes it ideal for a lot with limited space. It provides all the amenities to an ever-growing family.

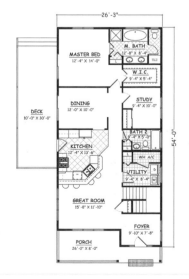

Main Level Floor Plan

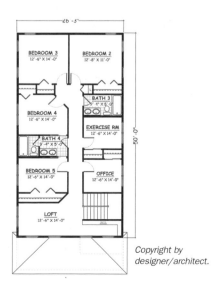

Copyright by designer/architect.

Upper Level Floor Plan

Plan #722073

Dimensions: 49'2" W x 47' D

Levels: 2

Heated Square Footage: 2,708

Main Level Sq. Ft.: 1,380

Upper Level Sq. Ft.: 1,328

Bedrooms: 5

Bathrooms: 4

Foundation: Crawl space, slab or basement

Material Take-off Included: Yes

Price Category: F

Images provided by designer/architect.

Features:

- **Kitchen:** You'll enjoy this well-designed space that features a double sink and both a range and a wall oven. Large cased openings give the room a touch of elegance.

- **Dining Room:** This dining room adjoins the kitchen, making family meals a joy. A double French door unit leads you into the backyard.

- **Master Suite:** Escape from the everyday in this wonderful master suite. Enjoy the large walk-in closet and the private bathroom with its double vanity and spacious shower.

- **Upper Level:** In addition to the bedrooms and bathrooms, this upper level is home to an office and a loft-like family room. Whether you need a place to work or to play, this home has the appropriate space.

The design of this home is ideal if you want a generously sized home with the perfect blend of public and private spaces.

CAD FILE AVAILABLE

Main Level Floor Plan

Copyright by designer/architect.

Upper Level Floor Plan

Plan #722051

Dimensions: 53' W x 30' D

Levels: 2

Heated Square Footage: 2,745

Main Level Sq. Ft.: 1,420

Upper Level Sq. Ft.: 1,325

Bedrooms: 5

Bathrooms: 4

Foundation: Crawl space, slab or basement

Material Take-off Included: Yes

Price Category: F

Images provided by designer/architect.

Optional Free Garage: If you would like an optional FREE 2-car garage plan, select one from page 8 or 9.

CAD FILE AVAILABLE

The covered porch, with its columns and brick accents, welcomes both friends and family into this wonderfully traditional-style two-story home.

Features:

• Kitchen: This L-shaped kitchen is designed with efficiency in mind. The room is open to the breakfast nook, helping to provide a continuous flow between the spaces.

• Breakfast Nook: A cased opening off the living room leads you into this cozy breakfast nook. Continuity is added by having the space also be completely open to the adjacent kitchen area.

• Master Suite: This lovely master suite, featuring a private bathroom and a large walk-in closet, will be a welcome respite after a long day. The bathroom features a whirlpool tub, dual vanities, and a separate shower, ensuring privacy and comfort.

• In-Law Suite: With a private bathroom featuring a large tub, two single vanities, and a separate shower, this roomy in-law suite provides additional comfort to your guests during their stay.

• Game Room: At the top of the main staircase is this open and airy game room, perfect for the younger members of the family to entertain their friends.

Main Level Floor Plan

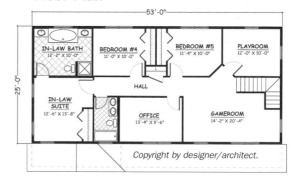

DECK
18'-0" X 8'-0"

MASTER BATH
12'-6" X 10'-0"

BEDROOM #2
11'-0" X 10'-0"

BREAKFAST NOOK
8'-4" X 10'-0"

KITCHEN
11'-0" X 10'-0"

HALL

MASTER SUITE
12'-6" X 18'-10"

STUDY
11'-10" X 10'-0"

LIVING ROOM
19'-4" X 13'-10"

W.I.C.

PORCH
34'-0" X 5'-0"

30'-0"

53'-0"

Upper Level Floor Plan

53'-0"

IN-LAW BATH
12'-2" X 10'-0"

BEDROOM #4
11'-4" X 10'-0"

BEDROOM #5
11'-4" X 10'-0"

PLAYROOM
12'-0" X 10'-0"

HALL

IN-LAW SUITE
12'-6" X 13'-8"

OFFICE
13'-4" X 9'-6"

GAMEROOM
14'-2" X 20'-4"

25'-0"

Copyright by designer/architect.

Plan #722021

Dimensions: 40' W x 48'9" D

Levels: 2

Heated Square Footage: 2,791

Main Level Sq. Ft.: 1,311

Upper Level Sq. Ft.: 1,480

Bedrooms: 4

Bathrooms: 3

Foundation: Crawl space, slab or basement

Material Take-off Included: Yes

Price Category: F

Images provided by designer/architect.

Features:

- **Covered Porch:** The front covered entry porch, featuring turned columns, is just the place to welcome family and friends home.

- **Family Room:** This family room is open to the kitchen and is bright and airy. It's sure to be the central gathering place of the home. Sliding glass doors open to a rear porch that spans the entire width of the house.

- **Bedrooms:** The upper level boasts two full-size bedrooms, each with walk-in closets. The lower level is home to the master suite and an additional bedroom that will make guests feel welcome.

- **Media Room:** This private retreat, located on the second floor, is wonderful for movie viewing or for relaxing with music.

This house, with its well-designed spaces, is truly a home you can make your own.

This charming two-story cottage style home is perfect for the family who values spending time together.

CAD FILE AVAILABLE

Main Level Floor Plan

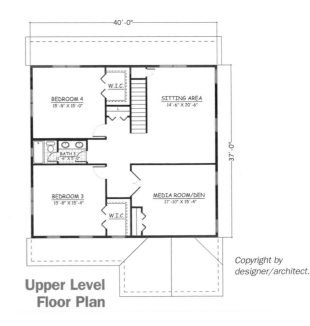

Upper Level Floor Plan

Copyright by designer/architect.

Plan #722023

Dimensions: 67'10" W x 58'2" D

Levels: 2

Heated Square Footage: 2,812

Main Level Sq. Ft.: 1,975

Upper Level Sq. Ft.: 837

Bedrooms: 5

Bathrooms: 3½

Foundation: Crawl space, slab or basement

Material Take-off Included: Yes

Price Category: F

This thoughtfully designed two-story traditional home, with its country-style front porch, welcomes friends and family home.

Images provided by designer/architect.

Features:

- Entry Foyer: This spacious foyer ushers you in, immediately making you feel comfortable.

- Living Room: Being open to the kitchen area, this cozy living room encourages more family time. The French door leading to the rear-covered porch expands the living area.

- Family Room: This gracious space on the upper floor will offer a more relaxing and quiet area for some family time. Separate from the central family area on the first floor,

it is the perfect area for family movie night, or perhaps a place for the youngsters in the home to entertain their friends.

- Kitchen: A well-placed center island creates additional counter space, along with an informal eating area that enhances this already thoughtfully designed kitchen.

- Master Suite: A spacious master suite, featuring two walk-in closets and private bath, will serve as a welcome haven after a long day. The private bath includes a separate shower, a private toilet room, a dual vanity, and a luxurious soaking tub.

Main Level Floor Plan

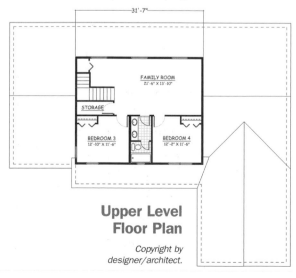

Upper Level Floor Plan

Copyright by designer/architect.

Types of Ceiling Treatments

There are many ways to enhance the ceilings in your home, ranging from simple surface upgrades to extensive framing projects that may add cost to your finished building price. And while some ceiling treatments are best installed when a house is being built, most can be added after you have built your new home if you need to balance your budget. Some of the least intrusive changes can produce dramatic results in how you experience a room. So if your budget is tight, include modest projects in your plans before considering more ambitious undertakings.

Paint and Wallpaper

Surface decoration has a great capacity for transforming the character of a room. While a plain white ceiling doesn't present much cause for excitement, a creative color scheme on the ceiling will certainly draw attention. In its simplest incarnation, this could mean simply painting the ceiling a color that complements or contrasts with the walls in the room. Or you might use one or more accent colors to create a border around the room, either adjacent to the walls or spaced some uniform distance toward the center of the room. A further elaboration of this idea might use a stencil to form the border—either one that is available commercially or one that you make yourself to reflect a personal theme.

This same concept can be executed using wallpaper instead of paint. You can apply wallpaper to the entire ceiling in a room or just create a border with a solid or patterned paper. There are even manufacturers of hand-printed wallpaper that offer elaborately figured papers designed specifically for ceiling applications. These can be assembled to form extremely intricate patterns that suggest paneling or painted scenes (Bradbury & Bradbury, www.bradbury.com). You should expect to pay a premium for these hand-crafted papers, but the results can be spectacular. And unless you have considerable experience hanging wallpaper, this kind of installation is best left to a professional.

There are also deeply textured and embossed wall covering products that can be used on ceilings. Two of the best known examples of these materials, in use since the late 1800s, are Anaglypta, made of recycled paper and cotton, and Lincrusta, made of molded linoleum. Both of these products are offered in a variety of patterns, textures, and sizes, and they must be painted after installation. Because these materials have such a long history of use, they can be an historically correct solution to a period-specific decorating dilemma. In addition, the heavy weight of these coverings makes them a great solution for covering small cracks. Of course, this only applies to surface defects and not serious structural problems.

You can also take painted treatments in a more creative direction by applying faux and textured finishes using a variety of techniques like glazing, color-washing, rag rolling, sponging, stippling, and marbleizing. And for the ultimate in painted ceilings, you can hire an artist to create a trompe l'oeil effect on the ceiling.

Go beyond plain white. Use vivid colors near or on the ceiling to draw the eye upward.

A wallpaper ceiling border can mimic the design used on the walls.

Suspended Ceilings and Acoustic Tiles

Many people associate suspended ceilings and tiles with commercial and office buildings. But these products have evolved in both material and design, and they present a valid option for home ceiling decoration, offering many choices of pattern and style, coupled with convenience and ease of installation. Both types of ceiling also offer superior soundproofing qualities when compared with either drywall or plaster.

Ceiling tiles can be applied directly to a plaster or drywall surface with adhesive, or you can first mount wood furring strips to the ceiling and then use staples to mount the tiles. Your builder may have a prefer-

ence. Although at one time this type of tile contained asbestos as one of its components, this has not been the case since the mid 1970s—today they are usually composed of wood-based fiber or recycled post-consumer and post-industrial products. Most tiles are sold as 12 x 12-inch squares with interlocking tongue-and-groove edges. A variety of styles and surface embossments is available, and most tiles will accept a painted surface, allowing you to create either a subtle or a dynamic look. Other tiles are offered with metallic coatings to mimic the look of a traditional tin ceiling.

Suspended ceilings are most suitable where you may need access above the ceiling. Basements are the most typical application in a home. To install one of these systems, you would hang metal tracks from

the ceiling joists using wires to create a grid. Manufactured panels are then laid into the grid to form the ceiling surface. The panels for a suspended ceiling are most often 2 x 4 feet or 2 x 2 feet, and they are offered in many different patterns, configurations, and colors. Some are flat, and others have recessed edges that allow them to drop below the surface of the metal tracks. There are also manufacturers of tin ceilings that sell metal panels that fit into suspended ceiling grids (American Tin Ceiling Co., www.americantinceilings.com). While suspended ceilings provide a relatively quick-and-easy way to install a finished ceiling in a basement or utility room, they provide the additional benefit of allowing easy access to pipes, heating ducts, and electrical wiring that typically run through or beneath the ceiling framing.

Suspended ceilings are a traditional ceiling treatment for basements, but the look of many newer products allow them to be used in more formal rooms as well.

Plank Ceilings

When you consider the popularity of hardwood flooring, the extension of the concept to the ceiling isn't a big leap. In fact, you can easily apply boards to a flat or sloped ceiling to create a warm and visually compelling atmosphere in a room.

There are many different wood materials suitable for this type of application. One of the most traditional choices is 4-inch-wide boards of Douglas fir with a beaded profile milled into the face of the stock. These boards have been used for porch ceilings and as wainscoting for well over 100 years, but they are equally suited for use as an interior ceiling. As with any solid-wood product, these boards can be painted or stained, or you can simply apply a clear finish to maintain the natural color of the wood.

Knotty pine boards are also quite popular for ceiling applications. Boards are available in a variety of widths, with tongue-and-groove edges that make installation quite simple. Some pine boards are sold with a beaded profile milled on one face and a plain surface on the opposite face. This gives you the opportunity to further customize the look of your ceiling by installing the boards to expose the face you find more attractive. You will also find a variety of packaged hardwood boards that are generally sold as wall paneling material, but you could certainly use them on the ceiling, as well. All of these products can be installed by either nailing them directly to ceiling joists or first installing furring strips over a drywall or plaster ceiling and nailing the boards to them.

Some manufacturers offer planks for ceilings that feature a prefinished laminate surface (Armstrong, www.armstrong.com). These usually have a core of medium-density fiberboard (MDF) and are installed using proprietary clips that fit into the grooved edges of the plank. The ceiling planks are available in a variety of wood-grain and painted finishes, eliminating the need to finish the material after installation.

Exposed roof planks, top, add a rustic touch to this attic bedroom.

Traditional plank ceilings, above, are made of wood, but new versions are made of medium-density fiberboard.

Soffits

A soffit is an area of lowered ceiling, usually adjacent to the walls of a room. The most widely known application of this concept is the boxed area, immediately above many kitchen cabinets, that fills the space between the cabinets and kitchen ceiling. However, this concept needn't be limited to a kitchen or to a cabinet installation. Soffits can be built in a portion of a room to create a sense of intimacy or dedicated purpose—such as for a reading nook or workspace. In addition, a soffit can be used to house recessed fixtures that can provide general lighting for a room or directed light for artwork or a particular task.

There are no specific dimensions pertaining to how a soffit is defined; it can extend down from the general ceiling surface as little as 1 inch or more than 1 foot, and it can extend out into the room by only a few inches or several feet. One of the interesting uses of soffits is to create a sense of expanding space in the center of a room. By lowering the ceiling on the perimeter of a space, you tend to experience the central area as being considerably more open—even if it is the same height as the ceilings throughout the rest of the building.

A soffit can be constructed with the traditional framing materials of two-by lumber and/or plywood. It can be faced with drywall, plaster, tile, metal, or wood, allowing you to to determine the degree of visual impact.

Soffits tend to make the center of the ceiling seem higher than it really is. This soffit houses recessed ceiling fixtures.

Beamed Ceilings

Beamed ceilings first appeared as a result of their structural function as supporting elements in post-and-beam construction. In a true beamed ceiling, the beams carry the boards that form both the ceiling and floor above; spacing and dimension of the beams are dependent on the load they must bear. While this type of construction is still used in some buildings, especially barns, it is relatively rare in residential design. More typically, homes are built using frame construction, in which nominal two-by lumber forms the core of the walls, floor, ceiling, and roof. In frame construction, intermediary support for the ceiling members is most often provided by interior walls, with only occasional use of visible beams—and these are usually sheathed in drywall or plaster to reduce their visual impact.

Decorative beams are meant to suggest their supportive cousins, but because they have no real structural function, their design can be entirely dependent on visual factors. For large rooms with high ceilings, beams can be larger and more closely spaced; smaller spaces with low ceilings usually work better with smaller, widely spaced beams. Beams that run across a long room tend to make the space feel wider, while those that follow the long dimension accentuate the room length. Beams can run directly between wall surfaces, or they can end at half-beams that abut the walls, suggesting supporting members at the perimeter. Likewise, you can construct one or more larger beams toward the center of the room that appear to support the cross-beams mid-span. For a simpler approach, you can limit the treatment to installing half-beams around the outside of the room, much like a cornice. You are not limited to using beams on only flat ceilings, and they can be particularly effective in rooms that feature sloped, cathedral ceilings. Beams can be oriented parallel with the rafters, following the slope of the ceiling, or parallel with the ridge board, to suggest structural purlins.

Structural beams are either solid timbers or laminated assemblies that must meet strict load-bearing requirements. In most cases, decorative beams are assembled from smaller pieces of softwood or hardwood lumber and trimmed with some kind of ceiling molding. They are constructed in a hollow, U-shaped form and hung on the ceiling from blocking strips. You then have the option of painting, staining, or clear-finishing the wood surfaces. This type of decorative beam would tend to be a prominent feature in a room. Alternately, you could face beams with drywall or plaster and then apply paint or wallpaper to them. This treatment would emphasize the structure over the beam surface and would likely be a more subtle presence in the overall room design.

For those who aren't interested in the mess or expense of installing real wood or drywall beams, there is another alternative: decorative beams of polyurethane, which feature surfaces that suggest rustic solid-wood beams but at a fraction of the cost and weight (www.fauxwoodbeams.com). Most of these beams are prefinished, allowing you to bypass the finishing steps, as well. As with decorative wood beams, these plastic "beams" are hung from blocks fastened to the ceiling surface.

Use beams in combination with other decorative ceiling techniques. Here, the bright white beams set off the color of the main ceiling area, top.

Beams appear to lengthen the room in the direction they run, above.

Images provided by designer/architect.

Plan #722036

Dimensions: 68'10" W x 44' D

Levels: 2

Heated Square Footage: 2,866

Main Level Sq. Ft.: 1,433

Upper Level Sq. Ft.: 1,433

Bedrooms: 5

Bathrooms: 4

Foundation: Crawl space, slab or basement

Material Take-off Included: Yes

Price Category: F

This comfortable two-story home features front and rear covered patios that will surely encourage you to spend many afternoons and evenings outdoors.

CAD FILE AVAILABLE

Features:

- **Great Room:** This gracious space immediately welcomes family and friends to the home upon entry. Open to both kitchen and breakfast area, this room will certainly be a gathering spot for all.

- **Kitchen/Breakfast Nook:** Plenty of counterspace in this kitchen will make mealtime prep easy. The sink is perfectly located in a wraparound countertop seating area, which will be the perfect place for the kids. Sliding glass doors grace this lovely breakfast nook and connect it to the rear patio.

- **Master Suite:** This lovely room, with its large walk-in closet and private bath, will be a place of comfort after a long day. The bath features a full-size tub, a separate shower, and dual vanities, offering you the privacy and comfort you seek.

- **In-Law Suite:** This space will surely make your extended family feel comfortable; it houses its own private bathroom.

Left Elevation

Right Elevation

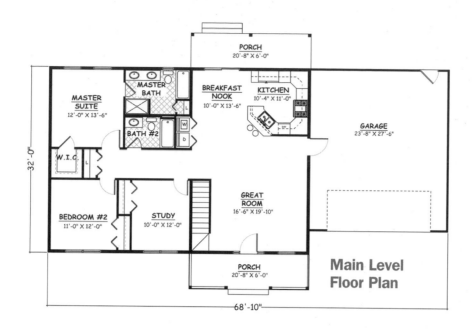

PORCH
20'-8" X 6'-0"

MASTER
SUITE
12'-0" X 13'-6"

MASTER
BATH

BREAKFAST
NOOK
10'-0" X 13'-6"

KITCHEN
10'-4" X 11'-0"

GARAGE
23'-8" X 27'-6"

BATH #2

W.I.C.

32'-0"

BEDROOM #2
11'-0" X 12'-0"

STUDY
10'-0" X 12'-0"

GREAT
ROOM
16'-6" X 19'-10"

PORCH
20'-8" X 6'-0"

**Main Level
Floor Plan**

68'-10"

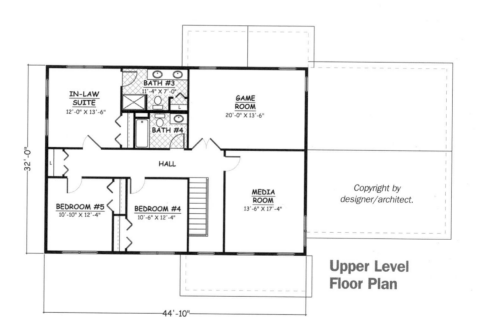

IN-LAW
SUITE
12'-0" X 13'-6"

BATH #3
11'-4" X 7'-0"

GAME
ROOM
20'-0" X 13'-6"

BATH #4

32'-0"

HALL

*Copyright by
designer/architect.*

BEDROOM #5
10'-10" X 12'-4"

BEDROOM #4
10'-6" X 12'-4"

MEDIA
ROOM
13'-6" X 17'-4"

**Upper Level
Floor Plan**

44'-10"

Rear Elevation

Plan #722002

Dimensions: 47' W x 40' D

Levels: 2

Heated Square Footage: 2,820

Main Level Sq. Ft.: 1,410

Upper Level Sq. Ft.: 1,410

Bedrooms: 5

Bathrooms: 4½

Foundation: Crawl space, slab or basement

Material Take-off Included: Yes

Price Category: F

This traditionally styled two-story home features large windows that will fill the interior with light.

CAD FILE AVAILABLE

Features:

- Foyer: Large windows and wonderfully understated front porch welcome you home.

- Living Room: This generously sized room is open to the foyer. The large walkway through to the kitchen and dining areas will come in handy when you are entertaining family and friends.

- Kitchen: This spacious kitchen, with ample pantry and a center island, provides plenty of counter space for the family cook. The open

design keeps everyone in close contact with one another.

- Guest Suite: This guest suite features a private bath with large tub and dual vanity. It will give your guests the privacy they deserve.

- Master Suite: Walk through the double doors into a calming retreat. Located on the upper floor, its large windows, private sitting area, large walk-in closet, and private bath will restore you after a long day. The private bath features a large tub for soaking, dual sinks, separate shower, and private toilet room, adding a luxurious feel to an already splendid room.

Copyright by designer/architect.

Main Level Floor Plan

Upper Level Floor Plan

Plan #722017

Dimensions: 52'4" W x 52' D

Levels: 2

Heated Square Footage: 2,842

Main Level Sq. Ft.: 1,664

Upper Level Sq. Ft.: 1,178

Bedrooms: 5

Bathrooms: 3

Foundation: Crawl space, slab or basement

Material Take-off Included: Yes

Price Category: F

Images provided by designer/architect.

A comfortable front porch welcomes you into this lovely home, offering a wonderful balance between public and private areas.

CAD FILE AVAILABLE

Features:

- **Family Room:** This wonderfully open space has room to spare. Featuring large windows and sliding glass doors to the rear deck, it will surely be the heart of the home.

- **Kitchen:** This kitchen is designed with a family in mind, featuring a large countertop workspace so preparing all meals will be quite manageable. A French door onto an expansive rear deck allows accessibility for dining outdoors.

- **Master Suite:** Set apart from the secondary bedrooms in the home, this space will be a welcome retreat after a long day. The gracious area offers a generously sized walk-in closet, sliding glass doors to the rear deck, and a private bath.

- **Upper Level:** In addition to three bedrooms with large closets, this floor features a full-size bath, library, and a moderately sized sitting room. While the first floor will certainly be the gathering spot for all, this upper level will offer a bit of refuge after a long day.

Spacious and thoughtful in its design, this home still remains affordable to build.

Copyright by designer/architect.

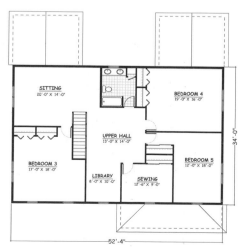

Main Level Floor Plan

KITCHEN 12'-0" X 15'-0"
DECK 19'-11" X 10'-0"
MASTER SUITE 15'-0" X 18'-0"
DINING 12'-0" X 13'-0"
FAMILY RM 22'-0" X 14'-0"
WIC
WORK BENCH 15'-6" X 5'-6"
BEDROOM 2 10'-0" X 13'-0"
ENTRY 7'-0" X 13'-0"
OFFICE 10'-6" X 13'-0"
PORCH 17'-0" X 6'-0"
GARAGE 23'-0" X 19'-0"
52'-0"
52'-4"

Upper Level Floor Plan

SITTING 20'-0" X 14'-0"
BEDROOM 4 19'-0" X 16'-0"
UPPER HALL 13'-0" X 14'-0"
BEDROOM 3 17'-0" X 18'-0"
LIBRARY 8'-0" X 10'-0"
SEWING 12'-6" X 9'-0"
BEDROOM 5 12'-0" X 18'-0"
34'-0"
52'-4"

Images provided by designer/architect.

Plan #722019

Dimensions: 60'6" W x 48' D

Levels: 2

Heated Square Footage: 2,860

Main Level Sq. Ft.: 1,885

Upper Level Sq. Ft.: 975

Bedrooms: 3

Bathrooms: 3

Foundation: Crawl space, slab or basement

Material Take-off Included: Yes

Price Category: F

This expansive two-story home features a smart mix of open public areas and private quarters that is sure to please every member of the family.

CAD FILE AVAILABLE

Features:

- **Covered Porch:** The centrally located front entry porch provides an elegant entrance into the home.

- **Dining Room:** The cased openings to this room give it a formal feel. It is also located near the kitchen and entry for the convenience of you and your guests.

- **Kitchen:** This modern kitchen is equipped with a center island and modern conveniences. It adjoins to the breakfast nook, which

features sliding glass doors that open to a covered rear porch. Another fine feature is the out-of-the way utility room accessible through a pocket door.

- **Master Suite:** This bright and spacious room is served by a private bath. The corner whirlpool tub invites one to rejuvenate after a long day. There's also a separate shower, a private toilet room, a dual vanity, and a walk-in closet.

- **Upper Level:** An additional bedroom and full bath, as well as a playroom and office, make the second floor a retreat for any generation.

Main Level Floor Plan

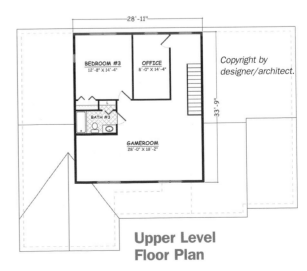

Copyright by designer/architect.

Upper Level Floor Plan

Plan #722020

Dimensions: 70' W x 48' D

Levels: 2

Heated Square Footage: 2,863

Main Level Sq. Ft.: 2,121

Upper Level Sq. Ft.: 742

Bedrooms: 4

Bathrooms: 3

Foundation: Crawl space, slab or basement

Material Take-off Included: Yes

Price Category: F

Images provided by designer/architect.

The open design of this traditional two-story home gives it a spacious feel, while the clean lines keep it affordable to build.

Features:

- **Covered Porch:** This large centrally located covered entry porch is just the place to greet guests.

- **Master Suite:** This architecturally designed room features a tray ceiling and French doors leading to the bath. The luxurious bath features a corner whirlpool tub, a separate shower, a private toilet room, and a double vanity.

- **Office Loft:** The second-floor landing becomes a loft that is designed to accommodate the family computer. Whether it's for games or keeping track of the family's finances, this space is sure to fit the bill.

- **Secondary Bedrooms:** Three additional bedrooms, two on the second floor and one on the first, provide plenty of space for the larger family. Two additional full baths provide comfort and convenience for all family members.

Main Level Floor Plan

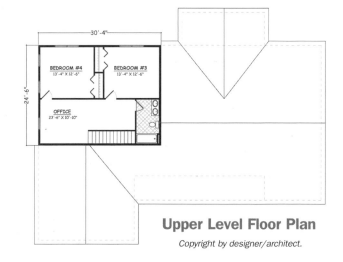

Upper Level Floor Plan

Copyright by designer/architect.

Images provided by designer/architect.

Plan #722049

Dimensions: 68'8" W x 29'6" D
Levels: 2
Heated Square Footage: 2,944
Main Level Sq. Ft.: 1,508
Upper Level Sq. Ft.: 1,436
Bedrooms: 5
Bathrooms: 4
Foundation: Crawl space, slab or basement
Material Take-off Included: Yes
Price Category: F

This expanded two-story home features brick accents and a hip roofline that gives it a traditional feel.

Features:

• **Great Room:** From the charming entry porch you step directly into this grandiose great room. Its open design and connection to both the public and private spaces in the home will make this the spot for all to gather.

• **Kitchen:** The open feel and ample counter space in this well-designed kitchen will make mealtime prep more enjoyable. This room also features a countertop eating area for morning breakfasts and after-school snacks. It is open to the dining room, allowing for interaction between family members and the cook.

• **Rear Deck/Grilling Porch:** With this covered grilling porch located off the kitchen area and the expansive rear deck connected to the dining room, dining outdoors will be a common occurrence.

• **Master Suite:** This lovely master suite features its own bathroom for privacy. The bathroom houses a tub, a separate shower, and dual vanities, which continue the comfortable feeling of an already delightful space.

• **Upper Level:** This upper level hosts an in-law suite, two additional bedrooms, and a full bathroom. Along with these rooms, the upper level has a several public areas, such as a playroom, a study, and a game room, which will be sure to please all.

CAD FILE AVAILABLE

Main Level Floor Plan

Upper Level Floor Plan

Copyright by designer/architect.

Plan #722026

Dimensions: 60' W x 49'2" D
Levels: 2
Heated Square Footage: 2,982
Main Level Sq. Ft.: 1,878
Upper Level Sq. Ft.: 1,104
Bedrooms: 4
Bathrooms: 4
Foundation: Crawl space, slab or basement
Material Take-off Included: Yes
Price Category: F

Images provided by designer/architect.

This spacious and versatile two-story traditional home is ideal for any family.

CAD FILE AVAILABLE

Features:

- Covered Porch: The covered entry porch is centered on the front of the house, providing a place to enjoy the outdoors and adding curb appeal.

- Kitchen: An island with snack bar is the high-light of this eat-in kitchen. Double windows at the sink and double French pocket doors that open to the foyer bathe this room in light.

- Office: Whether you work at home or just need a place to do family finances, this office locale will certainly fit the bill. Located just off the foyer and near a full bath, this office will make business visitors feel right at home.

- Master Suite: Located apart from the rest of the house, this master suite becomes a private retreat. It features a sitting area, large walk-in closet, a luxurious bath, and French doors that open to the rear deck. French doors provide an entrance into the bath, which includes a corner whirlpool tub, separate shower, dual vanities, and a private toilet room. It surely is a place to escape to after a long, hard day.

- Secondary Bedrooms: A first-floor guest bed-room and two additional bedrooms on the second floor complete the private areas of this home. The upper bedrooms share a full-size bath that has a private vanity and toilet for each bedroom, perfect for the teens in the family.

Main Level Floor Plan

Upper Level Floor Plan

Copyright by designer/architect.

Plan #722010

Dimensions: 85' W x 35' D
Levels: 2
Heated Square Footage: 3,123
Main Level Sq. Ft.: 2,038
Upper Level Sq. Ft.: 1,085
Bedrooms: 4
Bathrooms: 4
Foundation: Crawl space, slab or basement
Material Take-off Included: Yes
Price Category: G

Images provided by designer/architect.

This two-story home has an abundance of living spaces—something to suit any need.

CAD FILE AVAILABLE

Features:

- Covered Porch: This large covered porch is an ideal place for a swing or rocker.

- Living Room: This room features a large front picture window that makes this a bright and inviting space to entertain friends or just relax with the family.

- Kitchen: The center island with snack bar invites the family to join the cook, while the windows over the corner sink provide excellent views to the backyard. The pantry and adjoining dining room make the space complete.

- Mudroom/Utility Room: Conveniently located near the kitchen and with direct access to the garage and front yard, this space helps to make today's busy family life easier. Housing a washer and dryer, and featuring a storage cabinet, a hanging coat closet, and a built-in bench, this room allows the family to remove muddy shoes, store sporting equipment, or simply hang up their coat with ease.

- Master Suite: This retreat is a spacious room that has a luxurious bath that features a corner whirlpool tub, a separate shower, and a dual vanity. It's the perfect place to get ready on busy workday mornings or for relaxing on the weekend. The room also features a large walk-in closet.

Main Level Floor Plan

Upper Level Floor Plan

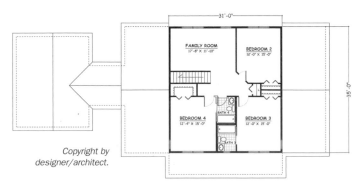

Copyright by designer/architect.

Plan #722045

Dimensions: 51'10" W x 54' D
Levels: 2
Heated Square Footage: 3,123
Main Level Sq. Ft.: 1,503
Upper Level Sq. Ft.: 1,620
Bedrooms: 5
Bathrooms: 4½
Foundation: Crawl space, slab or basement
Material Take-off Included: Yes
Price Category: G

CAD FILE AVAILABLE

While this expanded two-story home offers a variety of features, its lines are kept simple, making it easy to build.

Images provided by designer/architect.

Features:

- Covered Porch and Deck: These large areas are perfect for outdoor seating and dining spaces.

- Kitchen: Featuring a large built-in banquette, this kitchen invites the family to spend mornings together.

- Master Suite: This large and bright master suite is separate from the other bedrooms in the home, making it a private retreat. This suite also features a large walk-in-closet, a private bath, and sliding glass doors leading out onto the deck.

- Upper Floor: With its multiple bedrooms, guest suite, upper utility room, craft room, and media room, this floor has all that is needed to provide each member of the family the comfort and privacy they deserve.

- Guest Suite: This large guest suite, with its own bath featuring a private toilet room and a dual vanity, offers your guests all the comforts of home.

This home has features that will allow your family to grow and thrive within its walls.

Main Level Floor Plan

Upper Level Floor Plan

Copyright by designer/architect.

Images provided by designer/architect.

Plan #722074

Dimensions: 62' W x 39' D

Levels: 2

Heated Square Footage: 3,130

Main Level Sq. Ft.: 1,704

Upper Level Sq. Ft.: 1,426

Bedrooms: 5

Bathrooms: 4

Foundation: Crawl space, slab or basement

Material Take-off Included: Yes

Price Category: G

CAD FILE AVAILABLE

Optional Free Garage: If you would like an optional FREE 2-car garage plan, select one from page 8 or 9.

With such features as a wraparound front porch and multiple twin window units, this home evokes the charm of an old-fashioned farmhuse.

Features:

• Covered Porch: This expansive wraparound porch adds to the charm of this home while providing a relaxing place to sit and enjoy the outdoors. It also features French doors leading to two of the bedrooms.

• Dining Room: Located adjacent to the kitchen, this dining room has columns that flank the opening from the foyer, forming an elegant entrance. The sliding glass door that leads to the rear deck will invite the family to dine alfresco.

• Master Suite: Featuring a large walk-in closet and a private bathroom, this stylish master suite offers you a bit of respite from the everyday. Luxuriate in the corner whirlpool tub, and step out feeling relaxed and renewed. A French door leading to the front porch invites you to step outside to enjoy some fresh air.

• Secondary Bedrooms: Three additional generously sized bedrooms and an in-law suite complete the private areas of this home. The first floor bedroom has a private entrance to a full bathroom and a French door leading to the wraparound porch.

• In-Law Suite: This large in-law suite, featuring a private bathroom, will provide the occupants with all the luxury they deserve.

Left Elevation

Right Elevation

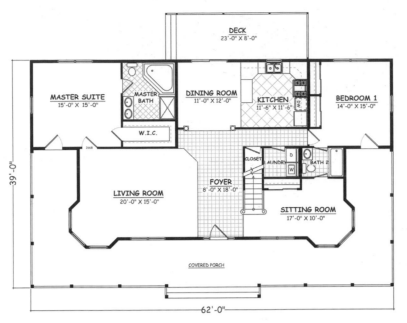

DECK
23'-0" X 8'-0"

MASTER SUITE
15'-0" X 15'-0"

MASTER BATH

DINING ROOM
11'-0" X 12'-0"

KITCHEN
11'-6" X 11'-6"

BEDROOM 1
14'-0" X 15'-0"

W.I.C.

2668

CLOSET

LAUNDRY

D

W

BATH 2

LIVING ROOM
20'-0" X 15'-0"

FOYER
8'-0" X 18'-0"

SITTING ROOM
17'-0" X 10'-0"

COVERED PORCH

39'-0"

62'-0"

Main Level Floor Plan

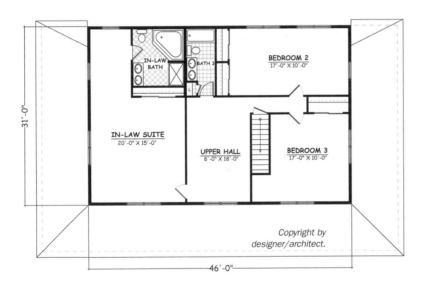

IN-LAW BATH

BATH 3

BEDROOM 2
17'-0" X 10'-0"

IN-LAW SUITE
20'-0" X 15'-0"

L

UPPER HALL
8'-0" X 18'-0"

BEDROOM 3
17'-0" X 10'-0"

31'-0"

46'-0"

Copyright by designer/architect.

Upper Level Floor Plan

Rear Elevation

Images provided by designer/architect.

Plan #722003

Dimensions: 72'6" W x 35' D

Levels: 2

Heated Square Footage: 3,150

Main Level Sq. Ft.: 1,996

Upper Level Sq. Ft.: 1,154

Bedrooms: 4

Bathrooms: 4½

Foundation: Crawl space, slab or basement

Material Take-off Included: Yes

Price Category: G

This traditionally styled two-story is filled with amenities for the most discerning of tastes.

CAD FILE AVAILABLE

Features:

• Covered Porch: This large covered porch provides a pleasing entry to this elegant home. It also has room for a small sitting area that is perfect for warm summer evenings.

• Dining Room: This spacious room is the perfect place for large family meals or festive gatherings with friends and family. Featuring sliding glass doors that lead to a large rear deck, the choice to dine indoors or outdoors will not be easily made.

• Kitchen: This roomy kitchen provides large countertop workspaces and has numerous cabinets for plenty of storage. A large pass-through to the dining room makes it easy to get dinner on the table.

• Master Suite: A set of double doors grants you entrance to this wonderfully private space. Separated from the other bedrooms in the home, this room houses many luxuries. With a private bath, walk-in closet, and a French door that leads to the rear deck, you will surely look forward to the respite that this room offers. The bath houses a dual vanity, a large tub, a separate shower, and private toilet room.

The elegant features and simple details within the home add to its character, while keeping it a home that is affordable to build.

Main Level Floor Plan

Copyright by designer/architect.

Upper Level Floor Plan

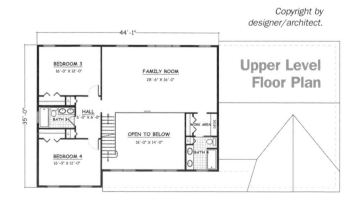

Plan #722016

Dimensions: 52'4" W x 52' D

Levels: 2

Heated Square Footage: 3,608

Main Level Sq. Ft.: 1,840

Upper Level Sq. Ft.: 1,768

Bedrooms: 5

Bathrooms: 3

Foundation: Crawl space, slab or basement

Material Take-off Included: Yes

Price Category: H

This delightful two-story home has a spacious layout designed for the active family.

CAD FILE AVAILABLE

Images provided by designer/architect.

Features:

• Covered Porch: The turned columns and decorative rail add charm to the covered entry porch.

• Kitchen: Large countertops and numerous cabinets will make meal prep easier. For outdoor dining, step through the French door and onto an expansive deck.

• Family Room: This wonderful space, which includes large windows and a set of sliding doors to the rear deck, will surely be a gathering place for all.

• Master Suite: Set apart from other bedrooms in the home, this generously sized master

suite features sliding glass doors to the outdoor deck. In addition the suite includes a private bath with an oversized tub, a separate shower, and a private toilet room.

• Upper Floor: This area features three additional bedrooms, a sewing room, a full bath, and a children's den. The children's den, which is filled with light and warmth from multiple windows, will surely provide many pleasant hours of fun.

With open areas and designated private spaces, this home will be sure to please every member of the family.

Main Level Floor Plan

Upper Level Floor Plan

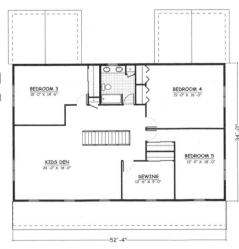

Copyright by designer/architect.

Plan #722005

Dimensions: 60' W x 47' D
Levels: 2
Heated Square Footage: 3,760
Main Level Sq. Ft.: 1,880
Upper Level Sq. Ft.: 1,880
Bedrooms: 4
Bathrooms: 4½
Foundation: Crawl space, slab or basement
Material Take-off Included: Yes
Price Category: H

The large front porch, spanning the width of the house, makes for a welcoming entrance to this traditionally styled two-story home.

CAD FILE AVAILABLE

Images provided by designer/architect.

Features:

- **Foyer:** This open and elegant foyer with its grand staircase welcomes you home.

- **Living Room:** A large picture window and sliding glass doors will certainly bring much sunlight to this wonderful room. Its tray ceiling and generously sized deck make this a place your guests will certainly enjoy.

- **Kitchen:** This spacious kitchen with large prep areas also features a countertop seating area that connects the kitchen to the dining room. This encourages extra family time while dinner is being prepared.

- **Library:** With built-in bookcases, and windows that flank the desk, all family members will certainly get use out of this delightful room on the second level.

- **Family Room:** Located at the upper floor, this room features a large front window and ample cabinet space, making this room a perfect place for family game night.

- **Master Suite:** Featuring private sitting room and large closets, this master suite envelops you in comfort. The private bath has such amenities as dual sink, private toilet, a large soaking tub, and separate shower. This amazing suite will certainly be a place of refuge after a long day.

Main Level Floor Plan

Upper Level Floor Plan

Copyright by designer/architect.

Images provided by designer/architect.

Plan #722004

Dimensions: 59'9" W x 50'5" D
Levels: 2
Heated Square Footage: 3,941
Main Level Sq. Ft.: 1,981
Upper Level Sq. Ft.: 1,960
Bedrooms: 3
Bathrooms: 3 Full, 2 Half
Foundation: Crawl space, slab or basement
Material Take-off Included: Yes
Price Category: H

This two-story home with its wrap-around porch has rustic, down-home country appeal.

Features:

- Foyer: This elegant and stately foyer with its grand staircase welcomes you home — connecting you to both the formal living and dining rooms.

- Living Room: With a boxed out window at the front and large windows at the side, this room is warm and inviting. It is the perfect place for entertaining guests.

- Dining Room: With windows mirroring those found in the formal living room, this wonderfully open space is the perfect place for large family meals or festive gatherings with friends. The room also features sliding glass doors that open out to a screened-in porch, allowing for dining alfresco in comfort.

- Kitchen: This spacious kitchen features a center island, large countertops, numerous cabinets, and a large pantry — making this kitchen a chef's dream. The space is also open to the dining room allowing for interaction while the chef is preparing the feast.

- Master Suite: Large windows and French doors that open onto the porch enhance the view from this wonderfully private space. The room also features such luxuries as a private bath, and two walk-in closets. In the bath you will find a dual vanity, a large tub, a separate shower, and a private toilet area.

Main Level Floor Plan

Copyright by designer/architect.

Upper Level Floor Plan

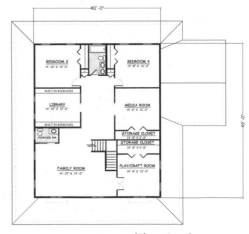

Plan #722075

Dimensions: 98' W x 31' D

Levels: 2

Heated Square Footage: 3,964

Main Level Sq. Ft.: 2,114

Upper Level Sq. Ft.: 1,850

Bedrooms: 5

Bathrooms: 4

Foundation: Crawl space, slab or basement

Material Take-off Included: Yes

Price Category: H

Images provided by designer/architect.

This thoughtfully designed two-story home features a plethora of amenities sure to please all members of the family.

Features:

• Great Room: Step directly from the front entry porch into this great room. A wonderfully open area, this room is sure to be the central gathering spot in the home. Its spaciousness, combined with the open floor plan leading back to the dining room, makes it a wonderful spot for entertaining and the perfect place for family to gather for an evening of fun.

• Kitchen: This spacious kitchen featuring a large pantry, ample counter space, and plenty of cabinet space will surely please the family chef. Large cased openings leading to both the dining room and the central hallway, along with a window above the sink, make this space feel bright and airy. The kitchen is also large enough to accommodate a small table and chairs, making it a perfect place for breakfast or a quick snack.

• Home Office: Located off the central gathering areas in the home is this lovely home office. The room allows for a bit of privacy for completing tasks such as the family finances, homework, or perhaps work from the office. With a private door leading to the hall bath, the office provides additional comfort and privacy.

• Upper Floor: In addition to the bedrooms and bath on this upper floor, there is also a sitting room and a playroom.

Rear Elevation

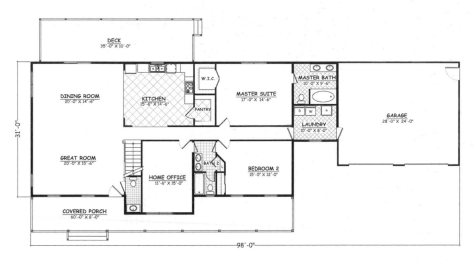

Main Level Floor Plan

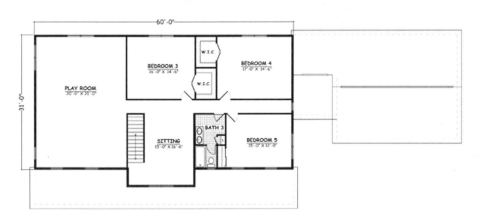

Upper Level Floor Plan

Copyright by designer/architect.

Left Elevation

Right Elevation

Plan #722018

Dimensions: 74' W x 44' D
Levels: 2
Heated Square Footage: 4,536
Main Level Sq. Ft.: 2,268
Upper Level Sq. Ft.: 2,268
Bedrooms: 6
Bathrooms: 3
Foundation: Crawl space, slab or basement
Material Take-off Included: Yes
Price Category: I

CAD FILE AVAILABLE

With an expansive deck at the rear and a covered porch spanning the front, this home enjoys an easy flow between outdoors and inside.

Features:

• Foyer: This entry foyer, with its grand staircase, welcomes both friends and family into the home.

• Family Room: Everyone will gather in this spacious room located directly off the foyer. The large cased opening at the rear of the room leads you toward the kitchen and dining room, allowing for an easy transition between rooms.

• Kitchen: The expansive cabinets, large pantry, and generous counter space making preparing family meals enjoyable. The area is open to the dining room, allowing for interaction between the chef, family members, and guests.t

• Master Suite: Featuring an oversized walk-in closet and private bath, this suite will be a welcome retreat after a long day..

• First Floor Bedroom: Set apart from the other bedrooms in the home, this room is the perfect area for your occasional guest. Close to a full bath, this room will allow your guests privacy during their stay.

• Upper Floor: Features an additional four bedrooms, a full bath, and a wonderfully open area that can be used as a game room and a library. The upper floor will surely be a gathering place for the younger generation in the home.

This home, with its spacious layout and grand outdoor amenities, is the perfect home for entertaining, as well as everyday family living.

Main Level Floor Plan

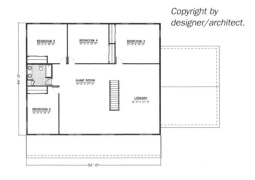

Upper Level Floor Plan

Whether you've always dreamed of building your own home or you can't find the right house from among the dozens you've toured, our collection of Easy-to-Build Expandable home plans can help you achieve the home of your dreams. You could have an architect create a one-of-a-kind home for you, but the design services alone could end up costing up to 15 percent of the cost of construction—a hefty premium for any building project. Isn't it a better idea to select from among the 150 unique designs shown in our collection for a fraction of the cost?

What Does Creative Homeowner Offer?

In this book, Creative Homeowner provides 150 home plans that you won't find in any other book or magazine. Our designs are affordable to build and expandable, so you can add on later. Whether your taste runs from traditional to country, farmhouse to Colonial, you are sure to find the best house design for your family. Our plans packages include detailed drawings to help you or your builder construct your dream house. **(See page 232.)**

Can I Make Changes to the Plans?

If you don't like any of the plans exactly as they are, Creative Homeowner offers three ways to help you achieve a truly unique home design. Our customizing service allows for extensive changes to our designs. **(See page 233.)** We also provide reverse images of our plans, or we can give you and your builder the tools for making minor changes on your own. **(See page 236.)**

Can You Help Me Manage My Costs?

To help you stay within your budget, Creative Homeowner has teamed up with the leading estimating company to provide, free, one of the most accurate, complete, and reliable building material take-offs in the industry when you buy your plans. **(See page 234.)** If you want an idea of costs before you commit to buying a plan, we can provide you with general construction costs based on the zip code for where you plan on building your new home. **(See page 236.)** Then you can decide whether you want to buy the plan later.

How Can I Begin the Building Process?

To get started building your dream home, fill out the order form on page 235, call our order department at 1-800-523-6789, or visit our Web site, ultimateplans.com. If you plan on doing all or part of the work yourself, or want to keep tabs on your builder, we offer best-selling building and design books at www.creativehomeowner.com.

Our Plans Packages Offer:

"Square footage" refers to the total "heated square feet" of this plan. This number does not include the garage, porches, or unfinished areas. All of our home plans are the result of many hours of work by leading architects and professional designers. Most of our home plans include each of the following:

Frontal Sheet

This artist's rendering of the front of the house gives you an idea of how the house will look once it is completed and the property landscaped.

Detailed Floor Plans

These plans show the size and layout of the rooms. They also provide the locations of doors, windows, fireplaces, closets, stairs, and electrical outlets and switches. Also included are full structural plans

Foundation Plan

A foundation plan gives the dimensions of basements, crawl spaces, and slab construction. Each house has a chioce of one of these three foundations.

Roof Plan

In addition to providing the pitch of the roof, these plans also show the locations of dormers, skylights, and other elements.

Exterior Elevations

These drawings show the front, rear, and sides of the house as if you were looking at it head on. Elevations also provide information about architectural features and finish materials.

Interior Elevations and Details

Interior elevations show specific details of such elements as fireplaces, kitchen and bathroom cabinets, built-ins, and other unique features of the design.

Cross Sections

These show the structure as if it were sliced to reveal construction requirements, such as insulation, flooring, and roofing details.

Frontal Sheet

Floor Plan

Foundation Plan

Roof Plan

Cross Sections

Stair Details

Elevation

Illustrations provided by designer/architect

Customize Your Plans in 4 Easy Steps

1 **Select the home plan** that most closely meets your needs. Purchase of a reproducible master, PDF files or CAD files is necessary in order to make changes to a plan.

2 **Call 1-800-523-6789 to place your order.** Tell our sales representative you are interested in customizing your plan, and provide your contact information. Within a day or two you will be contacted (via phone or email) to provide a list or sketch of the changes requested to one of our plans. There is no consultation fee for this service.

3 **Within three business days** of receipt of your request, a detailed cost estimate will be provided to you.

4 **Once you approve the estimate,** you will purchase either the reproducible master, PDF files, or CAD files, and customization work will begin. During all phases of the project, you will receive progress prints by fax or email. On average, the project will be completed in two or three weeks. After completion of the work, modified plans will be shipped. You will receive one set of blueprints in addition to a reproducible master or CAD files, depending on which package you purchased.

Modification Pricing Guide

Categories	Average Cost For Modification
Add or remove living space	Quote required
Bathroom layout redesign	Starting at $150
Kitchen layout redesign	Starting at $120
Garage: add or remove	Starting at $600
Garage: front entry to side load or vice versa	Starting at $300
Foundation changes	Starting at $220
Exterior building materials change	Starting at $200
Exterior openings: add, move, or remove	$75 per opening
Roof line changes	Starting at $600
Ceiling height adjustments	Starting at $280
Fireplace: add or remove	Starting at $90
Screened porch: add	Starting at $300
Wall framing change from 2x4 to 2x6	Starting at $250
Bearing and/or exterior walls changes	Quote required
Non-bearing wall or room changes	$65 per room
Metric conversion of home plan	Starting at $495
Adjust plan for handicapped accessibility	Quote required
Adapt plans for local building code requirements	Quote required
Engineering stamping only	Quote required
Any other engineering services	Quote required
Interactive illustrations (choices of exterior materials)	Quote required

Note: *Any home plan can be customized to accommodate your desired changes. The average prices above are provided only as examples of the most commonly requested changes, and are subject to change without notice. Prices for changes will vary according to the number of modifications requested, plan size, style, and method of design used by the original designer. To obtain a detailed cost estimate, please contact us.*

Architectural Seals

Because of differences in building codes, some cities and states now require an architect or engineer licensed in that state to review and "seal" a blueprint, or officially approve it, prior to construction. Delaware, Nevada, New Jersey, New York, and some other states require that all plans for houses built in those states be redrawn by an architect licensed in the state in which the home will be built. We strongly advise you to consult with your local building official for information regarding architectural seals.

Before Customization

After

Turn your dream home into reality with

a **Material Take-off** and  LOWE'S **FORPROS**

When purchasing one of the plans featured in this book, you get, at no additional cost, one of the most complete materials lists in the industry.

1 ▸ **What comes with a Material Take-off?**

Quote

• Basis of the entire estimate.

• Detailed list of all the framing materials needed to build your project, listed from the bottom up, in the order that each one will actually be used.

Comments

• Details pertinent information beyond the cost of materials.

• Includes any notes from our estimates.

Express List

• A combined version of the Quote with SKUs listed for purchasing the items at your local Lowe's.

• Your Lowe's Commercial Sales Specialist can then price out the materials list.

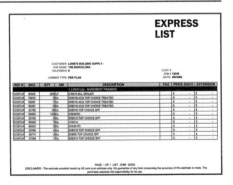

Construction-Ready Framing Diagrams

• Your "map" to exact roof and floor framing.

Millwork Report

• A complete count of the windows, doors, molding, and trim.

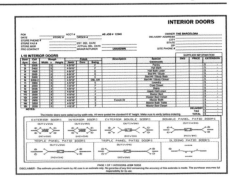

Man-Hour Report

• Calculates labor on a line-by-line basis for all items quoted and presented in man-hours.

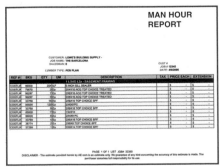

2 | Why a Material Take-off?

Accurate. Professional estimators break down each individual item from the blueprints using advanced software, techniques, and equipment.

Timely. You will be able to start your home-building project quickly—knowing the exact framing materials you need and how to get them with Lowe's.

Detailed. Work with your Lowe's associate to select with the remaining products needed for your new home and get a final, accurate quote.

3 | So how much does it cost?

Material Take-off pricing is normally determined by the total square feet of the home plan—including living area, garages, decks, porches, finished basements, and finished attics. For the collection in this book, the Material Take-off is included in the price of the home plans:

Square Feet Range	Price
Up to 5,000 total square feet	~~$345.00~~ Free

Call our toll-free number (800-523-6789), or visit ultimateplans.com to order your Material Take-off (also called Ultimate Estimate online).

4 | What else do I need to know?

When you purchase your products from Lowe's you may receive a gift card for $345, the regular price of a Material Take-off (even though it was included in your plan price) as an added value. Please go to **UltimatePlans.com** and select **Ultimate Estimate** located under "Quick Links" for complete details of the program.

The Lowe's Advantage:

What's more, you can save an additional 10% (up to $500.00) on your first building material purchase.* You will receive details on this program with your order.

Turn your dream home into reality.

*Good for a single purchase of any in-stock or Special Order merchandise only up to $5,000 (maximum discount $500). Not valid on previous sales, service or installation fees, the purchase of gift cards, or any products by Fisher & Paykel, Electrolux, John Deere, or Weber.

Decide What Type of Plan Package You Need

How many Plans Should You Order?

Standard 8-Set Package. We've found that our 8-set package is the best value for someone who is ready to start building. The 8-set package provides plans for you, your builder, the subcontractors, mortgage lender, and the building department.

Minimum 5-Set Package. If you are in the bidding process, you may want to order only five sets for the bidding round and reorder additional sets as needed.

1-Set Study Package. The 1-set package allows you to review your home plan in detail. The plan will be marked as a study print, and it is illegal to build a house from a study print alone. It is a violation of copyright law to reproduce a blueprint without permission.

Buying Additional Sets. If you require additional copies of blueprints for your home construction, you can order additional sets within 60 days of the original order date at a reduced price. The cost is $35.00 for each additional set. For more information, contact customer service.

Reproducible Masters

If you plan to make minor changes to one of our home plans, you can purchase reproducible masters. These plans are printed on bond paper. They clearly indicate your right to modify, copy, or reproduce the plans. Reproducible masters allow an architect, designer, or builder to alter our plans to give you a customized home design. This package allows you to print as many copies of the modified plans as you need for the construction of one home.

PDF Files

PDF files are a complete set of home plans in electronic file format sent to you via email. These files cannot be altered electronically; once printed, changes can be hand drawn. A PDF file gives you the license to modify the plans to fit your needs and build one home.

CAD (Computer-Aided Design) Files

CAD files are the complete set of home plans in an alterable electronic file format. Choose this option if there are multiple changes you wish made to the home plans and you have a local design professional able to make the changes.

Right-Reading Reverse

Plans can be printed in reverse—we can "flip" plans to create a mirror image of the design. This is useful when the house would fit your site or personal preferences if all the rooms were on the opposite side than shown. All plans in this collection are available in right-reading reverse; this feature will show the plan in reverse, and the writing on the plan will be readable. A $150.00 fee per plan order will be charged for right-reading reverse (regardless of the number of right-reading reverse sets ordered).

EZ Quote: Home Cost Estimator

EZ Quote is our response to a frequently asked question we hear from customers: "How much will the house cost me to build?" EZ Quote: Home Cost Estimator will enable you to obtain a calculated building cost to construct your home, based on labor rates and building material costs within your zip code area. This summary is useful for those who want to get an idea of the total construction costs before purchasing sets of home plans. It will also provide a level of comfort when you begin soliciting bids. The cost is $29.95 for the first EZ Quote and $19.95 for each additional one in the same order. Available only in the U.S. and Canada.

3-D Framer's Walk-Through

Step-by-step 3-D framing instructions from foundation sill plate to roof sheathing are available for all plans in this collection at a cost of $545. This plan-specific "slide show" will be deliverd in PDF format for easy viewing. The 3-D framer's walk-through enables you to "virtually tour" your dream house in the framing stage of construction. This is a valuable tool when framing the home, and it can save you time and money. It will show you stud lengths, plate heights, header size and location, plus girder size and location.

Lowe's Material Take-off (See page 234.)

Order Toll Free by Phone
1-800-523-6789
By Fax: 201-760-2431

Orders received 3PM ET, will be processed and shipped within two business days.

Order Online
www.ultimateplans.com
Mail Your Order
Creative Homeowner
Attn: Home Plans
24 Park Way
Upper Saddle River, NJ 07458

Canadian Customers
Order Toll Free 1-800-393-1883
Mail Your Order (Canada)
Creative Homeowner Canada
Attn: Home Plans
113-437 Martin St., Ste. 215
Penticton, BC V2A 5L1

Before You Order

Our Exchange Policy

Blueprints are nonrefundable. However, should you find that the plan you have purchased does not fit your needs, you may exchange that plan for another plan in our collection within 60 days from the date of your original order. The entire content of your original order must be returned before an exchange will be processed. You will be charged a processing fee of 20% of the amount of the original order, the cost difference between the new plan set and the original plan set (if applicable), and all related shipping costs for the new plans. Contact our order department for more information. Please note: reproducible masters may only be exchanged if the package is unopened. PDF files and CAD files cannot be exchanged and are nonrefundable.

Building Codes and Requirements

All plans offered for sale in this book and on our Web site (www.ultimateplans.com) are continually updated to meet the latest International Residential Code (IRC). Because building codes vary from area to area, some drawing modifications and/or the assistance of a professional designer or architect may be necessary to comply with your local codes or to accommodate specific building site conditions. We strongly advise you to consult with your local building official for information regarding codes governing your area.

Multiple Plan Discount

Purchase **3** different home plans in the **same order** and receive **5% off** the plan price.

 Purchase **5** or more different home plans in the **same order** and receive **10% off** the plan price.
(Please Note: Study sets do not apply.)

Blueprint Price Schedule

Price Code	1 Set	5 Sets	8 Sets	Reproducible Masters or PDF Files	CAD	Material Take-off
DD	$135	$155	N/A	$200	$500	included
A	$410	$470	$545	$660	$1,125	included
B	$465	$540	$615	$740	$1,310	included
C	$525	$620	$695	$820	$1,475	included
D	$575	$670	$745	$870	$1,575	included
E	$625	$730	$805	$925	$1,675	included
F	$690	$790	$865	$990	$1,800	included
G	$720	$820	$895	$1,020	$1,845	included
H	$730	$830	$905	$1,045	$1,900	included
I	$995	$1,095	$1,170	$1,290	$2,110	included
J	$1,190	$1,290	$1,365	$1,490	$2,300	included
K	$1,195	$1,295	$1,370	$1,495	$2,300	included
L	$1,240	$1,335	$1,410	$1,535	$2,400	included

Note: All prices subject to change

Lowe's Material Take-off (MT Tier)

Price	
~~$345~~	Free

Shipping & Handling

	1–4 Sets	5–7 Sets	8+ Sets or Reproducibles	CAD
US Regular (7–10 business days)	$18	$20	$25	$25
US Priority (3–5 business days)	$35	$40	$45	$45
US Express (1–2 business days)	$45	$60	$80	$50
Canada Express (3–4 business days)	$100	$100	$100	$100
Worldwide Express (3–5 business days)	** Quote Required **			

Note: All delivery times are from date the blueprint package is shipped (typically within 1-2 days of placing order).

Order Form
Please send me the following:

Plan Number: _____ **Price Code:**____ (See Plan Index.)

Indicate Foundation Type: (Select ONE. See plan page for availability.)
❏ Slab   ❏ Crawl space   ❏ Basement

Basic Blueprint Package

	Cost
❏ CAD Files	$_____
❏ PDF Files	$_____
❏ Reproducible Masters	$_____
❏ 8-Set Plan Package	$_____
❏ 5-Set Plan Package	$_____
❏ 1-Set Study Package	$_____
❏ Additional plan sets: __ sets at $35.00 per set	$_____

❏ Print in right-reading reverse: $150.00 per order
    *Please call all our order department
    or visit our website for availibility*
	$_____

Important Extras

❏ Lowe's Material Take-off	$___Free___
❏ 3-D Framer's Walk-Through: $545.00	$_____
❏ EZ Quote for Plan #_____at $29.95	$_____
❏ Additional EZ Quotes for Plan #s_____ at $19.95 each	$_____

❏ Free Detached Garage Plan: See plan page to
    determine whether your plan qualifies
    Detached Garage Plan Number _____
	$___Free___

Shipping (see chart above) $_____

SUBTOTAL $_____

Sales Tax (NJ residents only, add 7%) $_____

TOTAL $_____

Order Toll Free: 1-800-523-6789   By Fax: 201-760-2431
Creative Homeowner (Home Plans Order Dept.)
24 Park Way
Upper Saddle River, NJ 07458

Name _____
(Please print or type)

Street _____
(Please do not use a P.O. Box)

City _____   State _____

Country _____   Zip _____

Daytime telephone (_____)_____

Fax (_____)_____
(Required for reproducible orders)

E-Mail _____

Payment   ❏ Bank check/money order. No personal checks.
Make checks payable to Creative Homeowner

❏ VISA   ❏ MasterCard   ❏ American Express Cards   ❏ DISCOVER

Credit card number _____

Expiration date (mm/yy) _____

Signature_____

Please check the appropriate box:
❏ Building home for myself   ❏ Building home for someone else

SOURCE CODE   LA525

Index

For pricing, see page 237.

Index

For pricing, see page 237.

Material Take-off

The fastest, simplest way to estimate building your dream home — and it's FREE!

One of the most complete materials lists in the industry. Work with your Lowe's associate to get all the products you need.

LOWE'S FORPROS

To learn more, see page 234 or go to UltimatePlans.com and select Ultimate Estimate located under "Quick Links" for complete details on this program.

Copyright Notice

All home plans sold through this publication are protected by copyright. Reproduction of these home plans, either in whole or in part, including any form and/or preparation of derivative works thereof, for any reason without prior written permission is strictly prohibited. The purchase of a set of home plans in no way transfers any copyright or other ownership interest in it to the buyer except for a limited license to use that set of home plans for the construction of one, and only one, dwelling unit. The purchase of additional sets of the home plans at a reduced price from the original set or as a part of a multiple-set package does not convey to the buyer a license to construct more than one dwelling.

Similarly, the purchase of reproducible home plans (sepias, mylars) carries the same copyright protection as mentioned above. It is generally allowed to make up to a maximum of 10 copies for the construction of a single dwelling only. To use any plans more than once, and to avoid any copyright license infringement, it is necessary to contact the plan designer to receive a release and license for any extended use. Whereas a purchaser of reproducible plans is granted a license to make copies, it should be noted that because blueprints are copyrighted, making photocopies from them is illegal.

Copyright and licensing of home plans for construction exist to protect all parties. Copyright respects and supports the intellectual property of the original architect or designer. Copyright law has been reinforced over the past few years. Willful infringement could cause settlements for statutory damages to $150,000.00 plus attorney fees, damages, and loss of profits.